Suppletion in Verb Paradigms

Typological Studies in Language (TSL)

A companion series to the journal *Studies in Language*

General Editor   Michael Noonan

Assistant Editors   Spike Gildea, Suzanne Kemmer

Editorial Board

Wallace Chafe (Santa Barbara)
Bernard Comrie (Leipzig)
R. M. W. Dixon (Melbourne)
Matthew Dryer (Buffalo)
John Haiman (St Paul)
Bernd Heine (Köln)
Paul Hopper (Pittsburgh)
Andrej Kibrik (Moscow)
Ronald Langacker (San Diego)

Charles Li (Santa Barbara)
Edith Moravcsik (Milwaukee)
Andrew Pawley (Canberra)
Doris Payne (Eugene, OR)
Frans Plank (Konstanz)
Jerrold Sadock (Chicago)
Dan Slobin (Berkeley)
Sandra Thompson (Santa Barbara)

Volumes in this series will be functionally and typologically oriented, covering specific topics in language by collecting together data from a wide variety of languages and language typologies. The orientation of the volumes will be substantive rather than formal, with the aim of investigating universals of human language via as broadly defined a data base as possible, leaning toward cross-linguistic, diachronic, developmental and live-discourse data.

Volume 67

Suppletion in Verb Paradigms: Bits and pieces of the puzzle
by Ljuba N. Veselinova

Suppletion in Verb Paradigms

Bits and pieces of the puzzle

Ljuba N. Veselinova
Stockholm University, Sweden

John Benjamins Publishing Company
Amsterdam / Philadelphia

™ The paper used in this publication meets the minimum requirements
of American National Standard for Information Sciences – Permanence
of Paper for Printed Library Materials, ANSI Z39.48-1984.

Library of Congress Cataloging-in-Publication Data

Ljuba N. Veselinova
    Suppletion in verb paradigms : bits and pieces of the puzzle / Ljuba N. Veselinova.
       p. cm. (Typological Studies in Language, ISSN 0167–7373 ; v. 67)
    Includes bibliographical references and indexes.
       1. Grammar, Comparative and general--Verb. 2. Grammar, Comparative and general--Suppletion. I. Title. II. Series.

P281.V477 2006
415'.6--dc22   2006042985
ISBN 90 272 2979 1 (Hb; alk. paper)

© 2006 – John Benjamins B.V.
No part of this book may be reproduced in any form, by print, photoprint, microfilm, or any other means, without written permission from the publisher.

John Benjamins Publishing Co. · P.O. Box 36224 · 1020 ME Amsterdam · The Netherlands
John Benjamins North America · P.O. Box 27519 · Philadelphia PA 19118-0519 · USA

Contents

Acknowledgements   IX
Abbreviations and presentation conventions   XI

Introduction   XV
1. Preliminaries   XI
2. Organization of this book   XIII

CHAPTER 1
Previous studies on suppletion   1
1. Historical notes   1
2. Suppletion in contemporary linguistic theory (Chomsky and beyond)   4
    2.1 Defining the concept   4
        2.1.1 Relevant notions   4
        2.1.2 Kinds of suppletion depending on the kinds of linguistic signs it affects   9
        2.1.3 Diachrony vs. Synchrony   14
        2.1.4 Morphology of the suppletive forms   15
    2.2 Formal characteristics of suppletive forms   18
        2.2.1 Suppletion belongs to the lexicon = uninteresting   19
        2.2.2 Suppletion: "the problem child"   21
        2.2.3 Suppletion and Frequency   22
        2.2.4 Suppletion: a result, not a residue   26
3. Quo Vadis Domine   29

CHAPTER 2
Method   33
1. Sampling   33
    1.1 General issues   33
    1.2 The sampling method employed in this study   37
2. Ways to calculate frequencies of the suppletion types emerging from the data   40
    2.1 Counting genera instead of languages   40
    2.1 Weight values assigment   42
    2.2 Sources   45

4. Criteria for suppletion   46
   4.1 Grammatical category and its encoding.   46
   4.1 Form of the suppletive items.   47
   4.3 Use of the suppletive forms.   48
   4.4 Towards a typology of stem change in verb paradigms   48

CHAPTER 3
Some theoretical issues and a general overview of the data   51
1. Paradigm revisited   51
2. General overview of the data   58

CHAPTER 4
Tense–aspect suppletion I: Synchronic perspective   63
1. Introduction   63
2. Categorial suppletion according to tense and aspect   65
   2.1 Suppletion according to tense   65
      2.1.1 Semantic distinctions encoded by the suppletive forms   65
      2.1.2 Cross-linguistic distribution of categorial tense suppletion   66
      2.1.3 Lexemic groups with categorial tense suppletion   67
   2.2 Suppletion according to aspectual distinctions   68
      2.2.1 Paradigmatic relationship of the suppletive forms   68
      2.2.2 Semantic distinctions   72
      2.2.3 Cross-linguistic distribution of suppletion according to aspect   73
      2.2.4 Lexemic groups with categorial aspect suppletion   74
   2.3 Stem change which involves several tense–aspect categories   75
   2.4 Suppletive perfects   77
3. Non-categorial suppletion   78
   3.1 Cross-linguistic distribution   86
   3.2 Lexemic groups   87
4. Morphological analysis of the suppletive verbs   87
5. Summary of synchronic distribution of tense–aspect suppletion   89
   5.1 Summary of the sub-groups   89
   5.2 Verb meanings that occur with tense–aspect of suppletion   90
   5.3 Frequency of distribution in the samples   94

CHAPTER 5
Tense–aspect suppletion II: Diachronic and usage-based perspective   97
1. Introduction   97
2. Frequency and suppletion   98
3. Suppletion and analogy   106

4. Emergence of suppletion and general grammaticalization processes 115
   4.1 Suppletive copulas and the field of intransitive predication 116
   4.2 Historical information on copula verbs 120
   4.3 Grammaticalization of become as future copula 121
   4.4 Grammaticalization of position verbs to copulas 122
   4.5 Conclusion 126
5. Suppletion and lexicalization 126
6. Summary and conclusions 133

CHAPTER 6
Suppletive imperatives 135
1. A brief note on the functions and the marking of imperative 135
2. Suppletive imperatives from a synchronic perspective 136
   2.1 Semantic distinctions indicated by suppletive imperatives 136
   2.2 Types of stem change and form of suppletive imperatives 138
   2.3 Lexemic groups that occur with suppletive imperatives 138
   2.4 Frequency of distribution in the samples 139
3. Suppletive imperatives from a historical perspective 140
4. Summary and conclusions 145

CHAPTER 7
Verbal number and suppletion 149
1. Presentation of the data 151
   1.1 Semantic distinctions indicated by verbal number suppletives 151
   1.2 Form of verbal number suppletives 152
2. Lexemic groups that with verbal number suppletion 153
3. Frequency of distribution in the samples 156
4. Verbal number pairs: suppletive forms of the same word
   or separate words 158
   4.1 Verbal number and syntactic agreement 158
   4.2 Lexicalization, derivation and the concept of suppletion 163
   4.3 Emergence of agreement markers out of verbal number pairs 169
5. Summary and conclusions 174

Concluding remarks 175
1. Summary of the results and implications of the preceding chapters 175
2. Directions for future research 177

Appendix 1: The small sample 179
Appendix 2: Languages in the WALS sample 185
Appendix 3: Additional data 197
References 215

Index of languages   231
Index of authors   233
Index of subjects   235

Acknowledgments

This book is a revised and, hopefully, an improved version of my doctoral dissertation. My warmest thanks go to my former dissertation director, Prof. Östen Dahl, for all the ideas he shared with me and for his, apparently, limitless patience throughout the years. Many thanks also to Prof. Dr. Martin Haspelmath, for his insightful criticism, lengthy and patient discussions and the detailed comments on the first version of this work.

I have greatly benefited from the comments and suggestions of Prof. Maria Koptjevskaja-Tamm, Prof. Helen Aristar-Dry, Prof. Anthony Aristar, Bernhard Wälchli, Jennifer Spenader, Päivi Juvonen and Eva Lindström. Thanks also to Marcin Kilarski, Susan Robinson and Lamont Antieau for reading various parts of this work and improving my English. I am likewise grateful to Prof. Johan van der Auwera and Matti Miestamo for the discussions on various occasions and for sharing their work-in-progress with me.

I would also like to extend a collective THANKS to the WALS project (World Atlas of Language Structures) at the Max Planck Institute for Evolutionary Anthropology, Leipzig, Germany, as well as to the people who provided or checked data for a lot of the language investigated in this study. They are too numerous to be mentioned here but without their assistance, there would have been no data for some languages and a lot more mistakes in others. Without the generous help of the WALS project and its directors, I would never been able to gain access to many of the grammars used in this study. I thank them for this, and in general for giving me the opportunity to work on a linguistic atlas. The language consultants are duly mentioned in the text, and every reference to personal communication should be interpreted as a big and hearty thanks.

Needless to say, the people mentioned above are not in any way responsible for the shortcomings of this work.

For the financial support which made the revision work possible I thank the Anna Ahlström and Ellen Terserus Foundation, Stockholm University, Sweden for the postdoc stipend 2004–2005 and the English Department at Eastern Michigan University, Ypsilanti, Michigan, USA for the release time in fall 2005 when the manuscript was finalized.

For the good times we had together and in the hope of more to come, thanks to Anette Åkerström, Maria Rokova, Mike Perini, Grosshandlare Sigurd Gustafsson, Styrbjörn Järnegård, Ted Weisberg, Rebecka Weisberg, and again Jennifer Spenader and Susan Robinson. Thank you, folks, for always being there, regardless of space and time.

In conclusion, this work is dedicated to the people who raised me with lots of devotion and love, and spent many years worrying and wondering what I was up to and where. To my grandparents, Vera and Stefan Stoykovi, and my parents, Zhivka and Nikola Veselinovi.

Ann Arbor, December 22nd, 2005

Abbreviations and presentation conventions

Abbreviations

1	first person	ERG	ergative
2	second person	EXCL	exclusive
3	third person	F	feminine
ABL	ablative	FOC	focus
ABS	absolutive	FUT	future
ACC	accusative	GEN	genitive
ADJ	adjective	HAB	habitual
ADV	adverb(ial)	HEST	hesternal past
AGR	agreement	HOD	hodiernal past
AOR	aorist	IMM	immediate
APPL	applicative	IMP	imperative
ART	article	IMPF	imperfect
ASP	aspect	IPFV	imperfective
AUX	auxiliary	INCL	inclusive
BEN	benefactive	IND	indicative
CAUS	causative	INDEF	indefinite
COLL	collective	INESS	inessive
COMP	complementizer	INF	infinitive
COMPL	completive	INSTR	instrumental
COND	conditional	INTR	intransitive
CONTR	contrafactual	LOC	locative
CONV	converb	M	masculine
DAT	dative	MOD	modal
DEF	definite	N	neuter
DEM	demonstrative	NEG	negation, negative
DET	determiner	NMLZ	nominalization
DIST	distal	NOM	nominative
DISTR	distributive	NONLOCUT	nonlocutor person marker
DS	different subject	OBJ	object
DU	dual	OBL	oblique
DUR	durative	OCS	Old Church Slavonic
EMP	emphatic		

OPT	optative	RDP	Reduplication
PASS	passive	REC	Recent past
PERF	perfect	REFL	reflexive
PFV	perfective	REL	relative
PL	plural	REM	Remote past
POSS	possessive	RES	Resultative
PRED	predicate	SBE	subjective
PREP	preposition	SBV	subjunctive
PRES	present	SG	singular
PRET	preterite	SS	same subject
PREV	preverb	SUB	subordinate clause
PROG	progressive	SUBJ	subject
PROX	proximal/proximate	TNS	tense
PST	past	TOP	topic
PTCP	participle	TR	transitive
PUNC	Punctual	TS	Thematic Suffix
PURP	purposive	VV	Version Vowel

Other presentation conventions

< between two forms indicates that the form on the left resulted from the form on the right.

* used with a double meaning.
   (i) to indicate reconstructed and non-attested forms as for example Indo-European *bhu 'become'
   (ii) to indicate non-grammatical forms such as *goed.

The following row and column headings are used in tables where the cross-linguistic distribution of suppletion is presented

Small sample	94 independent languages
WALS sample	193 languages (genetically biased)
No	Number of languages where paradigms with non-categorial suppletion are found
Weight values sum	Sum of the weight values of all languages where verbal number pairs are found.
Total sum of weight values	70 (each phylum is assigned the value 1; there are 70 phyla in the sample)
n/a	Non-applicable
\	"out of"

Transcription

The presentation of the data follows the orthographic conventions employed in grammars of individual languages. Phonematic transcription is used very sporadically, only in cases where it is immediately relevant. It appears in IPA between slashes, e.g. /aipi:ei/.

Level tones are presented following IPA unless other wise indicated. Thus,

- ʺ Extra high
- ʹ High
- ˉ Mid
- ˋ Low
- ˵ Extra low

Introduction

1. Preliminaries

The term **suppletion** is typically used to refer to the phenomenon whereby regular semantic and/or grammatical relations are encoded by unpredictable formal patterns. Standard examples are expressions of comparative and superlative degrees of the English adjectives *good* and *bad*, or the present and past tense forms of the English verb *go*.

(1) English
    a.   POSITIVE   COMPARATIVE   SUPERLATIVE
         good   *better*   *best*
         bad   *worse*   *worst*
    cf. *fine*   *finer*   *finest*
    b.   PRESENT   PAST
         go   *went*
    cf. *dance*   *danced*

Suppletive forms can also be found in nominal inflection, as for instance the formation of plural forms illustrated below by Bulgarian *čovek* 'human being'.

(2) Bulgarian (Indo-European, South Slavic)
    SINGULAR   PLURAL   Gloss
    čovek   *xora*   'human being'
    cf. *kniga*   *knigi*   'book'

Examples similar to (1) and (2) above can be observed in many languages. Since they appear as notable exceptions to language-specific morpho-syntactic patterns, the mainstream view of suppletion is to consider the phenomenon as random and exceptional.

    The first question to ask is whether such a view is fully legitimate and empirically grounded, given that cases of suppletion are attested cross-linguistically, usually with one and the same lexical items, and in similar grammatical categories. One could argue that a certain phenomenon has to be more than just a marginal irregularity if it can be shown to recur in a variety of different languages. The systematic nature of this recurrence, however, has yet to be shown. A complete study of suppletion should cover instances of the phenomenon with all main lexico-syntactic categories, such as nouns, verbs, adjectives etc. The current study had to be restricted to suppletion in verb paradigms, mainly for practical reasons.

The examples above are somewhat deceptive in the sense that they present suppletion as a rather simple phenomenon. However, both its definition as well as setting its limits are far from unproblematic in several respects. In the short examples I gave here as introductory illustrations, I avoided any discussion of the form of the suppletive items; I was also deliberately vague as regards the nature of the morpho-syntactic pattern they "break": whether it is mainly **inflectional** or **derivational** or something in between the two. The use of the term **paradigm** was omitted as well. It is well known that these notions are not only crucial for any linguistic theory but also defiant of any general agreement. The definition of suppletion is directly amenable to them and as such has received different interpretations in theoretical works and grammatical descriptions. As we shall see in the following chapters, the very definition of something that appears fairly straightforward is a controversial issue in the pertinent literature.

My interest in suppletion came as a narrowing-down of a broader interest in the interaction of lexicon and grammar, specifically in grammaticalization, the process whereby lexical items become grammatical forms, or grammatical forms are further reinterpreted to acquire new grammatical functions. Suppletive forms have an unclear status in the grammar and lexicon of the languages where they are attested. The phenomenon they represent is of interest for several reasons. First, early generative work ascribes them to the lexicon without too many quibbles. However, since these same words/forms typically have a strong grammatical component in their meaning, and many of them (verbs in particular) are often used with a number of grammatical functions, one wonders if relegating them to lexicon is entirely correct. Besides, from a perspective where lexicon and grammar are seen as two ends of a continuum rather than two separate modules of a language system, suppletive forms truly represent the gray area between the two. Second, as already mentioned in the preceding paragraph, suppletion as a theoretical notion is typically considered a rather straightforward phenomenon but a closer look at the existing definitions reveals a number of problems and controversies. As regards typology, the theoretical notion of suppletion is rarely tried out on a number of different languages. Related to this is another fact which makes suppletion interesting, namely, that the cross-linguistic distribution of the phenomenon has not been properly investigated. Neither do we know much about ways in which suppletive forms arise.

In the course of the years spent with suppletive verbs (probably one too many), I came to think of them as the Hamlets of the verb kingdom: everybody thinks they are crazy; but are they really? Or is it our way of looking at them that veers off? In the play, Polonius, somewhat puzzled, makes the observation *Though this be mad-*

ness, yet there is method in't. This is basically what I am striving to show with this work. And if at the end the reader is even partially convinced that there is a system to suppletive verbs, the time and effort spent on them will not have gone in vain.

2. Organization of this book

The study is organized as follows. In Chapter 1, I discuss previous studies on suppletion, definitions and treatments of the phenomenon. The method employed in this project is presented in Chapter 2. The notion of **paradigm** is further discussed in Chapter 3, together with a general overview of the data on suppletive verbs found in the current language sample. Chapters 4 through 7 present the most common cases of suppletion according to grammatical categories such as tense–aspect, agreement categories such as person and number, imperative mood, and verbal number. The material on tense–aspect suppletion had to be split into two chapters since the issues which had to be discussed were too numerous and diverse to fit into a chapter of reasonable length. The book closes with a summary of the current findings and suggestions for future research. The main bulk of the collected data can be found in appendices, references to which are indicated in specific chapters.

CHAPTER 1

Previous studies on suppletion

This chapter presents the notion of suppletion in its historical context as well as the way it is understood in contemporary linguistic theory. Section 1 gives a brief presentation of the history of the term **suppletion**. Various ways to understand and define the concept are presented in section 2.1. Different ideas about placing suppletion in a theoretical context as well as explanations of the phenomenon are discussed in section 2.2. Section 3 outlines problems with existing theories and presents the issues pursued in this study.

1. Historical notes

The word **suppletion** is a derivative of the Latin verb *suppleō* 'fill up; make up a whole; make up for a loss, deficiency; add something that is missing in order to complete a whole'. Sources that discuss the history of the linguistic use of the term are not readily available. Encyclopedias of linguistics (Bright 1992; Asher and Simpson 1994) as well as dictionaries of linguistic and grammatical terms (Hartmann and Stork 1972; Trask 1993) present its modern use only; these are often biased towards one school of linguistic thought and omit any historical references. Nor do current journal articles or morphology textbooks present anything on this issue; therefore, textbooks on general history of linguistics, dictionaries of Classical and Medieval Latin and the Romance languages, as well as thesauri of English have been used as main sources for the information summarized below.

The notion of suppletion is not found in linguistic works prior to the late nineteenth century. However, among the works of linguistic antiquity, a close call is found in the work of Pāṇini who makes a distinction between regular and irregular forms of substitution. Thus he lists Sanskrit roots such as *dr̥s* 'look, gaze, behold' and *pásya* 'look, see' and quite a few others that appear to him as irregular alternations. Specifically, he notes that the root *dr̥s* is never used with the present/imperfective affixes but the root *pásya* is used instead (Deshpande 1992: 18–19).

The Classical Greek grammarians appear to have been little preoccupied with morphological structure per se. Dionysus Thrax (ca. 170–90 BC) is said to have used the notion of 'filling up' ἀναπληρόω /anaplēóō/ in his grammar of Greek with regard to particles 'filling up' the sense of specific verbs. Thus the idea of an item 'filling up' or adding to the sense of another seems to have been present in Antiquity.

However, the Greek idea of 'filling up' appears to describe the combination of two lexical items such as a verb and a particle, not the situation of one lexical item 'filling up/supplying' the missing forms in the paradigm of another as in the modern sense of the term "suppletion".

The Roman grammarians paid more attention to the latter phenomenon because they were more interested in morphology than the Greeks. Two schools of Roman linguistics need to be mentioned here: the **anomalists** and the **analogists**.

The anomalistic approach to language focuses on actual spoken or written language as the basis of grammatical descriptions. Patterns in language were assumed, but there were also gaps or anomalies that could not be integrated into any linguistic pattern. These were facts linguists had to accept.

The analogists had a more structural approach to linguistic studies. Their credo was that languages were basically regular. As much as they possibly could, they tried to force linguistic data into regular patterns in which everything was neatly systematized. Irregular forms were either forced into a regular pattern by one form of trickery or another, or simply altered to fit such a pattern. An example of this is Varro's[1] invention of the form *esum* 'I am' to make a regular paradigm of the present indicative conjugation of the Latin verb *esse* 'to be' which was *sum* 'I am', *es* 'thou art' and *est* 'he/she is' (Varro 1958: 519). Varro is not to be taken as representative of the analogists, though, as he never joined either the anomalist or the analogist tradition. He is the only Roman linguist who actually gives us a fuller survey of the arguments of these two directions within linguistic antiquity. Although he did borrow from both, his treatment of the anomaly vs. analogy controversy remains intimately connected with his more or less idiosyncratic theory about the structure of language. Anomaly was, for him, identical with voluntary derivation and analogy equally typical for natural inflection.

The Early Medieval grammarians followed the philosophical line of the Ancient Greeks, so we do not find much about linguistic structure in their work. Descriptions of Latin intended to be used as pedagogical materials do, however, make a note of the **substantive verb** *esse*. Other irregular verbs in Latin such as *īre* 'go' and *ferre* 'carry' are described as either **defective**, **anomalous**, or, in some cases, **primitive** , and usually their paradigms are listed apart from all other verbs. In the nineteenth century, Franz Bopp and later the Neogrammarians continue to use these notions.

Deshpande (1992: 21), and ultimately Osthoff (1899: 7–15), bring up the work of Delbrück which has to be mentioned in a chronological outline of the term suppletion. Although Delbrück does not use it under that name, the notion as such is lurking in the conclusion of his description of aspectual verb pairs in Sanskrit:

---

1. Marcus Terentius Varro (116 BC–129 BC)

> Semantically related roots, which cannot by themselves express all aspects (German *Aktionen*) merge together into one verb. The clearest division takes place between present and aorist. The future may follow either from the present root as in *atsyáti* from *ad* 'eat', [...] or the aorist root as *vakṣyáti* from *vac* 'speak'. The perfect is formed mostly from the aorist root as [...] *jaghāsa* from *ghas* 'eat. AORIST', but also from the present root as *jaghāna* from *han* 'strike. PRESENT'.[2]

The term "suppletion" gradually makes its way into grammatical descriptions and other linguistic works in the late nineteenth century (Osthoff 1899; Thomas 1899: 79). In grammars it was probably triggered by the preceding notion of a defective paradigm; e.g. if a verb **lacks** a form in a certain category, it is **supplied** by some other verb. Osthoff in his work *Vom Suppletivwesen der indogermanischen Sprachen* (1899) is the first linguist to give a definition of suppletion based on Indo-European material—examples, which by now, have become well known: Latin *bon-us* 'good' vs. *melior* 'better' or *ferō* 'carry' vs. *tulī* 'have carried'; English *am* vs. *are* vs. *is* etc.

In linguistic theory of the twentieth century, 'suppletion' came to be fully established as a concept with the advent of **structuralism**, where the relation between form and meaning as well as the understanding of paradigmatic relationships became very important for a synchronic language description. Thus we find it first defined by Bloomfield in *A Set of Postulates for the Science of Language*:

> 49. Def. If in a construction all the component forms are irregular, the whole form is *suppletive*.
> If *go* be taken as the stem of the verb, then the past *went* is suppletive. Under this definition *better* as comparative of *good* would not be suppletive, since the ending -*er* is regular; a definition that will include such forms can be made only within English (or Indo-European) grammar, after 'stem' and 'affix' have been defined for this language. (Bloomfield 1926: 161)

It appears that for Bloomfield suppletive forms are by definition unanalyzable wholes. According to the initial definition other exceptions which yield to morphological analysis can be described as suppletive only once language specific notions such as **stem** and **affix** have been explicitly defined; furthermore suppletion is reserved for unpredictable substitution of stems only. In his later work, Bloomfield expands the definition to apply to substitution of affixes as well.

> In the extreme case, an alternant bears no resemblance to the other alternants. In *ox: oxen* the bound form added in the plural is [-n] instead of [-iz, -z, -s]. If the language does not show parallel cases which warrant out describing the deviant form in terms of phonetic modification, an alternant is of this sort is said to be **suppletive**; thus [-n] in

---

[2]. The translation from German is my own. I also added translations to the cited Sanskrit forms. The original text runs as follows: "Bedeutungsverwandte Wurzeln, von denen die einzelne nicht alle Aktionen ausdrücken kann, vereinigen sich zu einem Verbum. Eine deutliche Scheidung findet nut statt zwischen Präsens und Aorist. Das Futurum folgt bald der Präsenswurzel, so *atsyáti* zu *ad*, [...] bald der Aoristwurzel, so [...]*vakṣyáti* zu *vac*. Das Perfektum wird meist aus der Aoristwurzel gebildet, so [...]*jaghāsa* zu *ghas*, aber auch der Präsenswurzel, so *jaghāna* zu *han*".

> *oxen* is a suppletive alternant of [-iz, -z, -s] because English grammar shows no phonetic modification of [-iz] to [-n]. In other instances it is the underlying form which suffers suppletion. Beside the ordinary derivation of *kind : kinder, warm : warmer*, and so on, we have *good : better*, where the underlying word *good* is replaced by an entirely different form *bet-*, which we describe, accordingly, as a suppletive alternant of *good*. In the same way, the infinitive *be* suffers suppletion, by [i-], in the third-person present tense form *is* [iz]. In *child*: *children*, a suppletive alternant *-ren* of the bound form is accompanied by a phonetic modification of the underlying word.　(Bloomfield 1933: 215)

Thus, Bloomfield's second definition of suppletion puts an emphasis on morphophonology in that suppletive forms are exceptions that in no way can be captured by existing morpho-phonological alternations in a certain language. Suppletion can apply to both affixes and stems, and finally, suppletive forms are not morphologically analyzable.

2. Suppletion in contemporary linguistic theory (Chomsky and beyond)

2.1 Defining the concept

Many works on suppletion do not elaborate the notion beyond the definition given in the introduction of this book. Although the notion appears quite straightforward, a closer look at the existing definitions reveals that (i) there exists disagreement as to what is to be considered suppletive and what is not; (ii) working definitions are at times inaccurate or even misleading with regard to describing the available language data; (iii) some criteria need to be stated more explicitly, others need to be discarded altogether before the concept is applied to data from a variety of languages. As this study is typologically oriented, the first step is to state language independent criteria as to what it is we are looking for since examination of cross-linguistic data tends to put the scholar in a jungle of bewildering facts.

2.1.1 *Relevant notions*

When studying suppletion we inevitably come to discuss concepts that are crucial to any linguistic theory, such as **word, morpheme, affix, paradigm**, inflection and **derivation, regularity, grammatical category**, just to name some of the more relevant ones. All of these have been subject to much discussion and each of the terms has received a slightly different interpretation in just about any textbook or tradition (Hartmann and Stork 1972; Matthews 1974; Anderson 1985; Malkjær and Anderson 1991; Bright 1992; Trask 1993; Asher and Simpson 1994; Aronoff and Anshen 1998; Stump 2001). The list of references can go on ad infinitum. Since doing justice to all of them is an impossible task, I will present some generally accepted versions of the central notions and concentrate on the working definitions used by Mel'čuk

(1994), as his work is one of the few that take a cross-linguistic perspective on suppletion and will therefore be referred to at length throughout this book.

2.1.1.1 Morpheme

The term **morpheme** was coined by the Polish linguist Jan Baudouin de Courtenay in 1880, who used it to refer to a set of minimal linguistic signs with identical semantic content. For instance, in English the minimal signs /-iz/, /-s/ and /-en/ are all associated with the meaning 'plural' and thus they are specific representations of the abstract PLURAL morpheme. Baudouin de Courtenay purportedly used **morpheme** in an ambiguous way, both for the abstract sign as well as for minimal signs (Mugdan 1994: 2546).[3] Mel'čuk (1994: 344) is in agreement with the original definition except that he explicitly reserves 'morpheme' for the abstract morphological unit and uses **morph** and **allomorph(s)** for minimal linguistic signs.

> 10. Morph, morpheme, allomorph [**Morph** is an elementary segmental sign. Different morphs belong to <= are **allomorphs** of > the same morpheme if and only if they are fully synonymous and distributed according to sufficiently simple rules contingent on word-internal context. A morpheme is thus not a sign, but a set of signs. A morph is said to **manifest** the morpheme of which it is an allomorph. Formally, *manifest/ be manifested* is represented by a bidirectional double arrow ⇔]   (Mel'čuk 1994: 344)

Base, **root**, **stem** and **affix** are different kinds of morphs. They are distinguished by the kind of meaning associated with them. Traditionally base, root and stem are said to carry lexical meaning while affixes carry grammatical/derivational meaning. Depending on its position with regard to the root, an affix can be realized as a **prefix** (preceding the root as in un-*true*); **suffix** (following the root as in *sing-er*); **infix** (coming in the middle of the root as in Tagalog sulat 'to write' vs. *s-um-ulat* 'ACTOR writes'); **circumfix** (occurring on both sides of the root as in Georgian *ori* 'two' vs. me-*or-e* 'second').

Base, root and stem are often used interchangeably; however, in more rigid traditions **stem** is reserved for the form of the root to which affixes (typically inflectional affixes) are added. Thus a stem may consist of one root as in English *dive*, a root and an affix as in *diver* or a combination of roots as in *skydive*.

2.1.1.2 Word

The notion of word has effectively proven to defy any universal definition. It is customary to give an operational definition based on the level at which the analysis is performed. So, for instance, a 'word' for the purposes of phonological analysis need

---

3. For a more comprehensive survey of the development of theoretical notions such as morpheme, morpheme alternants and allomorphs as well as the use of these terms in different linguistic traditions, see (Mugdan 1994)

not coincide with the 'word' as a grammatical unit or with the 'word' in the dictionary. Since the material analyzed in this study comes for the most part from grammars, we shall adopt the definition offered by Mugdan (1994: 2552):

> In traditional grammar, *give, gives, giving, gave,* and *given* are said to be 'forms' of one word. A 'word' in this sense can be understood as a set of linguistic signs that share the same lexical meaning (e.g. 'transfer to the possession of another') but differ in their grammatical meanings (give.PRESENT vs. give.PAST etc.). It is an abstract unit similar to morpheme and likewise has been allotted a term that ends in '-eme,' viz. **lexeme** (again an ambiguous term).

Word is thus understood as an abstract sign. It is often used interchangeably with lexeme; the term **grammatical** is often used synonymously with **inflectional**.

The definition used here thus puts an emphasis on meaning as the central defining feature of a word; it also presupposes that we know what the difference between lexical and grammatical meaning is. It is well known that this distinction is not as easy to make as it is often expected to be. Bybee (1985) defines grammatical/inflectional meaning in terms of its applicability and generality: grammatical/inflectional meanings (morphemes) tend to be general and thus applicable to a large number of other morphemes. Lexical morphemes, on the other hand, show a higher degree of specificity and are thus much more restricted in their combinatorial possibilities with other morphemes. Lexical and grammatical meaning are not discrete entities but rather two ends of a continuum. Just as it is hard to distinguish between lexical and grammatical meaning, it is equally hard to tell apart derivation from inflection. The problems are very closely related and the discussion of the lexicon vs. grammar continuum inevitably leads to a discussion of derivation vs. inflection. When we discuss lexical vs. grammatical meaning, our focus is on defining semantic content per se; when we discuss derivation vs. inflection, we focus on the processes that create expressions for lexical and grammatical meaning, respectively. The discussion of this issue continues in the section on derivational vs. inflectional suppletion (see section 2.1.2.2).

2.1.1.3 Paradigm

Mel'čuk (1994: 343–6) lists a number of working definitions of concepts used in his monograph; however, he does not include an introduction to the notion of paradigm. It appears to be substituted by definitions of lexeme and its forms as **allolexes**; grammatical meaning which is realized either as a **grammeme** "obligatory and regularly expressed meanings such as the nominal number or verbal tense in English"; **derivatemes** "meanings which, without being obligatory or always regular, are expressed similarly to grammemes—by the same type of morphological means, like affixes or alternations such as the agent (*-er*) or the abstract noun (**-ness**) in English". Mel'čuk states that for "the sake of simplicity" syntactic meanings are ignored.

Finally he introduces the notion of REGULARITY,[4] which is defined by the existence of (any) kind of rules regardless of their **productivity**. Thus he distinguishes DEGREES of regularity since not all rules in a language are equally productive. The notions outlined by Mel'čuk are generally adopted in my study as well.

Unlike Mel'čuk, however, I consider it important to introduce the notion of paradigm in a theoretical manner because the material investigated here uses paradigms presented in grammars. Moreover, there are authors who define suppletion exclusively within the limits of an existing paradigm, hence it is important to know what a paradigm is. Finally, when discussing the emergence of suppletion, we frequently refer to the notion of paradigm restructuring.

Carstairs-McCarthy (1998: 323) defines paradigm as the entire set of "actually or potentially distinct word forms belonging to a lexeme […] associated, […] with some morphosyntactic property or combination of properties". Each individual property or property combination within this set is called a 'cell'. A simple illustration of this are the forms of the English verb 'give'.

(1) English, adopted from Carstairs-McCarthy (1998: 324)
    PAST   *gave*
    NON-PAST THIRD SINGULAR   *gives*
    PERFECTIVE or PASSIVE   *given*
    PROGRESSIVE   *giving*
    BASIC (used in all other syntactic contexts) *give*

The traditional assumption is that all or nearly all members of the same lexico-syntactic category in a given language are inflected for the same inflectional properties. Carstairs-McCarthy (1998: 324) notes two kinds of deviations from this pattern:

(i) when a lexeme lacks expected forms.
(ii) when a lexeme shows some unexpected extra forms.

A lot of cases described as (i) can be easily explained by semantic or syntactic properties of the lexeme in question. For instance, weather verbs such as *rain* or *snow* in English typically occur only in impersonal constructions with a dummy subject such as *it rains/rained*. The use of such verbs in other constructions is generally ruled out.[5] A description of a verb such as *rain* that lists uses other than the impersonal as 'missing' is thus not justified. Carstairs-McCarthy reserves the term **defective paradigm** for cases where obvious semantico-syntactic motivation is not

---

4. The use of small capitals follows the original.
5. Metaphorical and/or ironic uses such as *You rained on this party* are of course possible. But such statements produce the desired effect exactly because they violate normal usage.

present as in the case of the archaic English verb *quoth* 'said' used in the past tense only to introduce direct quotations.[6]

Judging by the way (ii) is illustrated one is led to believe that Carstairs-McCarthy means by extra forms the "overpopulation of a cell". His example is the inflection of the Russian noun *les* 'forest' which shows two forms of the locative case, *v lesu* 'in the forest' and *o lese* 'concerning the forest'. Here we should also include the case where an "unexpected" category appears in a verbal paradigm. For example, in Irish most verbs do not have special forms in subordinate clauses. A few verbs, however, do show such forms; they are usually referred to as **dependent** forms in Irish grammars whereas the forms used in main clauses are labeled **absolute** forms. The verbs in question are *bheirim* 'give', *chím* 'see' and *deirim* 'say' partial paradigms of which are shown below compared with the regular *deinim* 'do'.

(2) Irish (Indo-European, Celtic) (Dillon and Ó Cróinin 1961: 203–07)

	bheirim	*chím*	*deirim*	*deinim*
	'give'	'see'	'say'	'do'
Absolute 1SG PRES	*bheirim*	*chím*	*deirim*	*deinim*
Dependent 1SG PRES	*tugaim*	*feicfead*	*abraim*	*deinim*

Since the verbs quoted above are the only verbs in Irish which make the distinction between absolute and dependent forms, the dependent ones can be considered "extra" forms in their paradigms.

With regard to morphosyntactic categories and the internal structure of paradigms, including stem allomorphy and suppletion, Bybee (1985), whose work will be discussed at length in the chapters to follow, offers a model that predicts which semantico-syntactic categories are most likely to be expressed inflectionally with verbs: Valence, Voice, Aspect, Tense, Mood, Number, Person of subject, Person of object and Gender. Of these, the most frequent is Mood, followed by Person, Number, Aspect and Tense; least frequent are Gender and Valence. She proposes the principles of 'relevance' and 'generality' to account for this distribution. The most frequent inflectional categories are those which are both highly relevant, in that their semantic content "directly affects or modifies" the semantic content of the stem (Bybee 1985: 13), and highly general, in that their semantic content is applic-

---

6. Incidentally, forms similar to *quoth* are cross-linguistically very common. cf. *inquit* in Latin (Östen Dahl, p.c.) are equally defective, that is, they are used only in third-person past and to introduce direct quotations. Östen Dahl (p.c.) and Maria Koptjevskaja-Tamm (p.c.) cite a quotative particle in Russian *mol* 'said' which historically comes from the verb *molvit* 'speak'; the form *mol*, however, has long ceased to be a verb and currently used as an evidential marker. Generally, it is very common for verbs meaning 'say' to show such "defective" paradigms and even evolve as quotative markers and complementizers of various kinds (cf. Heine and Kuteva (2002) for a relatively recent reference). So the 'lack' of forms in their paradigms may have a functional motivation too.

able to all or almost all verbs. Likewise, the principles of 'relevance' and 'generality' can be evoked when explaining the occurrence of allomorphy and suppletion in verb paradigms (Bybee 1985: 92). In her sample most cases of suppletion occur along aspectual lines, followed by tense and less commonly along mood lines; the number of cases of suppletion along person agreement lines is substantially lower.[7] Since both the relevance principle as well as Bybee's model of paradigm organization are used extensively in this work, they are presented in greater detail in the Chapter 3: 1, immediately preceding the general overview of the data.

2.1.2 *Kinds of suppletion depending on the kinds of linguistic signs it affects*
2.1.2.1 Affixal vs. stem suppletion
Although most definitions restrict suppletion to stem replacement (Matthews 1974; Rudes 1980), one could, with Bloomfield, include also affixal replacement, as in English plural suffixes, cf. Carstairs-McCarthy (1994: 354):

(3) English

	SINGULAR	PLURAL	
a.	*shop*	*shops*	/ʃɔps/
b.	*boy*	*boys*	/bɔiz/
c.	*ox*	*oxen*	/oksən/

In (3a) and (3b) the plural morphs /s/ and /z/ respectively are phonologically conditioned: /s/ after a voiceless consonant, /z/ after a vowel; /ən/ in (3c) is not conditioned by the preceding segments. Thus allomorphs of one and the same grammatical morpheme that are not phonologically conditioned are considered suppletive. According to Carstairs-McCarthy affixal suppletion is a much more widespread phenomenon than stem suppletion.

The notion of suppletion has also been stretched to cover relations between two forms of an idiom or between an idiom and a megamorph[8] as in (4c) and (4d) below.

(4) Russian, adopted from Mel'čuk (1994: 363)
    a. *govorit' krasno*   'talk magniloquently, to blarney'
    b. *krasnobaj*   'one who talks magniloquently, who blarneys'
    c. *molot' jazykom*   lit. 'to thrash with one's tongue' = 'to talk nonsense'
    d. *pustozvon*   'one who talks nonsense'

---

7. Bybee also quotes Rudes (1980) to confirm this observation; as we shall see below the generalizations offered by Rudes are based on his definition of suppletion which is not widely accepted.

8. Mel'čuk uses the term *megamorph* to refer to a semantically decomposable but formally indecomposable sign which may also include an affix (either derivational or inflectional). Generally, his term *megamorph* corresponds roughly to the more familiar term *portmanteau morph*.

Mel'čuk considers morph, megamorph and idiom to be MINIMAL SEGMENTAL signs. Moreover, in addition to stretching the limits of suppletion, Mel'čuk does so also with the notion of derivation. According to him, the noun in (4b) is a derivational correspondent of the idiom in (4d) "from a purely semantic point of view" (ibid: 363); as a consequence, the noun *pustozvon* in (4d) is to be considered suppletive with regard to the idiom in (4c). This is rather problematic, even according to his own criteria since for him a megamorph is a formally undecomposable linguistic unit; but the word *pustozvon* consists of two morphemes, *pusto-* and *zvon*, thus it does not satisfy the formal criterion for megamorph. Besides, it is questionable whether the process whereby a noun is derived from a corresponding idiom is a full fledged productive derivation in Russian.

As my study is concentrated on suppletion of stems, specifically stems in verb paradigms, I shall have little to say about all other kinds of suppletion. However, the reader should be aware of the kinds of linguistic signs the notion has been used to cover so far.

2.1.2.2 Derivational vs. inflectional suppletion

It is customary to distinguish between **inflectional** vs. **derivational** suppletion, although this suggests a sharp distinction between inflection and derivation, which, as I have already mentioned (cf. 2.1.1.2 *Word*), is notoriously hard to make, similarly to the distinction between lexical and grammatical meaning. That is, an exact boundary between inflection on the one hand, and derivation on the other, is usually impossible to set up.

The issue is, however, important for several reasons. First, certain kinds of suppletion are subject to a great deal of disagreement mainly because derivational suppletion is simply not accepted as such by a number of scholars. On the other hand, general works in linguistics refer freely to derivational suppletion. So there are conflicting views as to whether exceptions to derivational patterns may or even should be considered suppletive or not, but the issue is never overtly discussed. Second, it is not always entirely clear where one is to draw the line between suppletive forms related in a derivational way on the one hand, and separate lexical items on the other. In this respect, suppletion draws the limit of the possible word. The issue is, of course, as difficult as defining *word* in a universal, unambiguous way. I do not hope to arrive at a final and definitive solution here but an awareness of the problem is necessary. It will help us see where terminological battles and discrepancies come from, and I believe this problem can be used in an instructive way while we seek to understand the nature of suppletion. Bybee's (1985: 81–109) discussion of differences between inflection and derivation will be used as a starting point to further determine suppletion along the inflectional-derivational scale.

Bybee proposes the following criteria for the distinction of inflection and derivation: obligatoriness of the process, lexical generality, lexical specificity, and finally, the semantic relevance principle. None of these are absolute but rather, are valid to varying degrees. Thus inflection and derivation are seen in Bybee's model not as discrete expression types but rather as two ends of a continuum. For instance, any time an English verb is used, it has to be specified for tense either by means of ablaut as in *sing* vs. *sang* or by means of a dental suffix as in *dance* vs. *dance-d*. Tense is thus an obligatory category for English verbs (at least most English verbs; the modal verbs do not follow the tense requirement as closely). Tense is also rather general and its scope is the entire proposition (i.e. the entire proposition is specified for location in time). Thus, *go* and *went* are a case of inflectional suppletion according to tense because tense is an inflectional category for English verbs.

A derivational category, on the other hand, is typically optional; it may involve a change of lexical meaning as in *like* vs. *dis-like* or a change of lexical class as in **glory** vs. *glori-ous*. Members of a certain class may make use of the available derivational means, but they don't have to. This, however, is subject to a great deal of variation. Bybee (1985: 84) invokes the example of deriving adverbs from adjectives in English by means of the suffix *-ly*. The suffix has full lexical generality in the sense that any member of the category adjective can take it, and it may be argued that it is required by the syntax of the phrase where it is used. So, this kind of derivation comes very close to inflection: it is semantically general and it is required by syntax.[9] Thus, exceptions to it, such as *good* vs. *well*(*goodly*) may, according to Bybee, be thought of as suppletive (obviously she restricts the term suppletion to exceptions to inflectional patterns only).

Other kinds of derivation are more restricted. In English, some nouns may derive feminine forms by means of a suffix as in *tiger* vs. *tigr-ess*. This, however, does not mean that English nouns inflect for gender, but merely that gender derivation is possible for certain (usually animate) nouns in English.

Derivational suppletion is typically illustrated by exceptions to an otherwise regular pattern such as the case where the name of the inhabitant is derived from the name of a settlement, here illustrated by French.

(5) French, adopted from (Mel'čuk 1994: 381)

CITY	INHABITANT
Paris	*Paris-ien*
Berlin	*Berlin-ois*
London	*London-ien*

---

9. This statement may in fact become even stronger if we consider data from other languages. For instance in Swedish, adjectives are typically inflected for gender, non-neuter as in *en djup sjö* 'a deep lake' vs. neuter *ett djupt hav* 'a deep sea'; in the adverbial function only the neuter adjective can be used as in *Han sov djupt* 'he slept deeply/soundly' (Östen Dahl, p.c.).

CITY	INHABITANT
Bésançon	*Bisont-in*
Rodez	*Ruthén*
Fontainebleau	*Bellifont*
Le Puy	*Anic-ien/Ponot*

Another equally straightforward example of derivational suppletion would be exceptions to derivations of ordinal numerals as in *four* vs. *fourth* but *one* vs. *first*. However, exceptions to other kinds of derivation appear problematic as to whether they are to be described as separate lexical items or as derivationally related forms. For example, for Mel'čuk, the Russian nouns *byk* 'bull' and *korova* 'cow.FEM' are suppletive according to gender when considered against the background of a regular derivation of feminine nouns from masculine ones as in (6).

(6) Russian, adopted from (Mel'čuk 1994: 362)

	'elephant'	'tiger'	'donkey'	'cow'
MASC	*slon*	*tigr*	*osël*	*byk*
FEM	*slon-ixa*	*tigr-ica*	*osl-ica*	*korova*

One is immediately reminded of the quite similar derivational pattern in English and other Germanic languages (the English one was mentioned above). Following Mel'čuk's line of reasoning, *cow* and *bull* should be considered suppletive in English because they stand out as exceptions to the said derivational pattern. However, most English speakers tend to see *cow* and *bull* as two words that are related semantically, that is they refer to the same species but to rather different representatives of this species; thereby their referential content is different and thus it is more accurate to describe them as different words rather than derivationally related suppletive forms. As Mel'čuk admits in a footnote, it is not entirely settled whether *korova* and *byk* should be considered suppletive in Russian either. According to his own definition, it suffices that there exist SOME patterns in order to postulate suppletion so in this light such words should be considered suppletive. What Mel'čuk and other authors fail to note is that there are many cases which have an intermediate status between clear exceptions to inflectional patterns such as *go* vs. *went* and semantically related words such as *cow* vs. *bull*.

As we will encounter this problem again in Chapter 7 in the discussion of exceptions to patterns which derive verbal number pairs, a few other comments are in order. The issues at hand here are the productivity and scope of a derivational pattern, and implications for the nature of suppletion suggested by the difficulty of determining whether exceptions to derivational patterns are suppletive forms or different words.

Mel'čuk is not very consistent regarding the importance of productivity and scope of a derivational pattern when determining whether forms which appear as exceptions to it should be seen as suppletive or as different lexical items. These factors are important to him when postulating suppletion according to gender in Russian as gender derivation is widespread in this language; however it remains unclear how productive the derivation of nouns corresponding to idioms really is (cf. (4) above). The issue of productivity and generality of a derivational pattern is rarely discussed at length in relation to suppletion. Cases such as exceptions to derivation of ordinal numerals or the name of inhabitants from the name of settlements appear rather easy to classify as suppletion largely because the derivation, albeit optional, applies, or may be applied, to pretty much all members of the respective class. For example, it is probably not the case that all place names have a corresponding adjective in French but theoretically, all of them may have one. Besides, frequently used place names usually do have corresponding adjectives; those are typically derived in one and the same manner and exceptions to it appear as suppletive. Similarly, ordinal numerals are typically not derived for very high numbers; however, they are derived for lower ones, all in a similar straightforward manner.[10] Gender derivations of the kind illustrated in (6) are in many languages restricted to a certain class of nouns, usually semantically defined. According to Mel'čuk, in Russian the derivation illustrated above applies mostly to wild animals.[11] In English it is definitely restricted to wild animals and a few names of professions such as *waiter* vs. *waitress*, etc. So it appears that the more a derivational pattern is applicable to an entire lexical class, the stronger the paradigmatic relationship between the base of derivation and the derived item, and thereby, the exceptions are seen as suppletive. However, if the derivational pattern is very restricted, then exceptions to it do not appear as paradigmatically related, even in a derivational way, but rather as separate lexical items.

Derivational patterns and exceptions to them are instructive about the nature of suppletion in another respect. Namely, it is rarely, if ever, mentioned that suppletive forms may be seen as part of the gray area between lexicon and grammar. This aspect of suppletion will be emphasized further later in this work. When suppletive forms appear as exceptions to highly generalized inflectional patterns, they are closer to the grammatical end of the continuum; when they appear as exceptions to derivational patterns, they are, in varying degrees, closer to lexical end. As we shall see in the subsequent chapters, suppletion according to categories associated with verbs presents instances that can be placed at varying points on the grammatical-lexical scale.

---

10. The derivation of ordinal numerals is not cross-linguistically homogeneous but in a given language ordinals are always derived in one and the same way.

11. I believe this is not entirely correct as feminine derivations for names of professions exist as well, namely, *uchitel'* 'teacher.MASC' vs. *uchitel'nica* 'teacher.FEM' etc.

2.1.3 *Diachrony vs. Synchrony*

Bloomfield (see above) does not take diachrony into account when defining suppletion. There are authors though, such as Rudes (1980), who define as suppletive only those forms that are etymologically different.

Following Rudes the present tense forms of the verb 'be' in English *am/are/is* are to be considered **pseudo-suppletive** because they come from one and the same Proto-Indo-European root **es*. However, the present tense forms of the German verb 'be', cf. example (7) below, are to be analyzed and classified in a different way.

(7) German (Indo-European, West Germanic)

	SINGULAR	PLURAL
1	*bin*	*sind*
2	*bist*	*sinn*
3	*ist*	*sind*

The first and second person of the singular are suppletive with respect to all the other forms since they come from the Proto-Indo-European root **bheu* while all the others are etymologically derived form the Proto-Indo-European **es*. So according to Rudes, the German verb 'be' is to be classified as suppletive according to person and number in the present tense, while the same verb in English is to be considered pseudo-suppletive. Such a classification is, however, problematic. There are no morpho-phonological rules that derive the present tense person–number forms of this verb from one another in either language. Thus the alternation *am/are/is* is as isolated in the verb system of Enlgish as *bin/bist/ist* is in the verb system of German. This fact should be captured by a synchronic linguistic description. Considerations of the origin of the suppletive forms should be taken into account only when explaining how and why suppletion emerged.

The view whereby only etymologically different forms are defined as suppletive has been subject to criticism, cf. Mel'čuk (1994) but, except for Mel'čuk, it is rarely explicitly rejected. As Mel'čuk (1994: 355) puts it "etymological considerations should play no role in defining a theoretical concept". Further reasons for discarding etymology from the definition of suppletion are as follows: (i) Etymologies per se are often a question of dispute and frequently very uncertain. (ii) If we are to accept that only etymologically unrelated forms are to be considered suppletive, then we arrive at synchronically erroneous descriptions. (iii) A definition based on etymology makes a typologically oriented study practically impossible as historical information of this kind is not available for many of the world languages (Martin Haspelmath, p.c.).

2.1.4 Formal characteristics of suppletive forms
2.1.4.1 Phonological distance

A great deal of attention has been paid to the morphology of the suppletive forms as regards their degree of deviation from regular derivational or inflectional patterns. Thus, suppletion is seen as a **gradable** phenomenon. Dressler (1985) differentiates between **weak** and **strong** suppletion. Weak suppletion is exemplified in Dressler (Dressler 1985: 98) by forms such as *child* versus *children*, whereas an illustration of strong suppletion is the paradigm of the verb 'to be' in English. Similarly, Mel'čuk (1994: 344) regards suppletion as "a gradable relation between linguistic units which are semantically related in a regular way (that is, units which are supposed to appear in one and the same paradigm)". In his view there are two polar degrees of suppletion on the formal side: **formally strong**, or **genuine** suppletion, and **formally weak**, or **quasi** suppletion. These types reflect two ends of a continuum rather than an either-or opposition. Strong suppletion is usually easy to delimit as in the typical case there is no shared phonological material between the suppletive forms. Weak suppletion is harder to define rigidly because there is usually some phonological material shared between the suppletive forms, or they are produced by a phonological alternation which albeit restricted is still a valid one in the language, cf. "when getting formally weaker, suppletion gradually edges into regular enough alternations. There is a continuum of lowering formal suppletivity-from formally strong suppletion down to zero suppletion, with an infinity of intermediate cases" Mel'čuk (1994: 379).

2.1.4.2 Uniqueness

Since a sharp line cannot be drawn as to which weak suppletives should still be included in the lot, Mel'čuk introduces the criterion of ***uniqueness*** (1994: 367). The French third class verbs are often described in textbooks of French as irregular; but in fact, the phenomenon they represent makes them very similar to the class of strong verbs in languages such as English or Swedish (or any Germanic language for that matter), e.g. there exist inflectional patterns for them as well, albeit very restricted ones. Mel'čuk uses the verbs *pouvoir* 'can' and *mouvoir* 'move' to illustrate this point. If compared to a first class verb such as *demander* 'ask', such verbs appear irregular, cf. example (8), but a pattern can be described for them together with a dozen other verbs. Thus they are not to be considered suppletive.

(8) French (Indo-European, Romance), adapted from Mel'čuk (partial paradigms)

	demander 'ask'	*pouvoir* 'can'	*mouvoir* 'move'
1SG PRESENT	*demande*	*peux*	*meux*
1PL PRESENT	*demandons*	*pouvons*	*mouvons*

According to Mel'čuk's criteria, the alternation *i-* vs. *all-* in the French verb *aller* 'go' is suppletive because both the criterion of phonological distance and uniqueness are satisfied.

In cases of weak suppletion, it suffices with uniqueness alone for an alternation to be considered suppletive. For example, Mel'čuk considers the Russian forms *čelovek* 'person' vs. *ljud-i* 'persons, people' as suppletive according to nominal number as there is no formal resemblance between them so both criteria (phonological distance and uniqueness) are satisfied; on the other hand, *child* vs. *childr-en*[12] in English are phonologically similar but this particular alternation is said to be unique in English, therefore they are still suppletive, however less so than the Russian example. (For further discussion and the way this criterion was adopted here, consult Chapter 2: 4)

2.1.4.3 Analyzability /Segmentability of the suppletive forms

Although a great deal of attention has been paid to the degree of irregularity of suppletive forms in terms of their phonological distance, the extent to which they are morphologically segmentable seems to have been less important for scholars so far. Mel'čuk (1994: 365–275) makes a distinction between **radical suppletion** and **radical megamorph suppletion**, which at first glance seems to be doing the job, that is to differentiate between suppletive forms that are still analyzable in terms of a root/stem and affixes, and suppletive forms which are not analyzable at all. The category 'radical suppletion' appears to be reserved for cases where the stem change occurs according to a single inflectional category, and the individual forms in their specific paradigms can be segmented into stems and inflectional affixes (see (9) below). The category labeled 'radical megamorph suppletion' is less clear. Generally, it is said to cover cases where the suppletive forms are portmanteau morphs as in English *am* 'be.1.SG.PRES' vs. *was* 'be.1/3.SG.PAST'. However, the exemplification of radical megamorph suppletion in Mel'čuk's monograph shows that it is at best too broad as a category since it puts on a par cases that are by no means parallel.

The two categories, radical suppletion and radical megamorph suppletion, are illustrated as follows. Radical suppletion is illustrated by a number of examples both from noun and verb inflection, one of which is adopted in (9).

---

12. This is not to refute Mel'čuk's point as it is still valid but the application of his own criteria is not entirely waterproof. First, the morphological analysis whereby *childr-* is interpreted as a stem appears somewhat arbitrary. Mel'čuk never provides any arguments why *children* is to be segmented as *childr-en* and not as *child-ren*. Second, if we are to accept it, then the alternation *brother* vs. *brethren* needs to be taken into account, which in turn makes the case *child* vs. *children* less unique than Mel'čuk claims it to be. A better example would have been a verb that is really unique like the Spanish verb *decir* 'say', which has a completely idiosyncratic paradigm in the present tense albeit without prototypical stem change e.g. *digo, dices, dice, decimos, decís, dicen* cf. *comer* 'eat': *como, comes, come, comemos, coméis, comen*.

(9) Russian (Indo-European, East Slavic), adopted from Mel'čuk, (1994: 367)
    id-u go.PRES-1.SG.PRES 'I go'
    šë-l go.PST-1.SG.M.PST 'I went'

The example is consistent with the definition: *id-* and *šë-* alternate according to the inflectional category tense, while preserving the regular inflectional suffixes for those tenses in Russian. Other examples in this section are not entirely unproblematic.[13]

Radical megamorph suppletion is exemplified in (10), (11) and (12) below.

(10) French, (Indo-European, Romance), adopted from Mel'čuk (1994: 371)
                      être 'be'   *aller* 'go'
    1SG PRESENT *suis* /sui/ *vais* /ve/
    3SG PRESENT *est* /ɛ/   *allons* /alõ/

(11) German (Indo-European, Germanic), adopted from Mel'čuk (Mel'čuk 1994: 371)
                      sein 'be'
    1SG PRESENT *bin*
    2SG PRESENT *bist*
    3SG PRESENT *sind*

Examples (10) and (11) illustrate suppletion of verbal radical megamorphs according to person and number. Apart from *allons* above, none of the others can be further segmented into separate morphemes in any way and according to the definition of megamorph above, this is what we expect. However, consider the Russian example in (12).

(12) Russian, Mel'čuk (Mel'čuk 1994: 371)
                  'take'
    IMPERFECTIVE *brat'*
    PERFECTIVE   *vz'at'*

"The morphemic representation of the forms involved is as follows:"[14]

---

13. The Greek examples, one of which is *lé(+o)* vs. *(e+)íp(+a)* 'I say' present vs. past (Mel'čuk, 1994: 368) are cited to illustrate radical suppletion according to tense. First, such a description is somewhat misleading as the quoted Greek verbs change stems according to aspect rather then tense but this becomes clear only of one looks at the entire paradigms of these verbs; Mel'čuk never quotes whole paradigms. Second, the example shows some inconsistency as to the presentation of the forms: if the augment is posited for the perfective forms, it should be posited for the imperfective as well because it is definitely used there.

14. The presentation follows Mel'čuk. This author uses curly brackets for underlying stems and abstract meanings. The double arrow is used to formally represent the relation *manifest/be manifested*, cf. 2.1.1.1. *Morpheme* above.

{BR(+at')}, {IMPERF} ⇔ **br,**
{BR(+at')}, {PERF}   ⇔ **v/z'/**, etc."

Mel'čuk claims that *brat'* and *vz'at'* are radical megamorphs according to aspect because with them the root expresses the lexical meaning and the aspectual meaning "cumulatively", that is these meanings are, in his words "fused together". None of the verbs can take prefixes indicating aspect only. Prefixation is otherwise widely used to encode aspect in Russian (see further discussion on this issue in Chapter 4: 2.2). This is well and good, and still consistent with Mel'čuk's definition. The example is, however, confusing in other respects. First, positing the underlying stem as {BR} is purely arbitrary; it might as as well have been posited as {V/Z'}. Second, and more important, the whole category of radical megamorph suppletion appears problematic as it covers examples such as (10) and (11) on the one hand, and (12) on the other; thus it lumps together forms such as the person–number forms of the 'be' verbs in French and German, and verbs such as the Russian aspectual pairs *brat'* vs. *vz'at'* 'take', *govorit'* vs. *skazat'* 'say' (Östen Dahl, p.c.). Such a classification leaves out important language facts and puts on a par phenomena which are not entirely parallel. As it was mentioned above, the 'be' verbs in French and German not only have present tense forms which are morphologically unsegmentable; these verbs present stem alternations across several categories in the paradigm, and are on the whole complete isolates in the verb systems of French and German, respectively. The Russian aspectual verb pairs use one stem per category (IMPERFECTIVE vs. PERFECTIVE) but otherwise "behave" similarly to the rest of the verbs in Russian, without further complications in their paradigms. So the difference between the 'be' verbs in French and German and the aspectual verb pairs in Russian is significant and a typology of suppletion should make a stronger case of it than is done in Mel'čuk's work (Östen Dahl, p.c). In this study a distinction is proposed between **categorial** and **non-categorial suppletion** in order to make this distinction, cf. Chapter 2: 4.4 for definition and examples.

2.2 Treatments and explanations for suppletion

The phenomenon of suppletion has evoked different reactions among linguists. There is a strong tendency to regard it as something completely arbitrary and thus uninteresting; this is matched by an equally strong tendency to consider suppletion "marginal" and "accidental", and generally as non-functional historical residue. Some linguists see a psychological motivation for it in that suppletive items are very common words which express everyday notions; thus closeness to speaker[15] is

---

15. The notion is clarified and discussed in section 2.2.3.4 under the original German term *Nahbereit*.

said to be a crucial factor for the occurrence of suppletive forms. (It is often unclear whether the psychological motivation operates diachronically or synchronically, or on both levels). Other scholars explain suppletion generally in terms of frequency of use and economy of expression. Finally, an approach taken often in the 1990's is to view suppletion not as a residue but as a well motivated product of various processes of language change. Each one of these ideas is discussed below.

2.2.1 Suppletion belongs to the lexicon = uninteresting
2.2.1.1 Generative Grammar

Morphology was not a separate component of early generative grammar. Affixation and compounding were considered within the domain of syntax whereas the interpretation of strings of morphemes and accompanying syntactic features that resulted from the application of syntactic rules were treated as part of the phonological component (Hammond and Noonan 1988: 2). Given this, it is hardly surprising that suppletion is barely mentioned either as a phenomenon or a problem to any of the formal models which dominated the linguistic thought in the 1960s. Sporadic reference to forms such as *went* as the past tense of *go* occur only to relegate those to the lexicon, which at the time was considered the repository of all the arbitrary items of a grammar. Regardless of later developments within generative morphology the approach to swiftly do away with suppletive forms by assigning them to the lexicon persists even in later work, (cf. Mohanan 1986: 53, Scalise 1986: 105).

As morphology made its way back into formal models, (cf. Halle 1973), a great deal of attention was devoted to word formation rules and subsequently the separation of derivation and inflection as well as their relation to other components of the model, specifically the lexicon and the syntactic component. Aronoff (1976) was the first scholar to provide a comprehensive model of word formation within the generative tradition. His main innovation was to replace the morpheme with the word as the minimal unit of a generative morphology (Hammond and Noonan 1988: 5). He also introduced the notion of **blocking** (Aronoff 1976: 43) which "is the nonoccurrence of one form due to the simple existence of another". This notion was initially used to explain the non-application of otherwise fully productive derivational affixes. For instance, the suffix *-ity* in English regularly produces semantically related abstract nouns from adjectives of the form X*ous*; this kind of derivation, however, fails with certain adjectives although they have the appropriate form.

(13)　Adopted from Aronoff (1976: 44)
　　　various　variety
　　　curious　curiosity
　　　glorious　*gloriosity　glory

The derivation of **gloriosity* is blocked by *glory* which already exists in the speakers lexicon. In his later work Aronoff (Aronoff and Anshen 1998: 239) uses blocking to explain the occurrence of irregular plural forms such as *women* instead of the fully possible but non-occurring *womans* as well as the occurrence of suppletive forms in inflectional paradigms as in the case of *went* instead of **goed*. At first glance, the notion of blocking as well as the explanation it entails does hold a certain appeal, but it is still inadequate to fully account for suppletion. First, concerning language acquisition, Aronoff claims that first or second language learners of English would not produce the form **goed*. However, evidence from first language acquisition shows that English children tend to go through three distinct stages as regards the acquisition of such suppletive forms, namely: first they say *went*; at a later stage they make an overgeneralization and use *goed*, and at the third stage they start producing *went* again. Second, even if we are to accept that *went* blocks **goed* because it already exists in the mental lexicon, blocking does not explain emergence of suppletive forms. In this case, it remains unclear how *went* came to replace the previous suppletive form *ēode,* which was used in the Old and Early Middle English periods.[16]

Both in early as well as later models of generative morphology, suppletion is either ignored or at best assigned to lexicon, thus implicitly stating that no further explanation is necessary. The only notion from generative models that can possibly be taken as an account for suppletion is the phenomenon of blocking discussed above. Mainstream textbooks of morphology maintain and even reinforce these views. In Matthews (1974), suppletion is seen as a problem for regular inflection rules. Suppletive alternations are treated as simple entries in the mental lexicon, and as such they are considered to stand completely outside of the main conjugational patterns in a given language. The topic of suppletion *per se* is not allotted a detailed discussion anywhere in the book. Rather, it is touched upon in passing when problems for posited rules or definitions of inflection need to be identified. Similarly, Spencer (1991: 8) states that "there is a limit to phonological explanation in pretty well everyone's theory, and that limit is the phenomenon known as **suppletion**. This is illustrated by the type of alternation between *go* and its past tense form *went.*" In *Handbook of Morphology* (Spencer and Zwicky 1998) suppletion is mentioned only in passing in two articles, Aronoff and Anshen (1998) and Carstairs-McCarthy (1998).

Thus, in many versions of generative grammar, with its goal of constructing an adequate formal model of human language in which phonology, morphology, syntax and lexicon are seen as separate abstract components, the phenomenon of suppletion is considered so marginal and arbitrary that it is hardly a problem worth discussing. Rather, it becomes an acknowledged problem for another formal, though

---

16. For further examples on the emergence of suppletion despite existence of regular forms, consult Chapter 6:3, examples (137) and (138).

more semiotically (functionally) oriented school of morphology, namely Natural Morphology and related approaches, presented in the next section.

2.2.2 Suppletion: "the problem child"
2.2.2.1 Natural Morphology

Natural Morphology (hereafter NM), which flourished as a school in the 1980s, explored the concept of **markedness**[17] as first formulated by Nikolaj Trubetzkoy in 1931/(1969) for phonological systems and first applied to morphology by Roman Jakobson in 1939/(1971). The Natural Morphology school seeks to formulate principles of naturalness in morphological systems. Its domain is a specific class of universal characteristics of the human language faculty in the area of morphology. The major representatives of the school are Mayerthaler, Bittner, Dressler (Dressler 1985; Dressler et al. 1987) and Wurzel. The main universal principles, as articulated by Mayerthaler (1981: 23–35, 1987: 48–9), are as follows:

1. Principle of constructional iconicity/diagrammaticity
2. Uniform encoding: maximal when every form always has the same meaning and every meaning is represented by the same form.
3. Transparency: includes both semantic transparency—the notion of that the meaning of a word should predictable from the meaning of its constituent morphemes—and morphotactic transparency.

Fertig (1998: 1097) points out that suppletion violates all of these principles and thus, for Mayerthaler, it is quite 'unnatural':

> It always violates uniform encoding, at least as far as the stem is concerned, since the meaning of the lexical item is represented by a different form in each of the suppletive stems. Suppletion also violates "transparency" since each stem gives us information about grammatical categories as well as lexical identity. On the constructional iconicity scale, suppletive paradigms are, at best, less than maximally iconic (*good* vs. *better*), often minimally iconic (*much* vs. *more*), and sometimes even countericonic (*little* vs. *less*)".

Dressler (1985: 97–9) formulates an eight-point scale of morphotactic transparency. Point 'I' is most natural/least marked; point 'VIII' is least natural.

(14) Morphotactic transparencies scale, adopted from Dressler (1985: 98)

I	II	III	IV
Intrinsic allophonic PRs	PRs intervene e.g. resyllabification	Neutralizing PRs e.g. flapping	MPRs (no fusion) velar softening
excite + ment	*exist + ence*	*rid + er (AmE)*	*electric + ity*
excite	*exist*	*ride*	*electric*

---

17. For a brief discussion of this concept, consult Chapter 3: 1.

V	VI	VII	VIII
MPRs with fusion	MRs intervene, e.g. Great Vowel Shift	Weak suppletion	Strong suppletion (no rules!)
conclusion	*decision*	*childr-en*	*be, am, are, is, was*
conclude	*decide*	*child*	

Note: PR = phonological rule; MPR = morphophonemic rule; MR = morphological rule; AmE = American English

Following the scale above, suppletion is the ultimate example of "unnaturalness." NM predicts that the most unnatural techniques should be non-existent or marginal. According to Dressler this is certainly borne out with suppletion as it is supposedly restricted to languages with inflectional morphology; agglutinative languages such as Hungarian, Finnish and Turkish are said not to have any suppletion at all (Dressler 1985: 101). The latter statement, however, contains a gross mistake because as the data in Chapter 3 and subsequent chapters demonstrate, both Hungarian and Finnish have occurrences of verb suppletion though not as many as in, say, Lezgian or Irish[18] (consult also Appendix 3 on number of suppletive verbs per language). As for the more general correlation of agglutinative morphology with suppletion, Haspelmath (2000) provides empirical evidence that there are no valid statistical grounds for such a conclusion. Regardless of the fact that Dressler finds suppletion completely unnatural according to the morphotactic transparency scale, he still proposes a functionally oriented account for the existence of suppletion in terms of differentiation of items that are important for "man, for peasant economy" and in terms of economy of expression (Dressler 1985: 105, 107). Both of these approaches are discussed in greater detail below.

The "system-independent" principles outlined above have not passed without criticism either. It is in fact quite uncertain whether they are well grounded at all. Bybee (1985: 208) points out that the morphotactic transparency, the one meaning, one form principle applies rather sparingly in the languages from her sample while both allomorphy and suppletion are well attested.

Another line of thinking within formal morphology is represented in the work of Carstairs-McCarthy (1992, 1994) where suppletion is seen as a marginal phenomenon within morphological systems but is nonetheless considered interesting because of its diagnostic value when identifying paradigmatic relationships among the inflected forms of a word as well as a clue to the way they are stored in memory.

2.2.3 *Suppletion and Frequency*

The general view is that suppletion affects very common words, such as 'be', 'go',

---

18. The two languages with greatest number of suppletive verbs in my sample, 16 for Lezgian and 10 for Irish.

'come', 'eat', 'do'. Such words are not only common but they are also **high token frequency** items (as opposed to items that belong to a high **type-frequency** group). According to Crimmins (1994) the distinctions between token and type is attributed to philosopher C. S. Pierce. Crimmins uses the following questions to explain this notion: 'How many words are uttered in saying Home, sweet, home?' or 'How many digits are there in 499?'. Both questions have two possible answers: 'two' if types are counted; three if tokens are counted. Similarly to other basic notions, type and token lack a generally accepted definition, and the distinction is not always as easy to make as might be expected. In a very simplified fashion, one can say that types are properties, and tokens are instantiations of a given property/properties. When applied to morphology, type refers to a given conjugational class and tokens are particular forms that represent a class. For instance, there is a very large number of verbs in English which form past tense by adding a dental suffix /-ed, -d/. Thus the strategy of adding a dental suffix to form past tense is referred to as a type; all the verbs that form their past tense this way are part of a high type-frequency group due to the fact that they are numerous and constantly growing. High type-frequency items usually form a large number as a class, but the tokens (individual items) *per se* are not very frequently used. High token frequency items, on the other hand, show idiosyncrasies in their inflectional patterns but they are very frequently used in texts. Typical examples are the strong verbs in English together with the suppletive ones. Usually, in most discussions of suppletion and frequency, token, rather than type-frequency is meant.

2.2.3.1 "Historical junk"

It is very common to consider suppletion as a non-functional byproduct of processes such as sound change. Since it affects high token-frequency items, it is also considered "immune" to analogy because high token-frequency items are learned by rote and are thus resistant to analogical leveling. Versions of this view can be found in Nida (1963: 265) and Dressler (1985) and appear to be still current. For example Lass (1990: 81–2) while discussing the concept of **exaptation**[19] in language change, refers to suppletion as something "kept as marginal garbage, or non-functional/non-expressive residue (suppletion, 'irregularity')"; suppletive forms are completely non-functional; they are not considered among the grammatical forms which may adopt new functions. Similarly, Fertig (1998: 1069) quotes a relatively recent statement by Singh (1996: 22):

---

19. A concept Lass borrows from evolutionary biology. When applied to language data, it is used to cover cases where an old structure whose semantic content has become obsolete is re-adapted to express a new function.

> All that is left is suppletion but suppletion cannot possibly be a matter of morphology. That requires both formal and semantic similarity. The right metalanguage for morphology, in other words, is bound to expose exceptionality in morphology for what it really is: an artifact.

2.2.3.2 Non-traditional view: artifact does not mean non-functional

Bybee (1985: 92–3) generally agrees with the view that sees suppletion as a result of high token frequency. However, she points out that the forms which increased in frequency also underwent semantic change in the sense that they acquired more general semantic content. Since she sees all grammatical structure as a byproduct of language and historical change, suppletion fits quite well into her model (Fertig 1998: 1068). I will return to Bybee's ideas as well as the way they were further developed by Fertig (1998) later on in this book.

2.2.3.3 Suppletion and the economy principle

The notion of economy tends to be associated with two processes in language. Elements in language that are highly predictable in context tend to be eliminated, and elements that are used commonly tend to be reduced (Whaley 1997: 48).[20] I believe the latter process is meant when suppletion is accounted for in terms of economy.

The main proponents of an economic account for suppletion are Elke Ronnerberger-Sibold (1980) along with Wolfgang Dressler (1985) and Otmar Werner (1987). High frequency items tend to be short and since suppletive forms are typically high token frequency items they are claimed to be short as well. Furthermore, Ronnerberger-Sibold (1980, 1987) presents arguments from language production and processing: very frequent forms tend to be accessed directly rather than produced by rule; since suppletive forms tend to be among the frequent ones, they are also easy to access. In addition, the formal differences in suppletive paradigms make them easy to perceive. So the proponents of an economy account for suppletion still see the phenomenon as a result of high token frequency but they also find a functional motivation for it in terms of the psychological processes mentioned above.

Frequency of use and economy of expression definitely need to be brought into the picture when a full account of suppletion is sought. However, they cannot be taken to be the sole reasons for it. For example, Fertig (1998: 1079) points out that Werner never makes it clear how length is to be measured, "whether one should count segments, syllables, morae, milli-seconds or something else.". Likewise Fertig (1998: 1070) states that regardless of all efforts to make it look functional from a communication point of view, suppletion does not make much sense in the synchronic systems of the languages where it occurs. Finally, if we are to accept the

---

20. Whaley refers to Haiman (1983) when introducing this notion.

economy account point blank, we still fail to account for the less than universal occurrence of suppletion; such an account makes some languages look less functionally oriented/economical than others.[21]

I would also place Mel'čuk (1994) among the proponents of an economy account for suppletion although this is not the way he is typically cited. His work on suppletion is central for anyone interested in the phenomenon, but for whatever reason he is only one-sidedly quoted. Usually, only his initial statement is evoked, (cf. Aski 1995; Fertig 1998; Vincent and Börjars 1998) in which he refers to suppletion as "an extreme case of irregular alternation", that "violates an important linguistic (in fact semiotic principle): 'express the similar through the similar'" (Mel'čuk 1994: 342). Mel'čuk's position, however, is an ambiguous one but that is not explicitly recognized by most people who quote him. On the one hand, he appears to think of suppletion as an extreme case of morphological irregularity. On the other hand, his final conclusion puts him in a different light. He does seem to find suppletion quite natural by redefining the NM concept of naturalness to *linguistic naturalness* that somehow comes from within: "LINGUISTICALLY NATURAL = appearing spontaneously to fill some needs of the language" (Mel'čuk 1994: 392). This is what suppletion ultimately comes to be for him, "absolutely natural: it is never imposed on a language, but develops in it, as it were from within" (Mel'čuk 1994: 392). He goes on to further explain this emergence by stating that suppletion in fact produces "INDIVIDUALIZED—therefore more expressive, marking of some very basic distinctions"; according to him the emergence of suppletion also produces more compact expressions for high token frequency items. The explanation he offers for the development of suppletive forms effectively places him in the group above that considers suppletion economic from a communication point of view but his position is not far removed from from the view discussed in the section below either.

2.2.3.4 Suppletion and the closeness to speaker concept/Nahbereich
The idea that there are extra-linguistic reasons for the occurrence of suppletive forms was first articulated by Osthoff (1899). According to him the motivation for suppletion is the striving of primitive man to split and individualize things and phenomena which are close to her/him. This would explain why suppletion in Indo-European languages is encountered among words that express notions of everyday necessity, namely verbs such as 'be', 'give', 'go', 'see', 'take', 'carry', 'speak', 'hit'; nouns that indicate kinship such as 'father-mother', 'brother-sister', 'son-daughter'; degree of comparison for adjectives such as 'good' and 'bad' and for adverbs such

---

[21]. This issue borders on the question of linguistic complexity and calls for a longer discussion which lies without the scope of the current inquiry. The discussion on this issue is currently one of the hot topics in linguistic debate, see (Dahl 2005) for a recent reference.

as 'much'; ordinal numeral such as 'first' and 'second', personal pronouns and a few other words. Osthoff also points out that suppletion is used to differentiate domenstic animals on the basis of gender (e.g. 'ox-cow', 'ram-ewe') while it is not used in the same manner with wild animals (e.g. 'lion-lioness', 'tiger-tigress'.)

Osthoff's original idea was "revived" for the modern world by a few proponents of Natural morphology, namely Dressler (1985), Bittner (1988, 1996) and Wurzel (1990) and thus gained currency as the concept of **Nahbereich**. For these scholars suppletion is natural within a special, semantically defined domain of **Nahbereich** lit. 'a proximate/adjacent area'. Since human beings tend to differentiate more between things that are close by (physically or in some psychological sense) it is also natural to express/refer to them by highly individuated expressions such as the suppletive ones (Bittner 1988: 1, 41).

However, both Osthoff and his contemporary followers have received a great deal of criticism mostly because the notion of Nahbereich, albeit intuitively very attractive, is rather hard to delimit in any rigorous way. This is even recognized by Bittner himself; he attempts to salvage the account by stating that most suppletive forms are grammatical function words.

Fertig's (Fertig 1998: 1071–2) most important criticism of the Nahbereich account brings up the point that grammatical function words cannot in any way be defined as anything close to the speaker. "Bittner has no clear explanation for why grammatical function words should be suppletive beyond an ad hoc appeal to markedness reversal".

Markey (1985) articulates Osthoff's idea in somewhat different terms. For him the motivation behind suppletion is to be understood on a more cognitive basis: suppletive forms reflect basic "syntagmatic arrangements" that are deeply rooted in human cognition.

The hypothesis expressed by Markey can face criticism in a similar vein as the one addressed to proponents of the Nahbereich-account. Regardless of its strong appeal (at least for functionally oriented linguists) the categories labeled 'basic syntagmatic arrangements' are still very hard to define.

2.2.4 *Suppletion: a result, not a residue*

There are linguists who view suppletion as well motivated, though not solely due to frequency of use and economy of expression. For these scholars suppletion is a legitimate result of general processes of historical change. I will begin the analysis of their work by examining some of the lesser-known voices.

Gorbachevskij (1967) criticizes accounts based on frequency of use by pointing out that there are a lot of high frequency items in a language that are not suppletive. He proposes three different ways of emergence of suppletion (Gorbachevskij 1967: 28):

(i)   semantic convergence of two or more lexical items into one and the same paradigm.
(ii) semantic specification whereby certain members of a paradigm are replaced by members of another paradigm.
(iii) creation of suppletive forms as a result of sound change.

Unfortunately Gorbachevskij fails to sufficiently illustrate the three processes listed above, and, more importantly, to convincingly differentiate between (i) and (ii). As we shall see in the discussion of emergence of suppletion, his generalizations are basically valid, but what is missing is further specification of the semantic processes that lead to paradigm restructuring of the kinds outlined above.

The idea of **lexical convergence** and **lexical divergence** as processes that give rise to suppletive forms is further developed by Vera Koneckaja (1973). Lexical convergence is seen as the process of morphological and semantic change whereby two separate lexemes come together in one and the same paradigm, usually for semantic reasons, as for example, Old English *gān* 'go' and *wendan* 'turn, return' which currently supply the present and past tense forms of the Modern English *go*. Lexical divergence is the process whereby forms in one and the same paradigm become formally so distinct that they start to perceived as weak suppletives. However, once the semantic distinction which accounts for their paradigmatic relationship is lost, they start to be perceived as different words; Koneckaja gives the example of the split leading to differentiation of *may* vs. *might*. They were once two forms in one and the same paradigm, Old English *mæg* 'be able to, PRESENT, INDICATIVE' vs. *mighte* 'be able to, PRESENT, SUBJUNCTIVE' but in Modern English these forms have reached the status of two completely different modal verbs (albeit with defective paradigms).

The 1990s witness a proliferation of work devoted to finding a more functionally based explanation for suppletion, compared to the orientation to this topic in preceding decades. It is almost tempting to pair them up with Osthoff's study from 1899 and ascribe this "revival" to some kind of *fin de siècle* spirit (the true reason is most probably the general greater spread of functionally oriented approaches to language). Not only have linguists "rediscovered" the phenomenon as something that deserves attention but there are also quite a few empirically based claims that contradict the prevailing opinion of suppletion being something problematic and unnatural, surviving solely because of frequency of use.

Deshpande (1992) examines the emergence of suppletive verb pairs according to aspect in Sanskrit. Based on textual evidence from Vedic texts this author traces the gradual association of verbs (two or more verbs in each case) meaning 'give', 'speak', 'become', 'go', 'carry', 'eat' etc. with the aspectual category most appropriate for their meaning. Thus, he describes a form of reanalysis whereby two separate, though semantically similar, lexemes come to be associated each with a particular grammatical category based on their lexical meaning. Gradually, they become the only ones used in that function and thus start to be perceived as the sole expressions of the category in question. Deshpande (1992:41) concludes that "suppletion seems to originate in an accomodation between lexical expression of aspect and the available grammatical means.". As such it is not accidental, but rather a result from a regular semantic process.

Aski (1995) puts to scrutiny the rarely contested axiom that suppletive forms are resistant to analogical leveling. Based on data from Romance languages, she shows that suppletive paradigms are by no means excluded from synchronic phonological patterns or analogical changes affecting whole conjugational classes in a given language. The Romance verbs 'to go' are shown to have belonged to a rather restricted conjugational pattern (**morpho-phonological template** in Aski's, and ultimately, Nigel Vincent's, terms) in earlier stages of Romance as well as in Vulgar Latin. In later developments of Romance languages, these same verbs joined more "populated" templates in their respective languages. For instance, French *aller* 'go' while acquiring new suppletive forms, moved from a less populated to a more populated template. Viewed this way, suppletive verbs can be safely said to follow the same phonological changes as all other 'regular' verbs and are likewise accommodated in the appropriate phonological templates. I shall have occasion to return to this model and present it in further detail when discussing the development of suppletive forms (see Chapter 5:3).

De Haan (1997) studies the interaction of modality and negation from a typological perspective, but also shows that suppletion is one of the common strategies languages employ for negating modal verbs.

Fertig (1998) whose work was already abundantly cited above provides not only an excellent account of explanations for suppletion offered by proponents of Natural Morphology and theories based on frequency of use and economy of expression but he also identifies the issues that make them unsuitable for fully explaining the occurrence of suppletion. This scholar adopts the models proposed in Bybee (1985; Bybee et al. 1994) and develops them with regard to suppletion in some important ways. In particular, he proposes a distinction between "category specific suppletions" on the one hand, and "general suppletion" on the other (Fertig 1998:1078). Category specific suppletion results form the high relevance of one grammatical category to the meaning of a particular lexical item. General suppletion affects primarily grammaticalized and grammaticalizing words and can potentially be associated with any grammatical category, although it should still obey Bybee's semantic relevance hierarchy. As the subsequent chapters will show, this prediction is well borne out by the typological data from my study.

3. Quo Vadis Domine

As we saw above, all the definitions basically agree in that suppletion involves unrelated forms which otherwise stand in a paradigmatic relationship. What a paradigmatic relationship is, however, remains, largely unclear. Depending on the orientation of the analysis, affixal and stem suppletion may also be distinguished, and similarly, derivational vs. inflectional suppletion. It is common to view suppletion as a gradable phenomenon, reflecting the degree of deviation from existing morpho-phonological rules. However, little attention has been paid to the morphological structure of suppletive forms.

Subsuming suppletion under morphology, as is done in most treatments, is justified inasmuch as the study of paradigms is considered a matter of morphology; and suppletion presupposes the existence of some paradigms/patterns in order to be postulated. Vincent and Börjars (1998) have already objected to this view, showing that suppletion shares some characteristics with periphrasis. I will not be able to pursue this issue in any greater depth. In Chapter 3: 2, I list preliminary data that highlight suppletion within the domain of syntax.

The argument might seem trivial but it is never made explicit: namely, all definitions of suppletion pre-suppose well defined lexico-syntactic classes such as **noun**, **verb**, etc., each with well defined categories associated with it, and consequently paradigms. This seems to be somehow forgotten when we outline the distribution of suppletion. The observation that it does not occur in many languages is attributed to some general morphological type of the languages in question. No one appears to bring up the issue of way(s) morpho-syntactic classes are delimited in those languages where suppletion is absent.

When suppletion is referred to as "marginal", as is commonly done, there are two ways in which this could be the case: (i) it is marginal cross-linguistically, that is, it occurs in a very small number of languages around the world (cf. Dressler, Mel'čuk); (ii) it is marginal because there are typically very few suppletive items in the languages in which it occurs.

However, as is also widely acknowledged, suppletion affects high token frequency items, which are far from marginal since they are the ones most commonly used in texts and conversation of their respective languages. Consequently, phenomena associated with them cannot be marginal either. It is necessary to become more precise as to exactly what kind of marginality is ascribed to suppletion: suppletion is marginal with respect to type-frequency,[22] but it is almost the expected case with high frequency items in any language where it occurs and as such it is not marginal at all.

---

[22]. As we shall see further on, the emergence of the suppletive forms never invites to any kind of type. So "accusing" suppletion of low type frequency is simply misguided.

As regards the cross-linguistic marginality of suppletion: given that there is no good typological database of occurrence of suppletion in the languages of the world, the claim is not empirically grounded. The data used in the works mentioned above come mainly from Indo-European languages, with somewhat more varied sample found in Mel'čuk. In Mel'čuk's study 42% of the languages are Indo-European; Dressler's article provides references to Turkish, Hungarian and Finnish, all his other data coming from Indo-European languages. Durie (1986) presents a sample in which languages from North American Indian languages prevail. Thus the research so far does not present us with a typologically balanced sample that would allow for assessing the markedness or systematicity of suppletion in the languages of the world.

With regard to suppletion in verb paradigms, the works cited give the impression that there are three main types, namely suppletion according to (i) tense and aspect; (ii) person and number; (iii) verbal number alone. Rudes (1980: 1), regardless of the fact that out of the 14 languages he examines, 12 are Indo-European, claims there is evidence from "numerous languages" showing that there are two patterns that suppletive verbs may follow: suppletion by tense/aspect/mode, and suppletion by person/number in the unmarked present. Further, within a given language, he states, the pattern of suppletion tends to be the same for all suppletive verbs.

To this, the following objections can be made. First, lumping tense/aspect/mood in one pattern is overgeneralizing. There is cross-linguistic evidence that tense/aspect on the one hand, and mood (imperative in particular) on the other, show different genealogical and areal distribution. Second, suppletion according to person/number is not restricted to present tense only; it is admittedly more common within this category but there are languages where person/number suppletion occurs in non-present tenses as well. Third, Rudes' account ignores negation. There are numerous cases of suppletion according to polarity both in languages where negation is expressed syntactically and where it is expressed by means of affixes. A complete study of verbal suppletion should include suppletion according to polarity as well. Although I am unable to consider suppletion according to negative polarity in this study, it should not be left out when suppletion in general is discussed.

The generally accepted accounts for suppletion center around frequency of use of the suppletive items together with economy of expression which is closely associated with such items. Such accounts, however, give us only a partial story of suppletion. They still fail to explain why suppletion is more common with certain inflectional categories but less frequent with others, and they tell us nothing about the ways suppletion evolves.

When viewed from the perspective of Bybee's model where inflectional categories are correlated by the relevance they bear to particular lexical items and where grammar and lexicon form a continuum rather than two completely separate modules, suppletion suddenly finds its place in a language system. As it will be shown later in this work (cf. Chapter 5, Chapter 6: 3), the processes which create suppletive forms borrow features from both grammaticalization and lexicalization; the results they produce have, likewise, an intermediate status. This is why suppletion appears so unsystematic in the languages where it is found. This, however, does not mean that it cannot be described in a systematic way.

To summarize, the research published so far fails to address some significant issues concerning information about the distribution of this phenomenon among the world's languages, as well as its description from a typological and historical perspective. The present work is intended to fill some of these gaps. The database used here is, by the standards of modern typology, more diverse and better balanced than the data in previous studies with regard to the languages included in it. In addition to identifying types of suppletion which occur cross-linguistically, the study also brings to light areal phenomena regarding the occurrence of suppletive forms in verb paradigms. Furthermore, whenever possible I outline diachronic paths for the emergence of suppletive forms in verb paradigms and, finally, based on both synchronic and diachronic data, I suggest an explanation of how and why suppletion arises.

CHAPTER 2

Method

This chapter offers a discussion of the methodological problems pertinent to the current study. The main issues, presented in sections 1 and 2 respectively, concern the selection of languages to be investigated (sample design) and the interpretation of **frequency counts** emerging from the sampled data. The data sources used are discussed briefly in section 3. In the final section 4, I present the criteria adopted for identifying cases of suppletion in the investigated languages.

1. Sampling

The initial sample for this study was chosen according to the procedure used in Bybee, Perkins and Pagliuca (1994), to be discussed in more detail below. The final sample, however, was very much influenced by my participation in the World Atlas of Language Stuctures (WALS) project (http://www.wals.info), which led to increasing the size of the sample and substituting some of the initially chosen languages with ones included in the WALS sample.

1.1 General issues

Since any selection of languages (or any kind of data for that matter) is necessarily shaped by the research question(s) being asked, I will briefly restate the issues at hand. One of the primary goals of this work is to arrive at a typologically balanced database that shows the distribution of suppletion in the languages of the world. Apart from aiming to outline the occurrence of suppletion cross-linguistically, another goal of this work is to test whether suppletion can be correlated with areal phenomena as there has been no work on this issue.

Finally, a third goal was to determine, to the extent possible, how and why suppletion arises. To address this question, historical comparative studies had to be performed on several different language families, preferably ones that are well documented to make such work feasible.

Thus, for the synchronic part of the study, a sample that is both genealogically and geographically well balanced was necessary. For the diachronic part, case studies were carried out on data from Germanic and Slavic. Comparative evidence was also collected from several Arabic and Mixtec dialects.

The design of language samples for cross-linguistic work has by now become a theoretical issue in its own right. A wide variety of studies have been devoted to this topic, (cf. Bell 1978; Dryer 1989; Perkins 1989; Rijkhoff, Bakker, Hengeveld and Kahrel 1993; Maslova 2000, to name just a few.) In very broad terms, the following questions are central to the discussion in the sampling literature:

1. Quantity (size of the sample): how large should a sample be in order to be representative?
2. Quality: given the nature of human languages as a population to be sampled, what is a suitable method to use in order to arrive at the most representative sample? This question involves several separate, though related issues:
    a. How to avoid different kinds of bias, e.g. genealogical, geographic, cultural, bibliographic.
    b. How to arrive at a sample that would meet the requirement of mutual independence between units so that statistical tests performed on it would yield reliable results.
    c. How to take into account and represent the internal diversity or uniformity of particular linguistic groupings.[1]

Apart from these theoretical issues, practical issues that arise during a sampling procedure are choice of a suitable language classification and availability of reference sources.

The first issue that should be addressed is the choice of classification together with the question of sample size. Classifications commonly used so far are the ones by Voegelin & Voegelin (1978) Ruhlen (1987) or Grimes (1988). A revised edition of Grimes' classification is nowadays available online at http://www.ethnologue.com/; this classification was chosen since it is easily accessible, regularly updated and organized in a database. As regards the size of a sample, depending on the purposes of the inquiry, sample size will have varying degrees of importance and merit. Not surprisingly, opinions with regards to sample sizes vary widely. Although there is a strong tendency to work with very large samples nowadays, some scholars have argued that depending on the sampling technique, conclusions based on data from smaller samples are equally, if not more, valid as an analysis of fewer languages is presumable more thorough. (Keith Denning, p.c, among others). However, as Bell (1978) points out, in the long run, the very size of a sample does not really affect the validity of the conclusions. What is more important is how one selects the languages included in it. Perkins (1989) argues that samples sized from 50 to 100 languages are most appropriate for describing a variety of linguistic variables. A size of

---

1. This would, of course, represent a genealogical bias and thus come into conflict with the requirement stated in (2a) above (Martin Haspelmath, p.c.).

approximately hundred languages was aimed for in the initial stages of this study. Such a sample was designed according to a sampling procedure described below and covers 94 languages. It shall henceforth be referred to as the **small sample**. My participation in the WALS project led to the collection of data from an additional 99 languages. This latter group together with the initially chosen 94 languages forms the larger sample of 193 languages and is hereafter referred to as the **WALS sample**.

The issue of the quality of the sample is a more complex one and as stated above involves several different questions: choosing a sample that consists of independent units, avoiding different kinds of bias (genealogical, geographic, cultural and bibliographic), and finding a way to reflect the internal diversity of language families.

The problem of choosing a sample of independent units is probably the most difficult issue as regards sampling because it concerns the nature of the language population. In order for our conclusions to be statistically significant, we need data from a sample that includes independent languages. The procedure used in various disguises is to stratify a particular language classification based on the linguistic groupings listed there and select languages from it, typically also applying some form of mathematical calculus in order to obtain a certain representative number of languages from each group. Such samples are said to consist of independent languages. However, Dryer (1989) calls into question whether they really are such as there is some probability of existence of large, continent-size linguistic areas. Moreover there is always the distorting effect of large linguistic families.[2] So according to Dryer, all languages can be considered remotely related and thus non-independent members of a population. If this line of reasoning is correct, then conclusions about linguistic preferences for a certain feature based on comparative research cannot be checked by standard statistical tests for independent samples (Martin Haspelmath, p.c.). Dryer proposes a method of large size language sampling where whole linguistic groupings, in his terms **genera** of the size of Germanic or Romance are examined. For calculating frequencies of a linguistic feature, Dryer proposes to count the number of genera where it is found rather than the number of single languages; for assessing the linguistic preference for a certain feature, Dryer uses a binominal

---

2. A common praxis for sample design is to represent large language families such as Niger-Congo or Austronesian by a greater number of languages than smaller language families. This is done in order to achieve adequate geographical coverage of the languages of the world. However, such an inclusion does have a distorting effect when we try to assess the preference for a one linguistic feature over another in the following sense: generally, languages which are genealogically related will tend to, more often than not, show similar typological characteristics. So if we see a preference for certain linguistic features in a sample selected in the way just described, this may, in reality, just reflect the predominace and greater geographical spread of large language families, and not a genuine preference for the features in question (cf. Dryer 1989 for a more detailed discussion of this issue.)

sign test.[3] Since the method suggested by Dryer is used as one of the procedures to calculate the frequencies of different kinds of suppletion for languages in the WALS sample it is presented in more detail in section 2.1. of this chapter.

The work of Maslova[4] (2000) brings the discussion of testing typological universals to a considerably higher interdisciplinary level than any previous studies have done. Maslova proposes to view the current language population from a historical perspective of a substantial time depth (ca. 3,700 years ago; this date is, however, strictly hypothetical); she also introduces a mathematical approach for both sampling modern languages as listed in popular classifications as well as for testing typological universals. If we accept her hypothesis that the number of languages might have been substantially smaller if dated back to about 3700 years ago, it follows that modern languages might be genealogically much more closely related than it is usually assumed and as such they are not independent, hence not suitable for statistical methods or calculating any kind of frequencies at all. The hypothesis put forth by Maslova is thought provoking and ultimately very challenging; however, it is probably not unfair to say that her assumptions are rather strong. Besides, even if they were borne out, the time depth considered in her study lies way beyond the scope of the current project. While selecting a potentially misleading sample is definitely a possibility, this, in itself, is not a good reason to discard comparative work altogether.

In addition to the probability of languages being closely related on a deeper time scale, and thus not independent entities, they are most probably not independent geographically either. As Dahl (1985) points out, every time people try to avoid geographic bias, the assumption is that the languages spoken in one and the same area have been/are necessarily in contact and thus influencing each other. This is, however, far from true. Also, in Dahl's terms, it is significantly more difficult to avoid bias due to long term colonial effects. The latter observation is probably even more valid today given the availability of easily accessible mass media and general technological developments such as the advent of the Internet where the influence of English in particular is probably the most substantial one.

Thus, languages in general are, in some sense, deeply related in space and time, and a sample showing statistically significant linguistic preferences might be impossible altogether. Rijkhoff and Bakker (1998) seem to arrive at a similar conclusion. With such a prospect, one possibility for a typologist would be to quit conducting comparative projects and do something else since nobody likes to do work that is basically pointless. On the other hand, such realizations can be seen as use-

---

3. Sign tests are typically used with correlated samples.

4. Thanks to Maria Koptjevskaja-Tamm for showing the article to me even before it went to press, and also for the lengthy and detailed discussions on this topic.

ful warnings that prevent scholars from getting too carried way by the implications of their own work and from making claims that are too strong. This latter line of thinking is adopted in the current study.

1.2 The sampling method employed in this study

As may have become clear from the discussion above, human languages are a rather problematic population to sample; thus an unbiased, perfectly representative language selection is most probably an unattainable goal. Nonetheless, we can still try to do our best in selecting languages that are, within known limits, as diverse as possible in terms of genealogical relatedness and geographical distance. A number of sampling procedures have been proposed so far. I opted for the one used in Bybee, Perkins and Pagliuca (1994) for reasons to be explained below.

Bybee and her colleagues take the genealogical criterion as the main one for their language selection similarly to other sampling methods (see. for instance Rijkhoff, Bakker, Hengeveld and Kahrel 1993: 250). Unlike Rijkhoff et al. however, instead of applying one and the same procedure to all linguistic groupings, regardless of their size and levels of diversity, Bybee et al. do take into consideration both of these when calculating the number of languages to be included from each phylum. That is, the number of languages to be included from each phylum is calculated differently based on the number and size of subgroups within that phylum and the number of languages in the primary and secondary residues. This procedure was also found fairly easy to adapt and apply to a classification different from the one Bybee et al. used. For these reasons, the method used by Bybee et al. was adapted when designing the small sample used here.

Bybee et al. use the language classification by Voegelin & Voegelin (1978), and group the phyla listed there into several different categories depending on their size. The distinctions that Bybee et al. make are presented in Table 1. In a similar vein, I grouped the linguistic phyla listed in the Ethnologue into categories according to their size; see Table 2.

Table 1. Descriptive background of the universe of languages (adopted from Bybee et al. 1994: 305)

Number of languages in a phylum	Number of groups of this size in Voegelin and Voegelin (1978)	Category
1–6	56	Minimal
22–36	10	Small
50–122	6	Medium
155–323	6	Large
747–1,046	3	Macro

Table 2. Descriptive background of the languages in the Ethnologue

Number of languages in a phylum	Number of groups of this size in the Ethnologue	Category
1–6	43	Minimal
7–17	13	XSmall
22–36	16	Small
42–105	12	Medium
173–539	8	Large
1,236–1.446	2	Macro

Note: The figures are based on the online edition of the Ethnologue as of November 1998.

As shown in Table 2, the overall number of genealogical phyla in the Ethnologue is 94, out of which 56 are minimal groups or very small phyla with less than 22 languages, and 38 are phyla that cover more than 22 languages, with considerably varying sizes. The table does not list the language isolates, which are 31, and the 114 unclassified languages. At first, it was considered necessary to introduce the category XSmall for the groupings which cover from 7 to 17 languages. This extra category turned out to be moot for the final language selection since the procedure suggested by Bybee et al. for language groupings that consist of less than 20 languages was applied to these groups too.

Following Bybee et al., the minimal groups consisting of 1 to 6 languages together with the language isolates were all included in one set. The total sum of languages in the set was calculated (172 languages) and as they represented 2.5 % of all the languages in the Ethnologue, 3 languages from this group were chosen: Koasati (Muskogean), Ket and Basque. The second set of minimal groups, those consisting of 7 to 17 languages, was treated in the same way: that is the sum of all languages included here was calculated (139 languages) and as it represented 2.07 % of the languages listed in the Ethnologue, two languages from this group were selected, Central Yup'ik and Oneida. One language was chosen from the group of Pidgins and Creoles, namely Ndyuka, an English based Creole. All the other languages in the sample were chosen from the 38 larger phyla listed in the Ethnologue; phyla with fewer than forty-two members each contributed one language to the sample (see detailed list in Appendix 1); phyla with more than forty-two languages contributed more than one language each, with the number and affiliation of the selected languages depending on the sizes of the subgroupings within the phylum. For example, if a phylum has first-level or primary subgroups with more than twenty member languages, then one language was selected from each of these primary subgroups. If one of the primary subgroups is further divided into secondary subgroups of twenty languages or more, one language is selected from each of these subgroups. For instance, Austro-Asiatic is divided into the following subgroups, listed below with the number of languages in parentheses:

Table 3.

Maximal group / phylum	Primary subgroup	Secondary subgroups
Austro-Asiatic (180)	Mon-Khmer (156)	Aslian (19)
		Eastern Mon-Khmer (69)
		Monic (2)
		Nicobar (6)
		Northern Mon-Khmer (38)
		Palyu (1)
		Unclassified (4)
		Viet-Muong (17)
	Munda (24)	North Munda (15)
		South Munda (9)

One language was selected from the Eastern Mon-Khmer, one from Northern Mon-Khmer; as the residue in the primary subgroup was still larger than 30 languages, one language was chosen from the remaining secondary subgroups in Mon-Khmer, namely Viet-Muong. Finally, one language was chosen from the primary subgroup Munda.

Similarly to the classification in Voegelin & Voegelin, the two largest groupings in the Ethnologue are Austronesian (1236 languages) and Niger-Congo (1436 languages); both of these macro groups contain secondary and even tertiary subgroups that are still quite large. When choosing languages from these phyla, I picked one language from each subgrouping that was larger than 20 languages, regardless of the level of the subgrouping. This resulted in choosing seven languages[5] from the Austronesian phylum and 7 from Niger-Congo (see under relevant groups in Appendix 2). In the case of Austronesian, such selection is justified due to the fact that these languages are spoken on separate islands and cover a very wide geographical area. In the case of Niger-Congo, the groups cited by the Ethnologue are actually quite different from each other which warrants the inclusion of one language from each of them.

The number of languages arrived at after applying the procedure(s) above was at first 111. However, it became reduced to 102 after the search for reference sources was performed, and I opted to not looking for substitutes at that stage. The number of languages which were investigated from the small sample came to be 94.

The selection of languages was random in the sense that all languages listed in the Ethnologue had equal chances to be selected. However, the final inclusion of a language depended on the following criteria:

---

[5]. Ten languages were selected initially but seven were investigated. The WALS sample makes up for this since there are twelve Austronesian languages there.

- There are sufficient reference sources the language in question, in the sense that there is at least one grammar. If there was a dictionary or a text collection that was considered a plus and thus a language with those was be preferred over a language with just a grammar.
- If I had a choice between two languages spoken in the immediate proximity of each other and one of them could be substituted by a language spoken at a more distant geographic location, the latter was chosen.

Bybee et al. attempted to avoid bibliographic bias and along with it other kinds of bias (such as cultural). If they had a choice, these authors opted for languages the speakers of which are few and live in predominantly rural areas, for example, they chose Tigre rather than Arabic or Hebrew to represent Semitic). For my own selection process, this principle has been the most challenging to adhere to with any consistency. So the small sample is definitely bibliographically biased, especially for phyla from Oceania, South East Asia and South America. Also, well documented languages are crucial for this project. Thus, when sampling Semitic and Indo-European, Hebrew and Greek were quite deliberately included.

The languages included in the small sample of 94 languages, together with the sampling procedure are listed in Appendix 1; see Map 1. for an orientation on their geographic location.

2. Ways to calculate frequencies of the suppletion types emerging from the data

As discussed above, a perfectly representative sample is most probably within the realm of the impossible. Similarly, every frequency evaluation procedure is likely to be flawed in one way or another. One way out of this difficulty is to adopt a method in which we calculate the frequencies frequencies of types emerging from a sample in different (independent) ways and compare the results (Östen Dahl, p.c.). Thus four different counting procedures are employed here.

General frequencies in terms of per cent proportions were calculated on the smaller sample of 94 languages chosen by the sampling procedure outlined in Bybee et al. (1994) as well as for the languages in WALS sample. These frequencies are in turn compared with the results of two other counting methods.

2.1 Counting genera instead of languages

One counting method involves presenting the different kinds of suppletion per genera and geographical area, thus following Dryer (1989) and also Dryer (1992: 638) for the geographical areas. The procedure is outlined in (15).

(15) Counting procedure following the method suggested by Matthew Dryer (1989: 267–70)
   1. Group the individual languages from the sample into genealogical groups roughly comparable to Germanic and Romance in Indo-European.
   2. Divide the world into at least physically independent areas.
   3. Count the genera according to area.
   4. Count the number of genera for each of the relevant linguistic types within each continental area. (In our case the relevant linguistics features are different types of suppletion or the absence thereof).
   5. A genus is included (thus counted) in several types if it contains languages that show these types. So the sum of all genera in specific types per area does not have to add up to the total number of genera from a particular area.
   6. Determine how many areas conform to the hypothesis being tested. If all conform, then the hypothesis is considered confirmed.

Step 1 in the method is probably the most problematic one as Dryer himself points out. It is not always entirely uncontroversial to decide what a genus is and what it is not. As the literature is not always very explicit on this point the best one can do is make educated guesses in many cases. This is probably less of a problem for the current sample, however, as it is substantially smaller than Dryer's and the phyla included in it are relatively well studied. The genealogical groups assumed here are listed in Appendix 2 together with pertinent languages.

The procedure outlined above is illustrated by Dryer (1989: 269) by testing a number of hypotheses about linguistics preferences for various constituent orders and other linguistic features. In the example below the distribution of SOV is compared with that of the other very common constituent order SVO; Dryer's sample for this study consisted of 542 languages grouped in 218 genera.

(16) Distribution of genera according to areas in Dryer's sample

Africa	Eurasia	Australia-New Guinea	North America	South America	Total
45	52	30	60	31	218

(17) Distribution of SOV and SVO orders in the genera from Dryer's sample

	Africa	Eurasia	Australia-New Guinea	North America	South America	Total
SOV	22	26	19	26	18	111
SVO	21	19	6	6	5	57

The leftmost column lists the two types of constituent order. The numbers under each area indicate the number of genera containing languages of each type. For

Table 4. Distribution of the WALS sample in the areas suggested by Dryer (1992)

Area	Number of languages	Number of genera	Number of phyla
Africa	36	25	5
Eurasia	48	33	15
SEA and Oceania	23	18	4
Australia-New Guinea	26	24	6
N. America	33	26	18
S. America	27	24	22
Total	193	150	70

instance, there are 22 genera in Africa containing SOV languages and 21 genera containing SVO languages. The larger number for each area is enclosed in a box. Thus it can be seen that the number of genera containing SOV languages is greater than the number of genera containing SVO languages. Africa is the only area where the precedence of SOV genera over SVO is somewhat marginal; in the other four areas it is quite convincing. The example above illustrates the application of a binomial sign test. Dryer makes the analogy to the probability of flipping a coin five times and getting one and the same outcome each time. The chance of flipping a coin five times and getting five heads is one in thirty-two. On the assumption that the five areas are genealogically and areally independent, if there were not a linguistic preference for SOV over SVO order, then the chance for all five areas to contain more SOV genera would also be one in thirty-two. Thus since the number of SOV exceeds SVO in all five areas, the hypothesis is considered confirmed at a level of statistical significance less than .05.

This method is used to show the genealogical and areal distribution of different suppletion types found in the languages of the WALS sample. Table 4 presents the main geographical areas together with number of languages, genera and phyla from them. Since Dryer revises the geographical areas in his work of (1992), I am using his latter division of the world. The method remains the same otherwise.[6] In the subsequent chapters the results of the count using this method are referred to as **The Dryer Distribution**.

2.2 Weight values assigment

The fourth and final counting procedure uses a method suggested by Östen Dahl (p.c.). The languages in a sample are assigned different **weight values** depending on the degree of their genealogical relatedness. The weight values are then used to calculate frequencies for different types related to the sum of all weights, not to the absolute number of languages in the sample.

---

[6]. For six areas the chance becomes 1 in 64.

One of the main points with this procedure is to eliminate the influence large language phyla get in a sample of this kind. When making the preliminary language selection, one necessarily includes a larger number of languages from big language families such as Austronesian or Niger-Congo. So a simple count of languages in the end reflects a distribution where large language families still prevail, and thus the picture we get is most probably erroneous, as already discussed above.

Another aim (not necessarily secondary) of the current procedure is to "make up" for various biases arising during the working process. As mentioned above, the small sample became bibliographically biased. The historical-comparative work involved collecting data from closely related languages, quite the opposite of the initial sampling procedure, so the WALS sample became genealogically biased.

One way to solve the problem of calculating frequencies in a biased sample is to produce a much smaller, unbiased one, following Dahl (1985) who selected twelve independent languages out of the 64 that he used for his study. Such a number of languages could be picked out in the current study as well. They would include maximum two languages per continent, making sure that these two languages belong to completely different, independent families and report general frequencies based on this sample only. This however, involves a great deal of arbitrariness (Östen Dahl, p.c.). For example it is very easy to select languages that represent mere exceptions in their own continent, and again, end up with a somewhat skewed picture of the general distribution.

Another way out is, of course, to exclude the additional languages from the final count (which is done in the first counting procedure). The question is, since we already have the data, wouldn't it be wiser to actually try to make sense of them all? The procedure proposed by Dahl for assigning and then using weight values to the languages in the WALS sample involves the steps described in (18).

(18) Weighted sample procedure suggested by Östen Dahl.
1. Assign one and the same value, say 1, to all phyla in the sample.
2. For each phylum, divide 1 by n where n is the number of primary groups of this phylum included in the sample.
3. Apply 2 recursively to subsequent lower groups, until a reasonable depth in the family tree, or (desirably) specific language(s) level, is reached.
4. The value of the last division operation is assigned to a particular language(s) from that particular group.
5. Use the weight values to calculate frequencies of types as related to the total sum of weights, rather than absolute number of languages.

Some short examples of weight values assignment follow. The Altaic phylum is represented in the sample by three subgroupings, Mongolian, Tungus, and Turkic, so its n-value becomes 3, and 1 is divided by 3. Thus, the value 0.33 is assigned to each major subgrouping. Since in this case, each subgrouping is represented by one language only (Khalkha, Evenki and Turkish, respectively), the same value, 0.33 is assigned to each language. For the sake of getting the final sum 1, correctly, I have rounded off one of the values to 0.34 where the division is threefold as in the case above. Thus two of the languages get 0.33 and one 0.34.

The North-Caucasian family is also represented by three main branches, North-Central, Northeast, and Northwest; each one of them is assigned the value 0.33. The North-Central branch is represented by one language, Ingush; likewise, the Northwest branch is represented by one language only, Abkhaz, so both Ingush and Abkhaz get the value 0.33; the Northeast branch is represented by two sub-branches, Avaro-Andi-Dido and Lezgian; each of the sub-branches gets the value 0.33/2, that is 0.165; since each sub-branch is represented by one language only, these languages, Hunzib and Lezgian respectively get the value 0.165.

The weight values obtained this way are then used for calculating two kinds of frequencies.

The first one is the cross-linguistic frequency of a certain suppletion type. For example, in calculating the frequency of suppletion according to tense–aspect categories, the weight values of all languages where this kind of suppletion is found are summed up and their proportion in per cent is calculated out of the total of weight values sum which is 70.

The second way in which the weight values are used is to calculate the cross-linguistic frequency of verb meanings that occur with a certain suppletion type. For example all verbs that show tense–aspect suppletion are associated with the weight values of their respective languages. These weight values are added up and they become the sum total of all verb meanings that occur with tense–aspect suppletion (in this case 51.082, see Chapter 4: 5.2, Table 17.). If we want to check the cross-linguistic frequency of a verb meaning 'go' with tense–aspect suppletion, then the sum of all 'go' verbs is calculated and after that its proportion in percent of the total sum of tense–aspect meanings.

The weight values procedure eliminates the influence of large language families as well as of closely related languages as such languages end up with fairly low values. However, it probably gives far way too much prominence to smaller language families and language isolates. I did not try to make up for that by assigning lower values to minor language families; this is probably a conceivable step as the method develops. At its first application, all phyla regardless of size were assigned one and the same value, 1. The number of phyla in the WALS sample is 70, thus the sum total of weight values is 70. The weight values for the languages in the WALS sample are listed in Appendix 2.

The frequency of a certain type obtained this way is then compared with the frequencies calculated on absolute number of languages from the two samples as well as with the frequencies obtained from the genera counts. A similar comparison was carried out with the frequencies of lexemic groups that occur with a particular suppletion type.

3. Sources

The primary sources used to collect data for this study were reference grammars, dictionaries and other published monographs on individual languages. Nowadays it is commonly acknowledged that grammars are often less than perfect sources of language data since they tend to vary widely in scope and intelligibility. At the same time, work in typology can hardly be done without reference grammars and other descriptions of individual languages so such works remain an indispensable tool for a comparativist.

Grammars and equivalent descriptions were chosen for this project based on the assumption that suppletive paradigms are typically paradigms of very commonly used verbs and as such are bound to be reported in reference materials.[7] This is generally true but, not surprisingly, it is not a hundred-percent axiom. There are grammars where no suppletive paradigms were mentioned but after talking to individual authors it turned out that suppletive verbs actually exist and are among the most frequently used verbs; they were, for whatever reason, simply omitted from the description. Another serious problem is that there exist quite a few grammars where suppletive forms according to category X are reported but there is no good illustration of a proper paradigm (either regular or irregular or both). One then has to determine whether there is any regular expression for the said category which is a difficult task often resulting in rather arbitrary decisions. I tried to make up for this, to the extent possible, by talking to language experts, field workers or native speakers.

The secondary sources for the data collection were online descriptions published on the World Wide Web, or, as mentioned above, elicitation of data, via queries to various discussion lists with concentration on linguistics. Correspondence with grammar authors, field workers, as well as native speakers came to play a more decisive role at the final stages of this project. This however does not mean that I consulted both grammars and language experts for all 193 languages from the WALS sample. Experts were asked to help out with languages where the description did not provide answers to my questions; for some languages if an expert was available, I asked for confirmation of the data I collected from the published sources.

---

7. *Teach Yourself* books are often excellent sources of simplified facts on idiosyncrasies in inflection but they do not always provide a sufficient discussion of general verb morphology.

4. Criteria for suppletion

Based on the work discussed in Chapter 1, the following criteria were used when identifying cases of suppletion in the sampled languages.

4.1 Grammatical category and its encoding.

I. The unpredictable/irregular encoding of category X is referred to as suppletion as in English *go* vs. *went*.
II. Category X is otherwise regularly expressed by fairly well defined morpho-syntactic means as in English *dance* vs. *danced* or *sing* vs. *sang*. Both bound morphological and syntactic expressions are considered regular.

Both inflectional and derivational patterns are taken into account. As already discussed the distinction between them is, in many cases, very hard to make. I have taken the scope of a particular pattern as a main criterion on whether a paradigmatic contrast can be said to exist in a given language. The wider the scope of a given category, the more it looks obligatory, and thereby exceptions to this pattern appear to have a closer paradigmatic relation. As we shall see further on this criterion is not entirely watertight as some derivational patterns can be very widespread but the means by which they are expressed may show great diversity as regards their generality and scope (see Chapter 4: 2.2.1 on the derivation of aspectual pairs in Slavic languages).

Syntactic suppletion is rarely discussed explicitly.[8] However there exist a number of cases where an established syntactic pattern is not followed up and a separate lexical item is used instead. For example, in Cantonese there are several different strategies to negate a sentence predicate, most of which involve the particle *mh* (for non-past time reference), illustrated in (19).

(19) Cantonese (Matthews and Yip 1994: 250–2)
    a. *Gihn sām mh leng.*
       CL   shirt not nice
       'The shirt doesn't look nice.'
    b. *Gām-yaht ngóh mh gin haak.*
       today   I   not see client
       'I am not seeing any clients today.'

None of the common negative particles is used when the modal *yiu* 'need, have to' is negated as shown in (20).

---

8. For, to my knowledge first, serious discussions of this phenomenon, see Croft (1991), Palmer (1995) and de Haan (1997).

(20) Cantonese (Matthews and Yip 1994: 233, 234)
  a. *Ngódeih gām–máahn yiu chēut heu sihk.*
     we tonight need out go eat
     'We have to eat out tonight.'
  b. *Nī geui yéh msái joi gói la.*
     this h thing no-need again correct PRT
     'There's no need to correct this sentence again.'

Exceptions to syntactic patterns as the one above are considered instances of suppletion. As already mentioned (Chapter 1: 3), I will not be able to discuss syntactic suppletion in depth. However, preliminary data on this phenomenon are presented in Chapter 3: 2.

4.1 Form of the suppletive items.

I. I define formal irregularity by using purely synchronic criteria, e.g. etymologies are not taken into account when determining whether two forms are suppletive or not. Thus *am* vs. *are* vs. *is* are considered suppletive according to person–number regardless of the fact that all three are historically forms of one and the same Indo-European stem **es*. Suppletive forms are those which clearly do not conform to existing morpho-phonological patterns in language Z.

II. **Prototypical** cases of suppletion are those where there is no shared morphological material between the suppletive forms as in the already over-quoted example of *go* vs. *went*. They correspond to the NM notion of **strong** suppletion.

III. The **less prototypical** cases need to satisfy the criterion of *uniqueness* as introduced in Chapter 1: 2.1.4.2. They correspond to the NM notion of **weak** suppletion but I have split this category into two: the **truly unique** cases and the **borderline** cases both of which are illustrated below.

The truly unique cases are as illustrated by Ika in (21): the paradigm of the verb 'go' in this language consists of stems that clearly share morpho-phonological material; however they are not produced by any of the existing morpho-phonological rules and there are no other verbs that show even remotely similar alternations.

Verbs which form minor inflectional classes (typically such that consist of no more than two or three verbs) are considered borderline cases of suppletion as in Swedish in (22).

(21) Ika (Paul Frank, p.c.)

	'go'	'kill'
perfect	zož-aki	guak-aki
imperfective	zuei-n	guak-un
negative	zei-ʔ	guas-in (k → s by a regular process)
witnessed past	Zor-in	guas-in (k → s by a regular process)

(22) Swedish (own data)

	'go'	'get'
present	gå	få
past	gick	fick

My database claims to be exhaustive with regard to prototypical and truly unique cases of suppletion; however, I do not claim to have included all borderline cases in the languages examined in this study.

4.3 Use of the suppletive forms.

I. A suppletive form has to be obligatory in contexts that otherwise require marking of category X. That is, every time past tense is to be expressed for the English verb *go*, the form *went* has to be used.

II. If both a suppletive and a regular form are used for the expression of a certain category, this was coded as **alternation** as in (23).

(23) Bulgarian (own data)
'come'
idva-m   come.IPFV-PRES.1SG
idva-j   come.IPFV-IMP.2SG
ela   come.IMP.SG

III. Complementary distribution: the suppletive forms need to be in complementary distribution, e.g. one cannot be used instead of the other. For instance, using *went* in present tense contexts yields an ill-formed grammatical construction, and vice versa for the use of **goed* in the past.

4.4 Towards a typology of stem change in verb paradigms

A distinction is made between **categorial** and **non-categorial** suppletion.[9] Paradigms where the suppletive forms represent syncretism of several categories are

---

9. This distinction can be related to the distinction of general vs. category-specific suppletion offered by Fertig (1998) (cf. Chapter 1: 2.2.4) for more details on these notions.

considered cases of non-categorial suppletion. These two kinds are illustrated in (24) and . Here I gratefully acknowledge the contribution of Östen Dahl for bringing this issue to my attention and coining the terms.

(24)

	English 'go'		Finnish 'be'	
	PRES	PAST	PRES	PAST
1SG	go	went	ol-en	ol-in
2SG	go	went	ol-et	ol-it
3SG	goes	went	**on**	ol-i
1PL	go	went	ol-emme	ol-imme
2PL	go	went	ol-ette	ol-itte
3PL	go	went	**ovat**	ol-ivat

As it was discussed in Chapter 1: 2.1.4.3, a typology of suppletion should differentiate between cases where one and the same stem is used for all expressions of a category X from cases where suppletive forms actually conflate several categories and the paradigm is on the whole asymmetric. The English verb *go* uses one stem for all non-past tense forms, and another for the past. This is not the case with the Finnish verb *ollen* 'be', a partial paradigm of which is shown in (24). As we can see there are two (or three stems, depending on the analysis), and they are not evenly distributed according to category. The stem/form *on* is restricted to third-person singular present, *o-* is used for third-person plural present, and the rest of the forms are perfectly regular, with the stem *oll-* taking pertinent suffixes. Thus, it is not justified to postulate suppletion to either tense or person and number for this verb since there are just two forms that show irregularity and syncretism. As such the case is not identical with the kind of suppletion found in *go* which is why it has to be coded differently.

To recapitulate, the kind of stem change illustrated by the English verb *go* above is referred to as categorial suppletion according to tense. The kind of stem change shown by the Finnish verb *ollen* 'be' is labeled non-categorial suppletion. As we shall see in Chapter 4, these two kinds of stem change differ in several respects.

CHAPTER 3

Some theoretical issues and a general overview of the data

Paradigm as a theoretical notion was introduced in Chapter 1: 2.1.1.3 based on Carstairs-McCarthy (1998). In the first section of this chapter I introduce another, equally well known but for some reason relatively unexplored model, that of Bybee (1985). Bybee's model presents a different understanding of paradigm organization, irregularity in paradigms and ultimately suppletion. As already indicated, Bybee's work has greatly influenced the current study, which is why I discuss it here rather than in the background chapter. In the second section of this chapter I outline the types of suppletion according to grammatical category as they are observed in the current sample.

1. Paradigm revisited

In many morphological models from the generative tradition a paradigm is a group of inflectionally related words with a common lexical stem. It is a widely accepted practice to postulate an abstract underlying stem that typically has nothing or very little to do with the actual forms in a paradigm. The underlying stem is "realized" in the actual paradigm via the application of derivational rules that produce the existing surface forms. The focus of many formal models is the description (or the postulation of) these derivational rules and thereby the structure of each form in a paradigm. Since suppletive forms cannot be derived by formal rules, they appear as true problems for generative morphology and, as it was pointed out in Chapter 1, they are commonly relegated to the lexicon. For many formal morphological models (especially the early ones) one of the main questions a theory must address is what belongs to the mental lexicon and what can be described as rule-derived. Items that belong to the lexicon are generally of no interest for such models.

Bybee argues that determining which lexical items belong to the mental lexicon and which do not is too simplistic, and that such an approach does not accurately reflect language use and processing. According to Bybee's model, any form that is used may be represented in the lexicon, and the data from language processing she presents suggest that every time a form is used it leaves a trace in the mental lexicon of the speaker/hearer. The more a form is used, the stronger its representation in the mental lexicon. The question for Bybee, then, is not what is represented in the lexicon and what is not, but how strong is the form's representations and what are its connections to other forms.

Before we proceed with Bybee's model a brief comment on the notion of **markedness** is in order since it will be used below. The distinctions **marked** and **unmarked** values of a category were first developed for phonological systems by Nikolaj Trubezkoj in 1931 and first applied to morpho-syntactic categories and semantics by Roman Jakobson in 1939. The concept of markedness has since received a variety of interpretations and has been applied in rather different ways in virtually every school of linguistics. However, this is a topic in its own right and it is impossible to offer a full-fledged discussion here. In the presentation below the typological approach to markedness is followed[1]. The rudimentary treatment which follows below is intended only to give a very general orientation for those who might be unfamiliar with the concept.

A simplified summary of this important notion is the following: in the pair *cat-cats* the plural is the marked element because it has an extra morpheme. Conversely, *cat* is unmarked. The terms marked and unmarked are also utilized more broadly to refer to a default structure (unmarked) versus a structure that appears in limited circumstances (marked). In this broader sense, markedness is often based on pragmatic considerations. In typology, the frequency of a category and its values both in texts and cross-linguistically are also taken as indicators for the unmarked or marked status of a certain value(s). Thus there are three main criteria for identifying a value of a category as marked or unmarked: (i) structural; (ii) distributional and (iii) textual and cross-linguistic frequency. Not all three are applicable to all grammatical phenomena. Generally, the unmarked value(s) of a category tends to be expressed by a smaller number of morphemes and it shows a greater inflectional range and distributional applicability and greater textual and cross-linguistic frequency (Croft 1990: 92).

Since grammatical categories usually have more than one value, the binary distinction was soon developed into a **relative** one. This is to say that a value of a grammatical category is evaluated as marked when compared to one particular value X but unmarked when compared to another value Z. Thus markedness hierarchies can be postulated, for example, the values of the category of number: singular < plural < dual < trial/ paucal. The hierarchy is used to express generalizations such as that cross-linguistically, plural is marked with regard to singular but unmarked or less marked with regard to dual, and dual is less marked with regard to trial/paucal (Croft 1990: 66).

---

1. For a detailed introduction the reader is referred to the originators of the concept Trubezkoy 1969 and Jakobson (1939); a typological introduction is offered in Croft (1990, 64–94), and a treatment of markedness in formal and functional schools can be found in Battistella (1996). (This list is by no means exhaustive).

Jakobson observed that the unmarked member of a category might have a zero expression whereas marked members of a category rarely take a zero expression. Another characteristic of a marked member of a category is that it typically asserts the presence of a property while the unmarked member does not necessarily indicate the absence of that property; rather it may be neutral or ambiguous in this regard. For instance in the pair *pig-piglet*, *pig* is the unmarked member and it can refer to a pig of any size whereas *piglet* can be used to refer to a small /young pig only. With regard to verb categories, it will be noted below that present tense tends to be unmarked as opposed to past tense. The unmarked nature of a present tense follows from its various uses: present tense forms are commonly used with generic reference (that is no reference to a particular time) and present tense forms may be used for the so called 'historical present', that is to describe events which occurred in the past. Conversely, past tense is functionally more restricted than the present tense. Specifically, it is rarely used in non-past contexts, except for its use in hypothetical sentences.

Jakobson and later Greenberg observed that the unmarked member of a category tends to show more inflectional distinctions and more morpho-phonemic irregularities than the marked one. Jakobson's example is that in Russian, verbs in the present tense (the unmarked member of a tense category) show person–number distinctions while such distinctions are absent in the past tense (the marked member) as shown in (25). Russian verbs in past tense reflect the gender of subject but not person; only the masculine form is shown below.

(25) Russian

	PRESENT	PAST
1SG	čitaju	čital
2SG	čitaeš	čital
3SG	čitaet	čital

Greenberg (1966) observed that within a paradigm, the greater irregularity resides in the unmarked member of categories, which are also the most frequent. Thus alternations are more likely to be found in the present tense forms rather than past tense, in indicative rather than subjunctive forms. The data presented by Bybee (1985: 120–1) corroborate all of these observations.

As regards verb inflection, Croft (1990: 93), based on Greenberg's (1966) data and universals, makes the following observations. In person–number agreement, third person is less marked with regard to first which is less marked with regard to second. With regard to tense, present is less marked than preterit which is less marked than future; with regard to aspect, imperfective is said to be less marked than perfective. The indicative is less marked than hypothetical moods; the active voice is less marked than passive and mediopassive; positive polarity is less marked than negative polarity.

As it was stated above most formal models (Stump (2001) is not included here) are designed to postulate the derivational rules that "lead" to surface forms of a paradigm and have little or nothing to say about the relations which hold among the forms in a paradigm. Bybee makes an important contribution in this respect. She observes that paradigms are not unstructured lists but rather they tend to cluster around one or several forms, usually the most frequently used as well as semantically and formally unmarked ones.

Consider the partial paradigm of the Spanish verb *dormir* 'sleep' in (26).

(26) Spanish

	PRESENT	PRETERITE	SUBJUNCTIVE IMPERFECT	FUTURE / IMPERATIVE
1SG	duérmo	**dormí**	durmiera	
2SG	duérmes	dormiste	durmieras	duerme
3SG	**duérme**	**durmío**	durmiera	duerma
1PL	dormimos	dormimos	durmieramos	durmamos
2PL	dormís	dormisteis	durmierais	dormid
3PL	duermen	durmyeron	durmieran	duerman

The verb *dormir* above has a rather complex paradigm where three of the actual forms are used as bases for the derivation of other forms: *duérme* 3SG.PRES.INDIC, *dormí* 1SG.PRET.INDIC and *durmío* 3SG.PRET.INDIC.

It is hardly surprising that the 3SG forms of the present and preterit respectively are used as bases for the derivation of the other forms of the paradigm. The unmarked nature of 3SG has already been pointed out by Jakobson 1939 and Greenberg 1966. Specifically, Greenberg notes that if verbs tend to show person agreement at all, the third person will be the least marked, followed by the first person and then the second. This cross-linguistic generalization is corroborated by frequency counts from Spanish written and spoken sources (Bybee 1985: 58) where the most frequent verb forms are 3SG and SG in both present and preterit indicative. Those are exactly the forms that are most frequently used as bases for the derivation of other forms in Spanish paradigms.

Bybee uses the generalization with regard to marked and unmarked forms in verb inflection but also points out that it is not the only sufficient criterion for predicting which form(s) is most likely to be chosen as base(s). For making a correct prediction, she introduces the concept of lexical autonomy. Basic forms tend to be autonomous (a notion Bybee borrows from David Zager, and which is used to say that a form has its own lexical representation[2]). An autonomous form is more or

---

2. Lexical representation is related to the generative notion of what is in the mental lexicon and what is not.

less independent from other forms in the paradigm. That is, it can in various degrees function as a word on its own. Autonomous forms tend to be:

(i) semantically and formally unmarked, in the sense formulated by Jakobson (1939).
(ii) very frequent and thus learned and stored by rote.
(iii) morpho-phonemically irregular. "Even if a word is semantically marked, if it is so irregular that it cannot be derived from any other related words, it is autonomous" (Bybee 1985: 58).

So in Bybee's terms, two forms come to stand in a basic-derived relation "if one is autonomous and the other is less so, and if the two are closely related morphologically in both content and form" (Bybee 1985: 58). Some verbs have one basic form only. However, frequent paradigms may have several bases. The latter is especially true of suppletive paradigms. Bybee not only points out the existence of clusters in paradigms, but also shows that the degree of relatedness between forms may be stronger or weaker depending on the frequency of use of individual forms. So in her model, paradigms are not only semantically and formally related forms that cluster around one or several bases but forms show various degrees of closeness or distance from the base depending on their frequency of use and autonomous status. Both clustering around bases and relative autonomy of particular forms are reflected in the representation of the Spanish verb *dormir* in Figure 2.

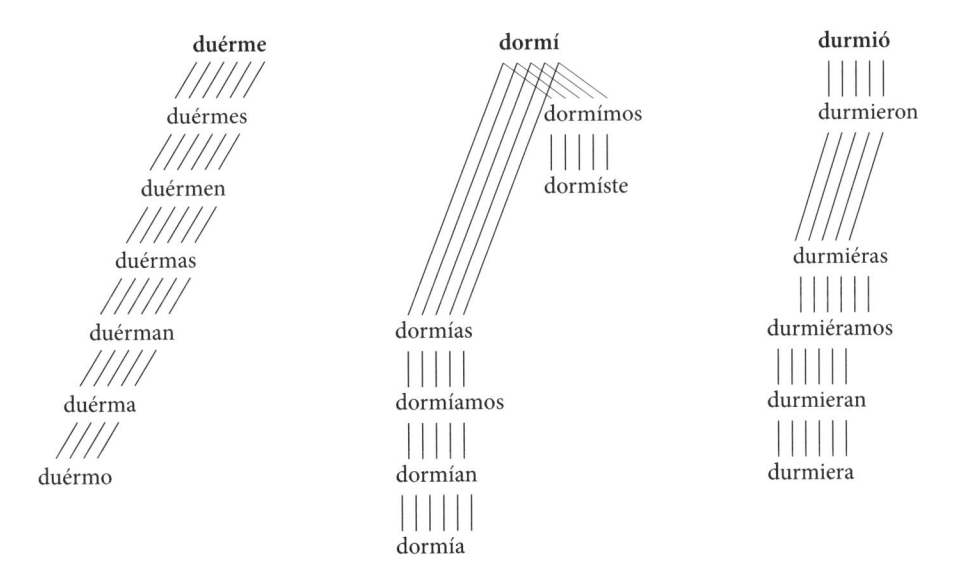

duérme
duérmes
duérmen
duérmas
duérman
duérma
duérmo

dormí
dormímos
dormíste
dormías
dormíamos
dormían
dormía

durmió
durmieron
durmiéras
durmiéramos
durmieran
durmiera

Figure 2. (Adopted from Bybee 1985: 124; the traditional Spanish orthography is used here rather than the one used by Bybee.)

In Figure 2 the inflected forms are listed in increasing frequency away from the bases to show that the more autonomous words (forms) are less closely related to the base word. In the diagram above the forms most distant from their respective bases are *duérmo* 1SG PRES INDICATIVE, *dormía* 1SG/3SG IMPERFECT and *durmiera* 3SG SUBJUNCTIVE IMPERFECT. Such a representation shows an aspect of the paradigm that is usually concealed in a mainstream formal model, namely, that the words at the bottom are in themselves fairly strong items and thus more independent from the base then the ones which are diagrammed close to it.

The observation that frequently used forms tend to be autonomous within a paradigm is very well illustrated by a suppletive paradigm. Consider the partial paradigm of the suppletive verb *ir* 'go' in Spanish.

(27)   Spanish

	PRES	PRET	SBV IMPFC	FUT	IMP
1SG	*voy*	fui	fuera	*iré*	
2SG	vas	fuiste	fueras	iráis	*ve*
3SG	*va*	*fue*	fuera	irá	vaya
1PL	vamos	fuimos	fuéramos	iremos	vamos
2PL	vais	fuistes	fuerais	iréis	*id*
3PL	van	fueren	fueran	irán	vayan

As we can see the choice of stems that are used as bases for the derivation of other forms in the paradigm still follows the noted cross-linguistic tendency: namely, they are all either 3SG or 1SG forms in the various tenses. So as regards choice of base, this suppletive paradigm is no exception to what is generally observed in languages. The paradigm of *ir* 'go' shows three additional autonomous forms, namely *voy* 1SG PRESENT, *ve* 2SG IMPERATIVE and *id* 2PL IMPERATIVE. A common verb such as 'go' is surely very often used in situations that require the imperative so it is not surprising that these forms have an independent status in its paradigm, cf. also Chapter 8 on suppletive imperatives).

As noted above, Bybee's model of paradigms diagrams the degree of relatedness among the forms in a paradigm. The degree of relatedness among forms of the paradigm is contingent on the morpho-syntactic category they express. The semantic categories relevant for verbs are arranged on a scale according to two parameters: the relevance of meaning of a certain category to the meaning of a verb stem and the way it affects the meaning of a verb. This scale has gained currency as the 'Relevance hierarchy' presented in (28).

(28)   Semantic relevance hierarchy (Bybee 1985: 124)

valence > voice > aspect > tense > mood > NAgr > PAgr > GAgr

NAgr = number agreement; PAgr = person agreement; GAgr = gender agreement

Bybee uses the hierarchy in two ways:

(i) To predict which categories are most likely to have an inflectional rather than derivational expression with verbs, and in connection to it, which categories would be expressed closest to the stem and which would tend to be further away from it.
(ii) To predict the degree of relatedness of forms within a paradigm and subsequently inflectional splits.

As regards (i), the categories on the left-hand side of the scale in (28) are very relevant for verbs but they also make the largest meaning change to the verb stem. So valence and voice rarely become inflectional but are rather derivational categories in many languages. Aspect also makes a great change in the meaning of a verb but it is more general than valence so it does become inflectional or nearly inflection in many languages. Tense and various types of agreement have the least semantic influence on the semantics of a verb, which is why they occur (a) at a greater distance from the stem than categories on the left hand side of the scale, and (b) they tend to become inflectional more often than other categories do.

As regards (ii), the semantic relevance hierarchy operates in the following manner: forms of different aspects of one and the same verb will be less closely related than the forms of different tenses and moods; forms of different persons and numbers, if they are in the same aspect or tense or mood, will be very closely related.

One of the most important predictions made by examining the degree of relatedness among forms in a paradigm is that inflectional splits are more likely to occur along major inflectional categories such as aspect and tense and less likely to occur along minor inflectional categories such as person–number agreement.

Bybee's model draws on data from cross-linguistic research, diachronic evidence of paradigm restructuring, text frequencies of categories for individual languages and experimental data from language acquisition and processing. Irregularity and suppletion are not isolated phenomena in her view. Rather the model accommodates them very well. Frequent paradigms are expected to have more than one autonomous form since forms that are used very often and in different functions may dissociate from other forms in the same paradigm. Thus autonomous forms tend to be both frequent and semantically/formally unmarked. Forms for different values of major inflectional categories that have a greater effect on the meaning of the verb stem are expected to differ more often than forms in one and the same category.

As we shall see in Chapter 4, suppletive paradigms generally conform to the cross-linguistic generalizations about markedness and autonomous forms in paradigms. The autonomous forms in suppletive paradigms are always those which are cross-linguistically unmarked with regular verbs.

2. General overview of the data

The data summarized below come from the 193 languages in the WALS sample. The types of stem change outlined above can be correlated with the kinds of semantic distinctions expressed by the stems. Non-categorial suppletion revolves around person–number of subject and tense–aspect as in French in (29).

(29) French (Indo-European, Romance)
    être 'be'

	PRES	IMPFC	FUT
1SG	*suis*	*étais*	*serai*
2SG	*es*	*étais*	*seras*
3SG	*est*	*était*	*sera*
1PL	*sommes*	*étions*	*serons*
2PL	*êtes*	*étiez*	*serez*
3PL	*sont*	*étaient*	*seront*

The verb *être* shows non-categorial suppletion because there is no single present stem that contrasts with the imperfect stem /ete/ and the future stem /sere/. Rather all person–number forms in the present are, in Bybee's terms, autonomous. In more traditional terms, they are portmanteau morphs that fuse the meaning of 'be' with the grammatical meaning of present tense and pertinent person–number reference.

The semantic distinctions of categorial (single category) suppletion cover a wide range of grammatical meanings, listed below with accompanying examples. The cases of suppletion are grouped into types according to grammatical category. Those that occur in a relatively large number of languages are called here **major** types, and the kinds of suppletion which occur in less than 10 languages are called **minor types**.

Major types

- Tense and aspect as in Irish and Modern Greek in (30) and (31) respectively.

(30) Irish (Indo-European, Celtic) (Dillon and Ó Cróinin 1961: 211)
    teim 'go'

	PRESENT	IMPERFECT	PAST	FUTURE
1SG	*téim*	*théinn*	*chuas*	*raghad*
2SG	*téann*	*théithéa*	*chuais*	*raghair*
3SG	*téann*	*théadh*	*chuaigh*	*raghaidh*

(31) Modern Greek (Indo-European, Hellenic) (Joseph and Philipaki-Warburton 1987: 187)
le(ā)ō 'say'

	IPFV	PFV
1SGPRES	*le(ā)ō*	
1SGPST	*eleāa*	*eîpa*
1SGFUT	*èa le(ā)ō*	*èa (ei)pō*
1SGPERF		*exō pei*

- Mood, specifically the use of a special form for the imperative as in Egyptian Arabic

(32) Egyptian Arabic (Afro-Asiatic, Semitic) (Mitchell 1962: 152)
'come'
ana geet	I come.PRV.M.SG
ana aagi	I come.IMPF.M.SG
taʔaala	come.IMP.M.SG
taʔaali	come.IMP.F.SG
taʔaalu	come.IMP.PL

- Verbal number as in Krongo

(33) Krongo (Niger-Congo, Kordofanian) (Reh 1985: 198)
'throw'
à-fà-anà	VERB MARKER-throw.SG.ACTION-SUFF
t-úufò-ònò	VERB MARKER-throw.PL.ACTION-SUFF

- Negative polarity as in Kanuri

(34) Kanuri (Nilo-Saharan, Saharan) (Hutchison 1981: 170–2)
mbéjí	'exist'
bâ	'not exist'

Minor types
- Person–number of subject as in Daga.

(35) Daga (Trans-New Guinea, Main section, Dagan) (Murane 1974: 70–1)

	PST	PRES
1SG	*ang-en*	*ang-ewan*
2SG	*ag-ean*	*ag-ewan*
3SG	*a-en*	*a-ewan*
1PL	*an-eton*	*an-ewan*
2PL	*ais-ean*	*ais-ewan*
3PL	*amo-n*	*amo-ewan*

- Person–number of object as in Usan.

    (36) Usan (Trans-New Guinea, Madang-Adelbert Range) (Ger Reesnik, p.c.)

	OBJ-hit-ss[3]	OBJ-hit-2/3.DS
1SGobj	ya-nam-b	ya-nam-a
2SGobj	na-nam-b	na-nam-a
3SGobj	wa-ram-b	wa-ram-a
1PLobj	inin-garam-b	inin-garam-a
2PLobj	anin-garam-b	anin-garam-a
3PLobj	i-garam-b	i-garam-a

    (37) Form of object (bound or free, definite or indefinite) as in Bukiyip below where suppletion is conditioned by the use of bound or free object.

    (38) Bukiyip (Torricelli), (Conrad and Wogiga 1991: 24)
    a. *ch-a-*wak *yabigw.*
    3PL.MIX.SUBJ-REALIS-eat soup
    'They are eating soup.'
    b. *ch-a-gw-**ah**.*
    3PL.MIX[4].SUBJ-REALIS-CLASS11PL.OBJ-eat
    'They are eating it.'

- Mood, specifically the used of a special form in subjunctive and similar moods, illustrated below by Finnish.

    (39) Finnish (Karlsson 1978)
    'be'
    ol-en be-1SG.PRESENT
    ol-in be-1SG.IMPERFECT
    ol-isi-n be-COND.PRES-1SG
    liene-n be.POTENTIAL-1SG

- Voice as in Malagasy

    (40) Malagasy (Austronesian, West Malayo-Polynesian, Borneo) (Keenan and Polinsky 1998: 590)
    'take'
    maka takes
    alain taken

---

3. SS = same subject of the following clause; DS = different subject in the following clause.

4. MIX indicates mixed gender.

- Honorific levels as in Korean

(41) Korean (Isolate, Asia) (Sohn 1994: 360)
   'eat'
   mek-ta   eat.PLAIN-INF
   capswu-si-ta   eat-DEFERENTIAL-INF
   tu-si-ta   eat-DEFERENTIAL-INF

As the data above suggest, verb paradigms involve a wide variety of phenomena: person–number agreement; tense and aspect categories; mood and modality, and together with them use of verbs in subordinate clauses; polarity (positive and negative); and voice and expression of politeness phenomena in the languages where the latter is grammaticalized. Within the limits of this study, I could only concentrate on a couple of these topics. Thus the kinds of suppletion discussed in detail in chapters 4 through 7 are suppletion according to tense–aspect categories, suppletive imperatives and verbal number suppletion. As we shall see, these types of suppletion can be further correlated with particular lexemic groups, language families, and geographical areas. Based on the data presented below, it will be argued that suppletion is not to be considered as an accidental and haphazard phenomenon, but rather that is it semantically, and, in some instances also pragmatically motivated. Suppletion examined from a typological perspective emerges as a gradient phenomenon not only according to form, but also according to the status of a category for which it is postulated. Thus some cases of suppletion are more prototypical than others, and on a grammatical-lexical scale, some cases of suppletion come closer to the grammatical end whereas others appear closer to lexicon. In general, the term suppletion is used to cover a wide variety of phenomena and this is not always obvious in the pertinent literature.

CHAPTER 4

Tense–aspect suppletion I
Synchronic perspective

1. Introduction

Suppletion according to tense–aspect categories is cross-linguistically the most widespread kind of stem change. In the current WALS sample it emerges as an areal phenomenon, concentrated mainly in western Eurasia, Meso-America and Papua New Guinea. As we shall see from the data presented below, specific patterns of suppletion according to tense–aspect categories can be correlated with particular lexemic groups and language families. The distribution of lexemes which tend to show tense–aspect suppletion is not random but can be shown to obey the relevance hierarchy presented by Bybee 1985. Furthermore, other interesting cross-linguistic patterns can be outlined, including a tentative implicational hierarchy for the likelihood of particular lexemes to use different stems in tense–aspect categories.

Different stems may be used to express the temporal situatedness of an event, typically, though not necessarily encoded as tense; in other cases, the alternating stems may be used to express the distinction between bound and unbound event typically, though, again, not necessarily, encoded as aspect. Within the broad domain of tense and aspect, the semantic distinctions made by suppletive verbs tend to follow general categories such as present:past:future or perfective:imperfective. However, different stems can be also used for the outline of finer grained tense–aspect distinctions, such as remoteness distinctions in the past or imperfect vs. preterite, and in some cases, perfect vs. other tense/aspect categories.

The paradigms which are the subject matter of this chapter show different kinds of complexity. In some of them the distribution of different stems follows established language specific tense aspect categories, as for instance the English verb *go* which uses one stem for the present tense and another, *went*, for the past. In other paradigms the different stems are not so neatly distributed as for in example the English verb *be* where several stems are, *am*, *are*, *is* are observed in the present and two completely different, *was* and *were* in the past. Paradigms of the latter kind are traditionally described as suppletion according to person–number categories, on the one hand, and suppletion according to tense on the other, but as already discussed in Chapter 1:2.1.4.3 this is not entirely correct. The stems included in the paradigm of the English verb *be* as well as similar verbs in other languages are portmanteau morphs which bundle up lexical meaning together with grammatical features such as person, number and tense in one and the same form. There is, however, no single stem either for a particular person or number or a tense category. Thus the term non-categorial suppletion was introduced in Chapter 2:4.4 to describe this particular kind of stem change. Cases where there is one stem per category are referred to as categorial suppletion.

The two broad kinds of stem change, together with subgroups, are presented in sections 2 and 3. In section 2, I describe the different subgroups of categorial suppletion: that is alternation of stems according to tense, aspect, more complex paradigms which involve both tense and aspect suppletion, and finally paradigms where there is a special form for the perfect. Paradigms which involve non-categorial suppletion are presented in section 3. The main points of the discussion for all groups are: paradigmatic relationship of the suppletive verbs, semantic distinctions outlined by the suppletive forms, cross-linguistic distribution, number of verbs per language, and finally, the verb meanings which occur with particular subgroups.

A note as regards the summary of the lexemic groups is probably most suitable here, since in the sections below we shall see several tables which present the quantitative distribution of verb meanings that occur with particular kinds of tense–aspect suppletion. In order to be made suitable for counting, some generalizing, and thereby simplification of the verb meanings reported in grammars was necessary. Generally, I chose the most common English gloss to refer to a particular lexemic group unless the source indicated a very specific meaning, in which case it was reported as such here as well. Thus for example, the verbs glossed 'be' may have different uses and thereby glossing in grammars 'be of identity', 'be of location', 'be, exist'. While those distinct senses are important in the discussion of suppletion of copula verbs (see section 4 of Chapter 5), for the general meaning counts of the synchronic distribution of suppletion, such verbs were glossed 'be/exist'. The verbs of motion, typically glossed as 'come' or 'go', 'go, walk' or in some languages 'come/go' are reported here under the joint heading 'come/go'. Unless the source was very clear as to a specific sense, generalizations similar to the one described for 'be/exist', come' and 'go'-verbs were applied to the position verbs 'sit', 'stand' and 'stay' as well as to verbs of speaking, doing and seeing, all of which can be translated by a great variety of different glosses in different grammars. The rest of the verb meanings are reported with the glosses from the original source. Consult Chapter 2:2.2 for details on the way weight values were used in the assessment of the frequency of lexemic groups with different kinds of suppletion.

As pointed out in Chapter 1:3, one of the deficiencies of previous studies on suppletion is the almost complete neglect of the morphological structure of the suppletive forms. In section 4 of this chapter, I discuss the morphological marking of suppletive forms, e.g. whether they can be described as verbs or not by language specific morphological criteria. The synchronic distribution of tense–aspect suppletion is summarized in section 5.

2. Categorial suppletion according to tense and aspect

2.1 Suppletion according to tense

2.1.1 *Semantic distinctions encoded by the suppletive forms*
The paradigmatic relationship of the suppletive forms which occur along tense lines is rarely questioned since tense typically is a category marked on all (or nearly all) verbs in the languages where it is observed as a category.

Within the domain of tense, suppletive forms are typically used to encode a binary contrast, as for instance, present vs. non-present as in Brahui in (42) or non-future vs. future as in Bengali in (43).

(42) Brahui (Dravidian, Northern) (Andronov 1980: 57–69, passim)
 'go'
 (*a*)*kā-va*   go-PRES/FUT.1SG
 ʔinā-ø   go-PST.3SG
 (*a*) *ʔinā-ra*   go-PST_PROG.3PL
 ʔin-ik   go-POTENTIAL FUT.3SG
 ʔina-ne   go-PST.PERF.3SG

(43) Bengali (Indo-European, Indo-Iranian, Indo-Aryan) (Dimock 1965: 191; Radice 1994: 50–5)
 'be present, exist'
 amiači   I be.1SG.PRES
 ami či-lam   I be-1SG.PST
 ami thak-bo   I stay-FUT = 'I will be'
 ami hɔ-bo   I become-FUT = 'I will be'

In a few cases suppletive forms may be used for making a three way distinction between past vs. present vs. future as in Georgian in (44).

(44) Georgian (South Caucasian) (Hewitt 1995: 446, passim)
 'be'
 v-ar   1SG-be.PRES
 v–i-kn-eb-i   1SG-VV-be.FUT-TS (FUT)-IND
 v–i-q'av-i   1SG-VV-be.AOR-IND

The use of suppletive forms to mark remoteness distinctions within tense is much less common. In the current sample, it is observed only in languages from New

66 Suppletion in verb paradigms

Guinea, illustrated below by (45) from Alamblak, a language spoken in the East Sepik Province, Angoram District, Papua New Guinea.

(45) Alamblak (Sepik-Ramu, Sepik), (Bruce 1984: 146)
'go'
kit-wë-r	go-PRES-M.SG
(yi)riah-r	go.FUT-M.SG
yifi-r	go.HOD-M.SG
r-i-ë-r	HEST-go-HEST-M.SG
yi-më-r	go-REM-M.SG

2.1.2 Cross-linguistic distribution of categorial tense suppletion

Tables 1 and 2 present counts on the cross-linguistic distribution of categorial tense suppletion. As discussed in Chapter 2, the frequency of a particular phenomenon is calculated here in four different ways. This is done in order to see if any significant differences would emerge, and ultimately, allow us to give a more realistic assessment of whether a certain phenomenon is cross-linguistically common or not.

As the figures in Tables 1 and 2 indicate, three out of the of the four ways of counting yield somewhat similar proportions for tense suppletion. The phenomenon occurs in about one fifth of the languages in both the small sample of 94 languages and in the WALS sample of 193 languages according to the raw count in Table 5. Likewise, the Dryer Distribution in Table 6, shows tense suppletion to occur in a little

Table 5. Language count

Small sample		WALS sample			
No	%	No	%	W	% of 70
21	22.24	39	20.21	7.24	10.34

Note: No. = Number of languages; W = Weight values sum; the total of weight values for the WALS sample is 70

Table 6. The Dryer Distribution

	Africa	Eurasia	SEA and Oceania	A–NG	N Am	S Am	Total
Yes	7	16	2	7	3	0	35
No	20	19	16	17	24	24	120

Note: Yes = presence of categorial tense suppletion; No = absence of categorial tense suppletion; Total number of genera = 150 (recall from Chapter 2: 2.1 that the number of genera does not necessarily add up since within one and the same genus, there can be languages with suppletion and without suppletion. So one and the same genus can be included in both yes and no groups).

more than one fifth of the world's genera. The result of the weight values calculus presents it as much less common as its frequency is down to one tenth of the total weights. Since three independent counting methods give very close results, it is probably safe to conclude that the proportion they yield is close to reality.

As regards areal distribution categorial suppletion according to tense is most clearly manifested in Eurasia as compared to other areas. However, this phenomenon is relatively well represented both in Africa and in Australia–New Guinea. In the current WALS sample, it is less common among the native languages of the Americas, South-East Asia and Oceania.

2.1.3 *Lexemic groups with categorial tense suppletion*

The number of suppletive verbs according to tense is typically one or two per language. The only exceptions are Irish with seven, followed by Suena with six; the latter is a language from the Morobe Province of Papua New Guinea. The exact number of suppletive verbs according to tense in individual languages is presented in Appendix 3.

The verb meanings found with this kind of suppletion are listed in Table 7. As the figures in Table 7 show, categorial tense suppletion is rather unevenly distributed

Table 7. Lexemic groups with categorical tense suppletion

Meaning	No.[a]	%	Weighed values sum	%
be/exist	24	34.3	4.62	34
go/come	17	24.3	2.29	17
sit/stand/stay	6	8.57	1.23	9
give	4	5.70	0.68	5
die	3	4.28	0.83	6
say	3	4.28	0.298	2
have	2	2.85	1.01	7
get	2	2.85	0.188	1
do	1	1.43	0.083	1
become	1	1.43	0.17	1
eat	1	1.43	0.125	1
fall	1	1.43	0.5	4
live	1	1.43	0.083	1
run	1	1.43	0.17	1
see	1	1.43	0.33	2
wake up	1	1.43	0.5	4
walk	1	1.43	0.5	4
Total	70	100.00	13.611	100

[a] No. For all verbs except 'be', this figure indicates number of languages since in most cases there is just one suppletive verb with a particular sense, say 'give' etc. In some languages, such as Mundari and Chamorro there are two copula verbs 'be of identity' and 'be, exist, have'; in each language both verbs show suppletion according to tense distinctions. Thus for the 'be/exist' group' the number of languages is 22 but the number of verbs is 24 as shown below.

among lexemic groups. By both counts, more than 30% of the verbs which use suppletive forms to encode tense distinctions are copula or copula-like verbs meaning 'be/exist'. Besides, the group of position verbs includes verbs which are regularly used as locative copulas in their languages. Since they are also used with their lexical meaning, I reported them separately but they could also have been counted together with the copula verbs. The other larger group consists of the verbs of motion, 'come' and 'go'. The rest of the verb meanings listed above show at best sporadic occurrences in the languages in this group. The proportions resulting from the weight values calculus confirm the ones produced by the raw count.

2.2 Suppletion according to aspectual distinctions

2.2.1 *Paradigmatic relationship of the suppletive forms*

Marking of aspect shows varying degrees of generality, obligatoriness and uniformity of expression. In this section I present paradigms where the stem change encodes bound vs. non-bound events. However, the specific categories where the stems are used are not always labeled as aspect (see data from Modern Eastern Armenian (53) and Burushaski (54) in section 2.2.2 below). Marking of aspect in Slavic languages is discussed in some detail since in these languages it appears to be a matter of word formation rather than inflection.[1] As we recall (cf. Chapter 1: 2.1.2.2), many scholars restrict the term suppletion to describe exceptions to inflectional patterns only. Hence, the paradigmatic relationship of the Slavic verbs found in aspectual pairs, and subsequently the use of the term suppletion to describe them requires a more detailed explanation.

There are 34 languages in the WALS sample where suppletive verbs according to aspect are observed (see section 2.2.3 below for further details on cross-linguistic frequency and areal distribution). In this group, there are 13 languages where the expression of aspect can be described as general enough in the sense that it applies to most of verbs in a specific language and its expression is more or less uniform. For instance, in Modern Greek, aspect is marked regularly on all verbs (with very few exceptions). The perfective stem is formed by the addition of a suffix, usually -s-, with accompanying morpho-phonemic changes as shown by (46).

---

1. See the discussion on the derivation-inflection continuum in Chapter 1: 2.1.1.2 and 2.1.2.2 for ways to define these notions.

(46) Modern Greek (Indo-European, Hellenic) (Joseph and Philipaki-Warburton 1987: 176)
'write'
γraf-ō   write.IPFV-1SG.PRES
e-γraf-a   AUGMENT-write.IPFV-1SG.PST
θa γraf-ō   FUT write.IPFV-1SG.PRES
θa γrap-s-ō   FUT write-PFV-1SG.PRES
e-γrap–s-a   AUGMENT-write-PFV.1SG.AOR

There are three verbs in Modern Greek, illustrated by 'see' in (47) which use completely unrelated stems for the expression of the imperfective: perfective distinction. They are thus paradigmatically related since the encoding of aspect is part of the inflectional system in this language.

(47) Modern Greek (Indo-European, Hellenic) (Joseph and Philipaki-Warburton 1987: 196)
'see'
blep-ō   see.IPFV-1SG.PRES
e-blep-a   AUGMENT-see.IPFV-1SG.PST
θa blep-ō   FUT see.IPFV-1SG.PRES
θa (i)d-ō   FUT see.PFV-1SG.PRES
e-id-a   AUGMENT-see.PFV-1SG.AOR

As mentioned above, in Slavic languages, marking of aspect is very much an issue of word formation. Data from Slovene, a South Slavic language, are used for the outline of basic facts of coding aspect in Slavic languages. It should be noted that a lot of details are omitted here since my focus is not Slavic aspectology. The literature on the subject is enormous; the reader is referred to Schuyt (1990) for a detailed presentation of the morphology of Slavic aspect, to Dickey (2000) for a relatively recent semantic analysis as well as to some older but excellent studies by Maslov (1984) and Dahl (1985).[2] Although Slovene is as representative as any Slavic language, there is a great deal of language specific variation as regards the expression(s) of aspect, so the data below should not be taken as valid for all Slavic languages.

In Slovene, as well as in the other Slavic languages, the opposition between imperfective and perfective aspect is expressed formally by prefixation (48a), suffixation (48b), stem modification (48c) and finally by using completely different verbs (48d) and (48e).

---

2. This list represents merely the books I have found most useful for the purposes of the current study. It is not exhaustive, and not even the tip of the iceberg of all the literature on Slavic aspect.

(48) Slovene (Indo-European, South Slavic) (Herrity 2000: 151)

	IPFV	PFV	Gloss
a.	kríti	po-kríti	'cover'
b.	kupo-vá-ti[3]	kupíti	'buy'
c.	za-pírati	za-préti	'shut'
d.	métati	vreči	'throw'
e.	praviti	reči	'say'

Thus most verbs in Slovene can be classified as either perfective or imperfective. Typically, they come in pairs but by means of what is commonly referred to as **secondary imperfectivization** an imperfective verb may be derived from a perfective one as in (49). The secondary imperfective verb may express iterative or delimitative action as *pokrivati* in (49), which may, apart from the unfolding action of covering, also mean 'cover a little'.

(49) Slovene (Indo-European, South Slavic) (Herrity 2000: 223)

IPFV	PFV	IPFV	Gloss
kríti	po-kríti	pokrí-va-ti	'cover'

Although the majority of Slovene verbs exist in correlated pairs or triples, a certain number of verbs have only one form which can be used in both perfective and imperfective aspects. Such verbs are commonly labeled as **biaspectual**; some examples of them are common verbs such as *rodíti* 'give birth to', *darováti* 'give, donate' *voščíti* 'wish, bid', to name just a few. Morphologically non-derived verbs tend to be imperfective but as can be seen from (48b) non-derived verbs, which are perfective, exist too. Their number is limited but by no means small. Finally, there are prefixed verbs as in (48c) without any non-prefixed counterparts.

Using prefixes as in (48a) to derive perfective verbs from their imperfective counterparts is a very widespread process, probably the most productive one amongst all mentioned above. It should be noted, however, that such prefixes are numerous and lexically conditioned. Furthermore, their function is very often semantic, that is, they not only change the aspect of a verb but also lead to a change of its lexical meaning as in (50). In such cases an imperfective counterpart of the prefixed perfective verb is (may be) created by means of suffixation.

(50) Slovene (Indo-European, South Slavic) (Herrity 2000: 204)

IPFV	Gloss	PFV	IPFV	Gloss
črtati	'draw a line'	podčrtati	podčrtavati	'underline'
		očrtati	očrtavati	'outline, sketch'

---

3. The stem to which affixes attach is *kup*V-.

Thus even from this very rudimentary presentation, it should become clear that the means for encoding aspectual categories in Slavic languages are very diverse, lexically conditioned and not particularly regular. So in this respect, verb pairs such as those illustrated by *metati: vreči* 'throw.IPFV:PFV' in (48d) and *praviti: reči* 'say.IPFV: PFV' in (48e) do not satisfy one of the criteria for suppletion stated in Chapter 2: 4, namely that the category according to which suppletive forms occur should be regularly expressed by fairly well defined morpho-syntactic means.

Making the imperfective–perfective distinction is, however, very pervasive in Slovene so the verbs which express it by separate lexical items appear like genuine exceptions to a widespread pattern. Although this pattern is not uniform, and consists, in fact, of numerous sub-patterns, the apparent non-use of any of them is still noted as an exception. Mel'čuk (1994) in his illustration of suppletion according to aspect readily reports the Russian aspectual pairs similar to the Slovene verbs above as suppletive according to aspect without offering any further discussion as to their paradigmatic relationship. It is worth mentioning that intuitions as to the paradigmatic relationship of such verbs vary (Maria Koptjevskaja-Tamm, p.c.).[4] In some descriptions they are called 'pairs', in others 'suppletive verbs according to aspect'. Native speakers, when consulted, readily produce pairs such as those in (48d) and (48e) as forms of the imperfective: perfective opposition for one and the same lexical meaning. However, since, in most instances of such pairs, we are dealing with polysemous verbs, their uses are typically numerous and the pairing of the verbs may be valid for a certain (even large) set of them, but not necessarily for all. In some cases we even observe a tendency for lexical split. For instance, the Russian verbs *klast'* 'lay.IPFV' and *položit'* 'lay.PFV' are typically reported in Russian grammars as suppletive according to aspect. However, the verbs match semantically only in their literal senses such as 'lay OBJECT SOMEWHERE' and similar. For more abstract senses of *položit'* such as 'put forth, suggest, propose, think' the regular imperfective *polagat'* is used. The distinction between a more literal and more abstract sense extends also to derivatives of these verbs as for instance *vkladyvat'/vložit' pis'mo v konvert* 'to place a letter into an envelope' and *vlagat':vložit' dushu vo čto-nibud'* 'to put one's heart into something'.

As noted already in Chapter 1, the scope and generality of a derivational pattern matter when one is to determine whether exceptions to it are to be seen as suppletive or simply separate lexical items. While the aspect in Slavic languages is clearly derivational in nature, it is also so widespread that it looks obligatory, (cf. also (Dahl 1985: 89.) Thus postulating suppletion according to the general imperfective: perfective distinction is justified for the observed cases in Slavic languages inasmuch as this distinction is so commonly coded on the majority of their verbs.

---

[4]. Thanks to Maria Koptjevskaja-Tamm and, indirectly to Alexej Shmelev, for the lengthy discussions on this topic as well as data from Russian.

2.2.2 Semantic distinctions

In the majority of the languages where suppletion according to aspect is observed, the suppletive forms express the main aspectual categories such as imperfective vs. perfective shown by Lezgian, a language from Dagestan, Russia, and Wichita, currently spoken by about a dozen people in west-central Oklahoma, USA.[5]

(51) Lezgian (North-East Caucasian) (Haspelmath 1993: 136)
 'do'
 awú-na do-AOR
 ijí-zwa do-IPFV

(52) Wichita (Caddoan) (Rood 1976: 73)
 'go'
 wa go.PFV
 hisha go.IPFV

There are languages such as Modern Eastern Armenian, Hindi, Bengali and Burushaski where the stem used in the aorist is also used in the perfect, and other categories associated with perfectivity. Thus an opposition is established between this stem and the stem used in tense categories associated with imperfective meaning. While aspect is not a category formally marked in these languages, following Dahl (1985), I have classified the suppletive stems as enconding an aspectual contrast rather than one of tense, which is why these languages are included in this group.

(53) Modern Eastern Armenian (Indo-European, Armenian) (Jasmine Dum-Traugut, p.c.)
 'come'
 gal come.INF
 gal-is come-PRES.PTCP
 gal-u come-FUT.PTCP
 ek-el come-PERF.PTCP
 ek-ats come-RES.PTCP
 ek-a come-AOR

(54) Burushaski (Isolate, Asia) (Lorimer 1935: 260)
 'come'
 jucha ba come be.1SG.PRES
 juch-əm come-1SG.FUT
 jucha ba-iyəm come be-1SG.IMPF
 daiyəm come.1SG.PST.PFV
 daiya baiyəm come.PST.PTCP be.1SG.PST= come.1SG.PERF

---

5. Historically the tribe ranged from Kansas into Northern Texas (Rood 1976).

Suppletive forms may be used to mark some less general aspectual distinctions but this is rather unusual. In the WALS sample such verbs are attested in Chalcatongo Mixtec, a language from Oaxaca, Mexico, and Mara, a Non-Pama Nyungan language from Northern Australia.

(55) Chalcatongo Mixtec (Oto-Manguean, Mixtecan) (Macaulay 1996: 170)
(Bybee 1985: 92–3)
'come'
nbíí come.HAB
bèì come.PROG
na-kii PFV-come

(56) Mara (Australian, Maran) (Heath 1981: 270)
'go/come'
-ḷini/jurā go.DUR
yuraŋī go.NON_DUR
aŋa go.PUNC.PST

The use of suppletive forms to indicate the imperfective vs. perfective distinction is the predominant case within suppletion according to aspect: out of the 84 verbs that show it in the current database, 78 verbs use suppletive forms in this way.

2.2.3 *Cross-linguistic distribution of suppletion according to aspect*

The different calculations of the cross-linguistic frequency of aspect suppletion are presented in Tables 8 and 9.

Table 8. Language count

Small sample		WALS sample			
No	%	No	%	W	% of 70
15	15.95	34	17.62	7.083	10.12

Notes: No. = number of languages; W = weight values sum; 70 = the total of weight values for the WALS sample

Table 9. The Dryer Distribution

	Africa	Eurasia	SEA and Oceania	A–NG	N Am	S Am	Total
Yes	2	11	0	2	7	1	23
No	23	22	18	22	15	23	123

Notes: yes = presence of categorial aspect suppletion; no = absence of categorial aspect suppletion; the total number of genera is 150.

Similarly to the counts for categorical tense suppletion, the proportions resulting from the raw counts (Table 8) are very close to the one resulting from the genera count (Table 9). As we can see, according to all three, categorical aspect suppletion occurs in around 15 percent of both languages and genera. The weight value calculus gives a lower frequency of ca. 10%. The proportions of both languages and genera with aspect suppletion is lower than that for categorical tense suppletion, which is contrary to what is commonly known, namely that paradigms are most likely to split along aspectual lines, cf. Bybee (1985: 92–3). I am afraid that at this stage I cannot offer a good explanation for this result. It should be noted that in terms of areal distribution, suppletion according to aspect shows concentration in two areas, Eurasia and North America, as opposed to tense suppletion which appears almost exclusively in Eurasia. Also, as it will become clear form section 2.2.4 below, most of the verbs in this group are full lexical verbs, as opposed to grammaticalizing or fully grammaticalized items, and languages with tense suppletion appear to have more of those, at least in the current sample.

2.2.4 *Lexemic groups with categorial aspect suppletion*
In individual languages, the number of verbs with aspect suppletion ranges between 1 up to as many as 9. In the majority of languages where such verbs are found they are between 2 and 4. The verb meanings which show this kind of suppletion are listed in the Table 10.

As the counts in Table 10 show, the two verbs which with the highest frequency both per number of occurrence, and weight values are the verbs of motion 'go' and 'come'. The proportion offered by the language count and the weight value calculus vary for other lexemic groups. Differences of 5% and greater appear in ***bold-italic*** in Table 10. For instance, a meaning such as 'give' has a low occurrence (3.6%) in the language count but relatively high weight value (9.32%). This shows that it occurs in languages which are not closely related. On the other hand, verbs such as 'take' and 'lay/put' show relatively high frequency in the language count but very low weight value sums. This points to the fact that these verbs show aspect suppletion in closely related languages. Indeed, most instances of aspect suppletion with these verbs are observed in East and West Slavic languages. While the results of the weight values calculus are still be taken with a certain amount of caution, in this case, the picture they present is not all that improbable. Given that we know that a verb such as 'take' occurs in closely related languages whereas verbs such as 'go/come' or 'do' or 'give' show suppletion according to aspect in genealogically and geographically distant languages, it is reasonable to conclude that cross-linguistically such verbs are more prone to show aspect suppletion than a verb such as 'take' where suppletion is essentially restricted to the Slavic family.

Table 10. Lexemic groups with categorical aspect suppletion

Meaning	No[a]	%	Weight value sum	%
go/come	19	22.62	4.702	33.99
take	10	*11.91*	0.568	*4.10*
say/speak	9	10.71	0.845	6.10
see/watch	7	8.34	1.282	9.27
do	6	7.14	1.051	7.60
lay/put	6	**7.14**	0.181	**1.31**
eat	4	4.76	0.540	3.61
give	3	**3.60**	1.290	**9.32**
carry	3	3.57	0.580	4.19
become	2	2.38	0.290	2.09
catch	2	2.38	0.028	0.23
die, (kill)	2	2.38	0.495	3.58
hear	2	2.38	0.136	0.98
throw	2	2.38	0.025	0.18
aim	1	1.19	0.014	0.11
beat	1	1.19	0.011	0.08
become cold	1	1.19	0.165	1.19
become, happen, go	1	1.19	0.500	3.61
cry	1	1.19	0.125	0.90
drink	1	**1.19**	1.000	**7.22**
move	1	1.19	0.007	0.05
Total	84	100.00	13.835	100.00

[a] For all verbs except 'go/come', this figure indicates number of languages since in most cases there is just one suppletive verb with a particular sense, say 'give'. In some languages, such as Pashto and Chalcatongo Mixtec, both verbs 'come' and 'go' are suppletive according to aspect, so the number 19 indicates the actual number of suppletive verbs with the sense 'come' or 'go'.

2.3 Stem change which involves several tense–aspect categories

Complex paradigms where different stems are used for the encoding of both tense and aspect categories are not particularly common but in a typology of suppletion in verb paradigms they need to be set apart from other verbs where separate stems are used for the encoding of either tense or aspect.[6] Such complex paradigms are exemplified below by Russian in (57) and Georgian in (58).

(57) Russian (Indo-European, East Slavic), (Maria Koptjevskaja-Tamm, p.c.)
 'come'
 prixož-u   come-1SG.PRES
 prixod-il come.IPFV-1SG.PST.M

---

6. Here I gratefully acknowledge the help of Maria Koptjevskaja-Tamm, who pointed out to me that such verbs should be put in a separate group.

	prišel	come.PFV.SG PST.M
	prid-u	come.PFV-1SG.PRES=come.PFV.FUT
	bud-u prixod-it'	be.FUT-1SGcome.IPFV-INF

(58) Georgian (South Caucasian) (Hewitt 1995: 446)
'say, tell'

v–e–ubn–eb–I	1SG-VV-tell.IPFV-TS-IND (=PRES.1SG)
v–e–ubn–eb–od–i	1SG-VV-tell.IPFV-TS-IMPF-IND (=IMPF.1SG)
v–u–txar–I	1SG-VV-tell.PFV-IND (=AOR.1SG)
v–e–t'q'v–I	1SG-VV-tell.FUT-IND (=FUT.1SG)

There are few other languages such as Ingush, a language spoken in Ingushetia (North Ossetia), Dagestan, Russia and Irish where some verbs use a different stem for just about every category in the paradigm.

(59) Ingush (North Caucasian) (Johanna Nichols, p.c.)
'give'

lu	give.PRES
luddy	give.FUT
lu-ora	give-IMPERFECT
d-alar	GENDER.CLASS-give.WITNESSED.PST
d-annad	GENDER.CLASS-give.NON_WITNESSED.PST

(60) Irish (Indo-European, Celtic) (Dillon and Ó Cróinin 1961: 211)
'go'

te-ann	go-3SG.PRES
rac-haidh	go-3SG.FUT
do chuaigh	PST.PARTICLE go.3SG.PST
do theídh	PST.PARTICLE go.HAB.3SG.PST
dulta	go.PST.PTCP

Only the present and the habitual past forms in the Irish verb 'go' are related by consonant gradation. The rest of the forms cannot be derived by any morpho-phonological rules of this language.

In my material such complex paradigms appear to be rare. In the WALS sample, they are concentrated in three branches of Indo-European: Slavic (7 languages), Romance (2 languages) and Celtic (1). Outside of Indo-European they are found in the languages of the Caucasus, Georgian and Ingush. Thus they amount to 12 languages.

Except for French, in all of the languages mentioned above, such complex paradigms are observed with the verbs of motion, 'come' and 'go'. Other meanings which occur in single languages in this group are 'be' (French, Spanish and Serbo-

Table 11.

Meaning	No.	%	Weight values	%
go/come	23	75	2.12	36
be/exist	3	10	0.26	4
say/speak/tell	2	6	2.00	33
do	2	6	1.33	22
give	1	3	0.33	5
Total	31	100	6.04	100

Croatian), 'do' (Ingush and Georgian), 'give' in Ingush 'say' and 'say to, tell', both in Georgian. This is presented also in Table 11.

2.4 Suppletive perfects

There are a few cases where the only irregularity in the paradigm is the use of a suppletive stem for the perfect as illustrated below by Pipil, a language from El Salvador.

(61) Pipil (Uto-Aztecan, Southern), (Campbell 1985: 94–5)
 'see'
 ni-k-ida-Ø   1SG.SUBJ-SG.OBJ-see-PRES   'I see it'
 ni-k-ida-k   1SG.SUBJ-SG.OBJ-see-PST   'I saw it'
 ni-k-its-tuk   1SG.SUBJ-SG.OBJ-see-PERF   'I have seen it'

I am aware of four other languages, Modern Greek, Serbo-Croatian, Macedonian and Bulgarian (curiously all from the Balkans) where a special form for the perfect is observed.

(62) Modern Greek (Indo-European, Hellenic) (Joseph and Philipaki-Warburton 1987: 196)
 'be'
 īmai   be.1SG.PRES
 imoun(a)   be.1SG.IMPF
 éxo staθ-i   have.1SG.PRES stand-PST.PTCP (=PERF.1SG 'be')

(63) Macedonian (Indo-European, South Slavic) (de Bray 1980b: 286–7)
 'go'
 id-am   go-1SG.PRES
 id-ev   go-1SG.IMPF
 po-jd-ov   PFV-go-1SG.AOR
 išol   go.PST.PTCP.SG.M

Suppletion of the form used for the perfect (typically a participle), however, observed in paradigms where other kinds of suppletion are present too as in the Germanic languages, illustrated below by Dutch.

(64) Dutch (Indo-European, West Germanic) (Donaldson 1981: 139)
'be'
ben	be.1SG.PRES
was	be.1SG.PST
geweest	be.PTCP

These languages are included in the group of non-categorial suppletion below so they are not counted here.

The number of languages with a special form only for the past participle is five (Serbo-Croatian, Macedonian, Bulgarian, Modern Greek and Pipil). The meanings are the verbs of motion 'come' and 'go' in the Slavic languages, 'be' in Greek, and 'see' in Pipil.

3. Non-categorial suppletion

The subject matter of this section are verbs which simply do not have an identifiable stem for all forms of neither a particular tense or aspect or a person–number category. In Chapter 3 I quoted the verb meaning 'be' from a well-known language, French *être*: *suis, es, est*, etc. In languages where paradigms of this kind are observed, they appear as complete isolates in their verb systems. However, when analyzed from the point of view of Bybee's model from 1985 (see Chapter 3: 1) such verbs appear a lot less idiosyncratic, especially in a cross-linguistic sense. First, they show only a clear tendency to follow familiar typological generalizations about verb paradigms. Second, it can be demonstrated that they share characteristics which make them similar to one another in the following respects:

(i) The choice of autonomous form(s).
(ii) The tense categories where autonomous forms occur.
(iii) The uses and function of such verbs in the languages where they are found.

The discussion below is focused on these three parameters.

As regards the first one, the choice of autonomous forms(s) in a paradigm, the paradigms relevant here can be classified into five broad groups. In the first group (Group I) I include languages where we find paradigms which consist of autonomous forms only in at least one tense. The second group (Group II) is very similar to the first one, the difference is that it includes paradigms which can be analyzed either as having a single-segment stem or as consisting of completely independent forms. In the third group (Group III), paradigms where one, or at the most two, autonomous forms are observed; those forms are typically 3SG and/or 3PL. In the fourth group (Group IV) I include languages where the autonomous form is first or second person. Finally, there is a small group of languages (Group V) where the stem change is conditioned by a combination of categories such as number and tense, and the category of person is irrelevant.

A typical paradigm from Group I shows forms which are completely distinct from each other in the sense that no language specific morpho-phonological rules can be postulated for their derivation. It is illustrated by the Basque verb *izan* 'be' in (65) below.

(65) Basque (Isolate, Europe) (King 1994: 363)

	PRES	PST
1SG	naiz	nintzen
2SG	zara	zinen
3SG	da	za
1PL	gara	ginen
2PL	zarete	zineten
3PL	dira	ziren

The forms are so different from each other that basic-derived relation is practically non-existent in the paradigm and thus all its forms are seen as autonomous.

Another example for non-categorial suppletion comes from Yimas, a language from the East Sepik Province of Papua New-Guinea. In this language, the subject-referencing prefixes are attached to the stem (*a*)*ya*- to build the forms of the copula verb. However, these prefixes undergo a great deal of metathesis and become infixed in some of the forms, often with unpredictable results. According to Foley (1991: 226), it is best to simply list the variant forms of the copula since they are highly irregular and are not accommodated by any morpho-phonological rules of the language.

(66) Yimas (Sepik-Ramu, Nor-Pondo), (Foley 1991: 226–7)
 'be

PERSON \ NUMBER	SG	DU	PAUCAL	PL
1	amayak	kapayak	paŋkrayak	aypak
2	amyak	kapwayak	paŋkrayak	(p)aypwak
3	anak	aympak	akrak	(p)apuk

Paradigms may exhibit different degrees of autonomy of forms. Consider the paradigm of the Dutch verb *zijn* 'be' in (67).

(67) Dutch (Indo-European, West Germanic) (Donaldson 1981: 139)

	PRES	PST
1SG	ben	was
2SG.INFORMAL	bent	was
2SG.FORMAL	bent/is	was
3SG	is	was
1PL	zijn	waren
2PL.INFORMAL	zijn/bent	waren
2PL.FORMAL	bent	was
3PL	zijn	waren

The forms in this paradigm show a great deal of syncretism, they are completely unpredictable which makes them independent from each other, in other words autonomous.

Other languages where verbs of the kind of Dutch *zijn* 'be' are observed are German, English, French, Hindi as well as Carib and Macushi, both Northern Carib languages spoken in the savannah areas of Venezuela, Guyana, Surinam and Northern Brazil.

(68) Carib (Carib, Northern) (Hoff 1968: 212)
maŋ 'be'

	PRES	PST
1SG	wa	wa:koŋ
2SG	ma:na	ma:koŋ
3SG	maŋ/na	kina:koŋ
1PL	kita:toŋ	kita:tokoŋ
2PL	mandoŋ	ma::tokoŋ
3PL	mandoŋ	kina:tokoŋ

The second group includes paradigms of the kind of Slovene verb *biti* 'be' in (69).

(69) Slovene (Indo-European, South Slavic), (Herrity 2000: 167, passim)
biti 'be'

	PRES	PST M[7]	FUT
1SG	sem	bil sem	bo-m
2SG	si	bil si	bo-š
3SG	je	bil je	bo
1DU	sva	bil sva	bo-va
2DU	sta	bil sta	bo-sta
3DU	sta	bil sta	bo-sta

---

7. M refers specifically to the singular forms of the past tense.

1PL	smo	bili smo	bo-mo
2PL	ste	bili ste	bo-ste
3PL	so	bili so	bo-do

Compare the present tense paradigms of two other Slovene verbs in (70a–b).[8] The verb *délati* 'do' in (70a) belongs to the so called **thematic** conjugation and is completely regular; the verb *védeti* 'know' in (70b) belongs to a restricted set of verbs called the **athematic** conjugation and show certain irregular features.

(70) Slovene (Indo-European, South Slavic), (Herrity 2000: 159, passim)

	a. *délati* 'do'	b. *védeti* 'know'
	PRES	PRES
1SG	déla-m	vé-m
2SG	déla-š	vé-š
3SG	déla	vé
1DU	déla-va	vé-va
2DU	déla-ta	vé-sta
3DU	déla-ta	vé-sta
1PL	déla-mo	vé-mo
2PL	déla-te	vé-ste
3PL	déla-jo	vé-do/vé-jo

As we can see, the present tense of the Slovene verb 'be' in (69) consists of irregular forms only. The form *je* 'be.3SG.PRES' is completely unrelated to all the other forms, and what they have in common is just the initial segment *s-*. One possible analysis is to identify the initial segment *s-* as a possible stem and state that the person–number suffixes of the thematic conjugation, as illustrated in (70a), are added to it. However, it is questionable whether such an analysis holds any plausibility. Most probably, speakers perceive and remember such forms as they are, without further analysis. Similar verbs exist in other languages as well. In this sample they

---

[8] Some characteristics of the Slovene verb system are as follows. Generally, verbs in Slovene have a synthetic present tense. The other tenses, such as the future, past and the pluperfect are expressed analytically with the auxiliary *biti* 'be' and the *-l* participle. So, for instance, for the verbs cited above first-person singular of past tense will be *vedel sem* 'known be.1SG.PRES' = 'I knew' and *délal sem* 'done 1SG.PRES' = 'I did'; for the future *vedel bom* 'known 1SG.FUT' = 'I will know' and *délal bom* 'done 1SG.FUT' = 'I will do'. In the present tense, each Slovene verb inflects in accordance with one of five conjugations. The first four are called thematic since a thematic vowel (*-a-*, *-i-*, *-je-* or *-e-*) precedes the person–number suffixes, illustrated by *délati* in (70a). The fifth conjugation includes a limited number of so-called athematic verbs in which the person–number affixes are added directly to the root of the verb without the presence of an athematic vowel, illustrated by *védeti* 'know' in (70b).

appear to be predominantly Indo-European: Modern Eastern Armenian, Modern Greek, seven Slavic languages, and finally Spanish. The only non-Indo-European language in this group is Brahui, a Northern Dravidian language from Pakistan. Bybee (1985: 121) refers to this phenomenon in her discussion of the correlation of high frequency with high degree of synthesis or fusion. She finds this correlation both on lexical and paradigmatic level. Highly fused stem and affix combinations occur among the most frequent lexical items. With the exception of Spanish, all of the languages, mentioned above, the verbs which show this kind of synthesis include the verb 'be', which is one of the most frequent and multi-functional verbs in any language that has it.

The paradigms included in Group III are illustrated by Fur, a Nilo-Saharan language from Northern Sudan in (71a) and (71b) and Finnish in (72). What such paradigms have in common is that the autonomous forms there are confined to a few cells and unlike the paradigms in (65)–(69) above they have not taken over the entire paradigm. Typically, such single occurrences of autonomous forms are express the third person, either SG or PL or both.

(71) Fur (Nilo-Saharan, Fur) (Angelika Jakobi, p.c.)

a. 'be' b. 'go'

	PRESENT	PAST	PRESENT	PAST
1SG	àŋ	ààŋá	ànnì	íò
2SG	ɟàŋ	ɟààŋá	ɟànnì	ɟíò
3SG	**ìì**	ààŋá	**dúítì/dúì**	**ɲàŋá**
1PL	kàŋ	kààŋá	kànnì	kíò
2PL	bàŋ	bààŋá	bànnì	bíò
3PL	**gé**	**kèìŋ**	kànníà	kéŋè

(72) Finnish (Finno-Ugric, Finnish), partial paradigm (Karlsson 1978)
olla 'be'

	PRESENT	IMPERFECT
1SG	ol-en	ol-in
2SG	ol-et	ol-it
3SG	**on**	ol-i
1PL	ol-emme	ol-imme
2PL	ol-ette	ol-itte
3PL	**ovat**	ol-ivat

Group IV includes paradigms where the autonomous form(s) is either 1 or 2 person.

(73) Hungarian (Finno-Ugric, Ugric) (Olsson 1992: 180–1)
'go'

	PRESENT
1SG	*mëgyëk*
2SG	*mész*
3SG	*mëgy*
1PL	*mëgyünk*
2PL	*mëntëk*
3PL	*mënnek*

The fifth group (Group V) includes paradigms from two languages only: Ingush (North Caucasian), Northern Tepehuan (Southern Uto-Aztecan). The stems in those paradigms involve categories such as tense and number, rather than tense and person–number as in the groups above.

(74) Ingush (North-Caucasian) (Johanna Nichols, p.c.)
'go'

	PRES	FUT	WITNESSED.PST	NON-WITNESSED.PST
SG	*d-uoda*	*ghogvy/ghorghvy*	*d-axar*	*d-axaad*
PL	*d-olx*	*ghogby*	*b-axar*	*b-axaab*

Thus the verb 'go' in Ingush above, does not have a single stem for the present tense but rather two stems, one used with singular subjects and the other with plural.

We now turn to the second parameter of the description of "messy" paradigms, namely their occurrence in specific tense categories. Paradigms which show non-categorial suppletion are observed in both present, past, very seldom in the future. As shown in Table 12 below, the cross-linguistic distribution of such paradigms in specific tenses is uneven. The most common case is that such paradigms are restricted to the present tense as in (69) from Slovene above. The occurrence of irregular paradigms of this kind in both present and past tenses as in Basque, (65) above, is much less common. Finally, there are two languages, Maltese and Fur, which have verbs where the irregularity is restricted to past tense only (see examples (75) and (77) and discussion below).

Table 12 presents a summary of the description of non-categorial suppletion with regard to occurrence of autonomous forms in the paradigms and the tenses where autonomous forms are observed. As the table demonstrates, it is largely the present tense where a uniform stem is missing and autonomous forms are observed. The greater part of paradigms with non-categorial suppletion consist of autonomous forms only (cf. groups I and II above).

A closer examination of the data cited above shows all paradigms with non-categorial suppletion, the third-person singular tends to be the least marked form

Table 12. Distribution of autonomous forms in tense categories

Groups according to the choice of autonomous forms		No.	Tense categories where autonomous forms are observed				
			PRES	PRES & PST	PRES & FUT	PST	FUT
I	All autonomous	13	8	4	1	–	–
II	Single-segment stem	11	8	3			
III	3 autonomous	9	7	2		2	–
IV	1 or 2 autonomous	6	6	–		–	–
V	Tense and Number only	2	2			1	–
Total	41[a]		31	9	1	3	–

Note: No. = number of languages

[a] The actual number of languages where non-categorial suppletion is found is 39. However, in Spanish, Hungarian, Ingush and Fur there is more than one such verb. These verbs fall into different groups which is why these languages are included in the count of different groups as well.

in the sense that it is the shortest and structurally simplest form in the paradigm.

Observations of tendencies such as those described above are per se not new, neither in the typological literature, nor in the much smaller world of suppletion. Mayerthaler (1981: 105) notes that in a number of West Indo-European languages, the verbs meaning 'be' have suppletive paradigms and that the third-person singular of these verbs is formally very simple. He quotes the paradigms of the verbs 'be' from German, Latin, Old Icelandic and Portuguese. According to him, it is a notable fact that even such strongly suppletive paradigms conform to general markedness hierarchies which state that the unmarked present tense shows more morpho-phonological irregularities than the marked tenses. However, since by his own definitions, such paradigms are, "contra-iconically" coded, they remain anomalous in his view.

Unlike Natural Morphologists, Bybee does not presuppose "one-form-one-meaning transparency principle". On the contrary, she predicts that verbs with multiple functions will have paradigms where forms easily dissociate from each other. In the group discussed here, most of the verbs with paradigms where the forms show various degrees of autonomy are used with various grammatical functions in their respective languages. In fact, there is a clear correlation between a paradigm that consists of exclusively (or nearly exclusively) of autonomous forms only and the auxiliary status of the word expressed by it. In my database there are 65 verbs which show non-categorial suppletion. Out of them, 47 are auxiliaries of some kind in their languages; 35 have complex paradigms of the kind illustrated for groups I, II and III above.

In Bybee's 1985 model irregularity/autonomous forms in the paradigms of auxiliaries and other grammaticalizing words are expected. That is, they are close to what is normal in language, rather than against it. This differs from various accounts of suppletion which make it look functional from a communication point of view. Bybee does not say anything as regards the communicative value of autonomous forms in paradigms; she simply observes that multifunctional and frequently used forms tend to dissociate from each other even within one and the same paradigm. In fact one would wonder why linguists would expect for a verb such as 'be' or a grammaticalizing 'go' to have a structure identical to verbs such as 'clean' or 'dance' when their scope of use and function are completely different.

There are verbs with non-categorial suppletion (cf. (75) and (77) below) which are not auxiliaries. However, a motivation for the structure of their paradigms can still be suggested.

(75) Maltese (Afro-Asiatic, Semitic) (Borg and Azzopardi-Alexander 1997: 357)

	PERFECT	IMPERFECT	IMPERATIVE
1SG	għidt	ngħid	–
2SG	għidt	tgħid	għid
3SGM	**qal**	jgħid	–
3SGF	**qalet**	tgħid	–
1PL	għidna	ngħidu	–
2PL	għidtu	tgħidu	għidu
3PL	**qalu**	jgħidu	–

Most of the forms in the paradigm above are derived from a single base -għ(i)d-. The only exceptional forms are the third-person forms of the perfect, which is used as perfective and past. However, it is not at all surprising that exactly those forms are different. They are certainly the most frequent forms in the entire paradigm, if one thinks about the most common uses of a verb such as 'say'. In fact, it is cross-linguistically very common that third-person forms of 'say' verbs detach from the rest of their paradigms and evolve into quotative and even evidential markers. A number of grammars report a defective verb 'say', illustrated here by Diola-Fogny, a language, from Senegal. In this language there is a defective verb -ɛn 'say' which is used to indicate that a quotation or a reported statement is to follow:

(76) Diola-Fogny (Niger-Congo, Bak) (Sapir 1965: 44)
kɔnɛ ko-kʉlɨ-koli
ku-ɛn-ɛ ko-kʉlɨ=koli
3PL-say-FOCUS 3PL-afraid-RDP
'They said they were afraid.'

Similar examples from both Indo-European and non-Indo-European languages are numerous, and I shall have occasion to return to the issue of 'say' verbs in section 5 of chapter 5.

In Fur, the verb 'kill', shown in (77), has different stems for present and past. Its paradigm is further complicated by the fact that the third-person singular of the past tense has a special form which is completely different from the other two stems of the paradigm.

(77) Fur (Nilo-Saharan, Fur), (Angelika Jakobi, p.c.)
'kill'

	PRESENT	PAST
1SG	ììrù	àwì
2SG	ɟììrù	ɟàwì
3SG	íírù	**fùì**
1PL	kììrù	kàwì
2PL	bììrù	bàwì
3PL	kììrɛ̀	kàwiŋè

Again, if we think about the most frequent way a verb such as 'kill', would be used, it is most probably the use when one reports the fact that somebody killed something or somebody. So from a functional perspective, a special form for the 3SG PAST is fully motivated.

3.1 Cross-linguistic distribution

Estimates of the frequency of non-categorial suppletion are presented in Tables 13 and 14. According to language counts in both samples, as well as the count based on genera such complex paradigms are found in about one fifth of the languages examined here. The frequency based on the weight values count is substantially lower,

Table 13. Language count

Small sample		WALS sample			
No	%	No	%	W	% of 70
21	22.34	39	20.21	9.60	13.71

Note: No. = number of languages; W = weight values sum; 70 = the total of weight values for the WALS sample

Table 14. The Dryer Distribution

	Africa	Eurasia	SEA and Oceania	A–NG	N Am	S Am	Total
Yes	3	14	1	3	4	2	27
No	24	19	17	21	22	22	126

Note: Yes = presence of non-categorial suppletion; No = absence of non-categorial suppletion; total number of genera is 150 but this is not surprising since most of the languages with non-categorial suppletion are Indo-European (in this sample).

3.2 Lexemic groups

The lexemic groups which occur with non-categorial suppletion are listed in Table 15. What was already said is only substantiated here by figures: namely more than half of the verbs in this group are either 'be' or verbs of motion; and the greater part of them are used with grammatical functions of some kind.

Table 15.

Meaning	No.	%	Weight values	%
be	31	47.69	7.29	43.47
go/come	12	18.46	2.03	12.10
say	5	7.69	2.42	14.40
give	3	4.62	1.23	7.60
have	3	4.62	0.38	2.20
die	2	3.07	0.50	2.91
eat	2	3.07	1.01	6.00
do	1	1.54	0.06	0.36
hit	1	1.54	0.17	1.00
kill	1	1.54	0.17	1.00
look	1	1.54	0.17	1.00
shoot	1	1.54	0.17	1.00
strike, swear	1	1.54	0.17	1.00
think so, guess, hope	1	1.54	1.00	5.96
Total	65	100.00	16.77	100.00

4. Morphological analysis of the suppletive verbs

It is typically pointed out that suppletive forms are generally unanalyzable wholes, that is portmanteau morphs. However, what seems to go without further discussion is the fact that there are different degrees of irregularity with regard to their morphological marking. There are suppletive forms which, by language specific criteria, show completely regular verb morphology in terms language specific marking; there are suppletive forms which strongly resemble regular verbs but show some marking which sets them apart the regular verbx in language X, and finally there are suppletive forms which have nothing to do with regular verbs at all. A few brief illustrations are given below.

The forms of Modern Greek verb *blepō* 'see' (cf. (47) above) show completely regular verb morphology and the only irregularity in the paradigm is the change of stem according to aspect. The Georgian verb 'be' is has nearly all the markers, which a regular verb in Georgian has in the non-present tenses, cf. (78) and (79) below, and thus its paradigm is only slightly different from the rest of Georgian verbs. The Swedish verb 'be', on the other hand, shows hardly any resemblance to a regular Swedish verb, in either past or present, cf. (80).

(78) Georgian (South Caucasian) (Hewitt 1995: 446, passim)
'be'
v-ar   1SG-be.PRES
v–i-kn-eb-i   1SG-VV-be.FUT-TS (FUT)-IND
v–i-q'av-i   1SG-VV-be.AOR-IND

(79) Georgian (S-outh Caucasian) (Hewitt 1995: 283, passim)
'fall over'
v–i-kc-ev-i   1SG-VV-fall over-TS-IND = fall over.PRES
mo–v-i-kc-ev-i   PREV-1SG-VV-fall over-TS-IND = fall over FUT
mo–v-i-kc-i   PREV-1SG-VV-fall over-IND = fall over AOR

(80) Swedish (Indo-European, North Germanic), own data
'be'
a. är   be.PRES
   var   be.PST
b. dans-ar   dance-PRES
   dans-ade   dance-PST
c. skriv-er   write-PRES
   skrev   write.PST

In Table 16 I summarize the observations as regards the morphological characteristics of the verbs examined in previous sections. The row headings indicate the sub-groups of tense–aspect suppletion. Under the column entitled **Verb**, I indicate the number of verbs that actually have verb morphology. In the column **Not-Verb**, I indicate the number of verbs with one or more forms in their paradigms that have nothing in common with language specific verb morphology.

Table 16. Morphological characteristics of suppletive forms

	No.	Verb	Not-Verb
Aspect suppletion	84	84	
Complex paradigms and /or suppletive perfect	18	18	
Tense suppletion	70	53	17
Non-categorial suppletion	65	8	57

Note: No. Total number of verbs in a particular sub-group

As the figures show, all of the suppletive forms discussed under aspect suppletion are morphologically regular verbs. This is, however, not the case for most of the verbs under non-categorial suppletion as well as with some of the verbs in the group of categorial tense suppletion. This difference in form is matched by the function and use of these words in their respective languages. Suppletive verbs according to aspect are typically full lexical verbs. The majority of the verbs with non-categorial suppletion are typically used with several grammatical functions: they are copulas or auxiliaries for various tenses, aspects or moods.

5. Summary of synchronic distribution of tense–aspect suppletion

5.1 Summary of the sub-groups

The different groups of tense–aspect suppletion presented above can be summarized as follows:

1. Languages with non-categorial suppletion   39
2. Languages with tense suppletion   39
3. Languages with aspect suppletion   34
4. Languages with a special form in the perfect only   6
5. Languages with complex paradigms where the stems   12
   change according to several tense–aspect categories

If a language has more than one suppletive verb, it falls into several of the groups above. There are languages which have verbs with non-categorial suppletion only; similarly there are languages which have suppletive verbs according to tense only, and finally languages only with suppletive verbs according to aspect. However, in this sample there is no language where there are verbs with complex paradigms only of the kind discussed in section 2.3 or with verbs where the only suppletive form is the one for perfect.[9] So, based on the data here, we can postulate an implicational relationship between the kinds of tense–aspect suppletion, shown in (81).

(81) Implicational hierarchy for types of tense–aspect suppletion

Non-categorial suppletion   Suppletive perfect
Tense suppletion   >   Suppletion according to several tense–
Aspect suppletion   aspect categories

---

9. Rama, a Chibchan language from Nicaragua might have a suppletive perfect for the verb 'be' and that would be the only case of tense–aspect suppletion in the language. However, the data I currently have for this language are insufficient which is why I have exlcuded it from the cases of tense–aspect suppletion presented here.

This presents suppletion as a much more orderly phenomenon then previously thought, in that we can postulate that if a language has verbs where stems change according to several tense–aspect categories or perfect, it is bound to have suppletive verbs according to a single tense–aspect category only or non-categorial suppletion. As we shall see below, an implicational hierarchy can be also postulated for the verb meanings found with tense–aspect suppletion.

The data is plotted the data on two maps, presented in Appendix 3. On Map 2, I plot languages with non-categorial suppletion only. On Map 3, the languages are grouped as follows:

- ◆ Languages with suppletive verbs according to tense   39
- ● Languages with suppletive verbs according to aspect only   16
- ■ Languages with suppletive verbs according to tense and   15
  aspect, complex paradigms and/or perfect
- ○ Languages without categorial tense–aspect suppletion   123

5.2 Verb meanings that occur with tense–aspect of suppletion

The summary of the verb meanings encountered with tense–aspect suppletion is presented in Table 17. Both ways of calculating the frequency of occurrence of lexemic groups with tense aspect suppletion give fairly similar results. The verbs of motion together with the verbs meaning 'be, exist' constitute about half of all suppletive verbs according to tense–aspect. After them the frequency of the other meanings drops substantially. Discrepancies between the count of absolute meanings and the one based on weight values are probably most significant for meanings such as 'take' and 'lay, put' discussed above in section 2.2.4.

Tense-aspect suppletion is clearly attested more often with certain lexemic groups than with others. In fact, the counts above can be used further for working out implicational hierarchies for this phenomenon. Based mainly on weight values proportions, a hierarchy stated in (82) could be postulated.

(82) Lexical hierarchy for tense–aspect suppletion (I)

1	2	3	4	5
≥ 20%	≈10%	6–5%	≈ 3%	3–2%
be >	say >	do >	eat >	sit
come		see	die	have
go		give		

The hierarchy states that if a language has a suppletive verb from stage 5, it is bound to also have a verb from the group from the stages 4, 3, 2 and 1. Similarly, if a lan-

Table 17. Lexemic groups with tense–aspect suppletion

Meaning	No.	%	Weight Value	%
come/go	59	24.90	11.142	21.81
be/exist	56	23.62	12.035	23.55
say/speak	19	8.02	5.565	10.89
give	11	4.64	3.530	6.91
see/watch/look	10	4.23	2.752	5.39
take	10	4.23	0.568	1.11
do	10	4.22	2.524	4.94
die	7	2.97	1.825	3.57
eat	7	2.97	1.675	3.28
sit/stand/stay	6	2.54	1.230	2.41
lay/put	6	2.54	0.181	0.35
have	5	2.12	1.390	2.72
bring/carry	3	1.26	0.580	1.14
become	3	1.26	0.460	0.90
get	2	0.84	0.188	0.36
hear	2	0.84	0.136	0.26
catch	2	0.84	0.028	0.05
throw	2	0.84	0.025	0.05
drink	1	0.42	1.000	1.96
think so, happen, guess	1	0.42	1.000	1.96
become, happen, go	1	0.42	0.500	0.99
cry	1	0.42	0.125	0.24
fall	1	0.42	0.500	0.99
wake up	1	0.42	0.500	0.99
walk	1	0.42	0.500	0.99
hit	1	0.42	0.170	0.33
kill	1	0.42	0.170	0.33
run	1	0.42	0.170	0.33
shoot	1	0.42	0.170	0.33
strike, swear	1	0.42	0.170	0.33
become cold	1	0.42	0.165	0.33
cry	1	0.42	0.125	0.25
live	1	0.42	0.083	0.16
aim	1	0.42	0.014	0.02
beat	1	0.42	0.011	0.02
move	1	0.42	0.007	0.01
Total	237	100.00	51.089	100.00

guage has tense–aspect suppletion with a verb from stage 3, it will necessary have tense–aspect suppletion with a one verb from stage 2 and stage 1. After a check of how well it actually works with the languages in the sample, it turned out that the hierarchy in (82) needs a bit or re-working. The version which presents more accurately the observed data in is presented in (83).

(83)   Lexical hierarchy for tense–aspect suppletion (II)

1	2	3	4
be	say	give/(take)	become
come	do	sit	have
go	see	die	
		eat	

As it will become clear from Map 4 in Appendix 3, there are still a couple of languages which appear as counter examples to it in that they have suppletive verbs in stage 4 but not from stage 3. Skipping stage 1 is relatively rare. In fact, there is only one language, Oneida, a Northern Iroquoi language from Upstate New York and southern Ontario, Canada, where the only suppletive verb is 'say', that is, stage 1 above is skipped.

Of course, the explanatory value of such implicational hierarchies calls for a lengthy discussion which I cannot offer here. But the very fact that such implications can be wrought shows that suppletion is more than just a haphazard phenomenon. A proper motivation for the hierarchies presented above is yet to be suggested. What I can offer at present are mere speculations.

As indicated by the counts above, the greater part of the verbs with tense–aspect suppletion consists of verbs such as 'be/exist' as well as the motion verbs 'come' and 'go'. Verbs with these meanings are used with grammatical functions in many languages. The 'be' verbs fall into the group of non-categorial suppletion as well as in the group of tense suppletion. The verbs of motion appear almost evenly distributed among all the subtypes of tense–aspect suppletion presented above: 12 languages in non-categorial suppletion, 17 in tense suppletion, 16 in aspect suppletion and 12 in complex paradigms where the stems change according to both tense and aspect category. This distribution can hardly be an accident. Verbs such as 'come' and 'go' commonly evolve into auxiliaries of some kind, hence their presence in the group of non-categorial suppletion. Furthermore, both aspect and tense are very relevant to an action such as motion, hence lexical expressions which are highly compatible with one tense–aspect category but incompatible with others are fully expected. Where suppletion occurs with lexical items that show no tendency to become grammatical markers in their respective languages, suppletive verbs are found in categories which are highly relevant to the meaning of a verb. The greater part of the occurrences of suppletion with verbs such as 'say', 'do' or 'see' are observed in aspect categories, and those are certainly relevant to the meanings of these verbs. Thus it is quite natural to find specific lexical item, which express these notions and differ solely on their Aktionsart. What the hierarchy in (83) states is that the first items to show suppletion in a language are those which are most prone to evolve as grammatical markers. However, it seems also possible to correlate suppletion with general lexicalization hierarchies.

The work of Åke Viberg in (HyltenstamViberg 1993) on lexical organization from a cross-lingusitic perspective is very relevant here. Based on frequency counts in 11 European languages, Viberg (1993: 346) identifies the nuclear lexical items in semantic fileds such as Motion, Possession, Production, Verbal Communication, Perception, Cognition and Desire. His generalizations appear also valid for non-European languages as well according to to his preliminary data. Nuclear verbs are typologically least marked, which is also reflected in lexicalization hierarchies. To give a short and simplified example, (Viberg 1993: 347), originally Viberg (1984), presents a marked hierarchy for verbs of perception, present here in (84):

(84) Viberg's hierarchy for verbs of perception
SEE > HEAR > FEEL > TASTE, SMELL

The hierarchy states that if a language has only one verb of perception, the basic meaning its basic meaning is 'see'. If a language has two verbs of perception, their basic meanings will be 'see' and 'hear'. The least marked verb in a semantic field, which in the case of perception is 'see', tends also to be the most frequent one in a specific language. Based on frequency counts, similar lexicalization hierarchies can be postulated for the other broad semantic fields mentioned above.

Except for the verbs 'sit', 'eat' and 'die', the verbs listed in the suppletive hierarchies above are practically identical with the verbs Viberg identifies as nuclear in their respective semantic fields. So the verbs most prone to show suppletive forms in their paradigms are not just very common words. They are the verbs which are typologically least marked lexical items within their respective semantic fields. As such they share a number of features cross-linguistically such as a tendency to be lexicalized in a great number of languages, a tendency to show irregular inflection as well as to give rise to grammatical markers, a richer array of syntactic possibilities and more possibilities in word formation., cf. Viberg (1993: 350) for further details.

5.3 Frequency of distribution in the samples

The estimates of the cross-linguistic frequency of tense–aspect suppletion is presented in Tables 18 and 19. The proportion resulting from the raw count of the small sample is very similar to the one yielded by the Dryer Distribution: a little more than one third of the languages and the genera. This might mean either that the small sample does not consist of as independent languages as I claim, or that the WALS sample is not so bad after all.

The proportion based on the weight values procedure presents tense–aspect suppletion as a less common phenomenon. If one is to trust the figures above about one fourth of the languages in the WALS sample have tense–aspect suppletion. However, what the weight values proportion really shows is that tense–aspect suppletion is

Table 18. Language count

Small sample		WALS sample			
No	%	No	%	W	% of 70
33	35.11	75	38.86	17.590	25.12

Note: No. = number of languages; W = weight values sum; % of 70 (the total of all weight values)

Table 19. The Dryer distribution of tense–aspect suppletion

	Africa	Eurasia	SEA and Oceania	A–NG	N Am	S Am	Total
yes	8	22	3	10	9	3	55
no	20	11	15	14	19	21	100

Note: Yes = presence of tense–aspect suppletion; No = absence of tense–aspect suppletion; total of genera in the sample is 150

favored in some language families and not at all favored in others. This is shown in more detail in Table 20 where I present its distribution in language phyla. Tense-aspect suppletion is attested in 25 out the 70 phyla in the WALS sample. The phenomenon is clearly associated with phyla such as Indo-European, both North and South Caucasian, Oto-Manguean in Meso-America, Carib in South America and Sepik-Ramu from Papua New Guinea.

As regards areal distribution, tense–aspect suppletion is concentrated in Eurasia. This is not to say that it is completely absent from other parts of the world. As it will become clear from Map 3 in Appendix 3, two hotbeds are observed in Meso-America and Papua New Guinea. The only three Australian languages where tense–aspect suppletion is attested are in Northern Australia.

To conclude, the synchronic distribution of tense–aspect suppletion presents the phenomenon as systematic in several respects.

- There is a strong tendency to find it with grammatical and grammaticalizing items.
- Where it occurs with full lexical items, the categories with suppletive stems are highly relevant to the meanings of these verbs.
- Some language families favor it whereas others don't. Describing it as unnatural would make whole language phyla seem unnatural, which is a bit far-fetched.
- There are clear areal patterns in its distribution among the languages of the WALS sample.

This concludes the discussion of suppletion in tense–aspect categories as it is found in the modern languages of the world. In the next chapter I present various hypotheses and case studies on the emergence of suppletive forms in paradigms.

Table 20. Distribution of tense–aspect suppletion in language phyla

Phylum	No \ To
Afro-Asiatic	3 \ 13
Australian	3 \ 11
Austro-Asiatic	1 \ 5
Austronesian	2 \ 12
Barbacoan	1 \ 1
Basque	1 \ 1
Burushaski	1 \ 1
Caddoan	1 \ 1
Carib	3 \ 3
Chibchan	1 \ 2
Dravidian	2 \ 2
East Papuan	1 \ 2
Indo-European	25 \ 25
Iroquoian	1 \ 2
Khoisan	1 \ 2
Na-Dene	1 \ 2
Niger-Congo	2 \ 12
Nilo-Saharan	3 \ 8
North Caucasian	4 \ 4
Oto-Manguean	3 \ 3
Sepik-Ramu	2 \ 2
South Caucasian	1 \ 1
Trans-New Guinea	4 \ 9
Uralic	2 \ 3
Uto-Aztecan	4 \ 9

Note: No = number of languages with some kind of tense–aspect suppletion; To = total number of languages from that phylum included in the sample

CHAPTER 5

Tense–aspect suppletion II
Diachronic and usage-based perspective

1. Introduction

In this chapter I present case studies which trace the development of suppletion in tense–aspect categories. Based on the data presented in them I highlight characteristics of the emergence of suppletion which so far have passed without notice. Specifically, I argue that suppletive paradigms result from a variety of processes, so historically they represent different phenomena which in a synchronic analysis become subsumed under one and the same label.

Since many accounts for the existence of suppletion evoke high frequency of use as the motivating factor, a discussion of this issue is presented in section 2 below. Typically, in accounts of suppletion, the term frequency refers to high token frequency. Related to these views are observations that suppletive forms are completely immune to analogical leveling (cf. Chapter 1, section 2.2.3.1). There is evidence, however, that the emergence of suppletive forms actually follows analogical processes, rather than resisting them. The issue of emergence of suppletion as a result of analogical processes and type, rather token frequency is discussed in Section 3.

The emergence of suppletion is, in some cases, similar to grammaticalization as lexical items undergo loss of referential meaning and start to be used with a relational function; see section 4 on the creation of copula verbs.

In other cases, the evolution of suppletion is related to a semantic shift which is close to lexicalization, that is specification of meaning or contextual use is involved. Case studies on this subject are presented in section 5.

Suppletive forms may result from erstwhile regular morpho-phonological processes which at some point have ceased to be productive, cf. (Mel'čuk 1994: 392–3). As I am not going to be able to discuss this particular development in detail, I offer a brief discussion here. When a phonological or a morpho-phonological process declines in productivity and ultimately becomes fully defunct, traces of it can be seen in lexical items to which it was applicable and which were /are frequently used. Strong verbs in Germanic languages are considered as cases of weak suppletion, especially by Natural Morphologists (see also Chapter 1, section 2.2.2). In earlier stages of Germanic, however, they were perfectly regular. As ablaut ceased to be a regular morpho-phonological process, the verbs that continued to use it for the formation of their past and perfect participles started to be perceived as irregular. Similarly the alternation *are: is* in English was once upon a time an instantiation of a regular sound change. This phonological process lost currency a long time ago and thus the forms are seen as completely autonomous. However, as discussed in Chapter 4:3 above (Non-categorial suppletion) such autonomy of forms is encountered mainly with words which have a grammatical function, and in Bybee's (1985) view, they gain independence in connection with the process whereby the word in question acquires its grammatical function. It is my impression that, more often than not, cases of non-categorial suppletion result from the "irregularization" of an erstwhile regular pattern. Thus categorial and non-categorial suppletion are different phenomena, both synchronically and diachronically. Diachronically, non-categorial suppletion seems to originate from the "disintegration" of a paradigm; categorial suppletion, on the other hand, appears to result from the merging of paradigms of distinct lexical verbs. Speculations about the nature of such processes as well as motivations for them are presented in the sections below.

2. Frequency and suppletion

Frequency of use is often pointed out as one of the main factors for the creation and maintenance of suppletion, (cf. Dressler 1985; Mel'čuk 1994). As already stated in Chapter 1:2.2.3, typically, token-frequency is meant whenever suppletion is correlated with frequency of use.[1] This, however, is done in very general terms only and leaves room for a lot of specification. As Corbett, Hippisley, Brown and Marriott (2001), point out, it is often unclear when frequency is correlated with irregularity, what exactly is meant by frequency: is it that a particular word, say, *go* in English is very frequent (in that the sum of all of its forms is substantially greater than the sum total of the forms of other verbs) or is it the case that the form *went* is very frequent in relation to past tense forms of other verb and within the paradigm of *go*. In the same study, Corbett and his colleagues (2001) demonstrate that there is a relation between irregularity and frequency but it is more complex than previously thought. Specifically, these authors find that irregularities in Russian noun inflection which involve a split between singular and plural forms tend to occur with nouns which are used frequently in the plural. However, the irregularity of individual forms in a subparadigm (either singular or plural) does not appear to be directly related to its frequency. This suggests, in their view, that an individual irregular cell does not stand out from its subparadigm in terms of frequency (Corbett et al. 2001:220).

---

[1] For the distinction between token- and type-frequency, please consult Chapter 1:2.2.3.

Chapter 5. Tense–aspect suppletion II: synchronic and usage-based perspective

For the purposes of this study, I examined frequency counts for English (Leech et al. 2001), Spanish, *Corpus del Español*, (Davies, M. 2004. http://www.corpusdelespanol.org/), Russian (Steinfeldt 1965), Turkish (Pierce 1963) and Chinese (Suen 1986); in the first three languages, there is tense–aspect suppletion, while in Turkish and Chinese, there is none. The counting techniques used to obtain the results presented below differ substantially; thus a comparison between the frequency counts is probably not warranted in a strict mathematical sense. However, if we are to compare the frequency structure of different languages, we almost have to allow for such "layman" comparison as doing frequency counts typically involves complex procedures; conducting precise counts on different languages and corpora is simply not feasible within the time frame of a single project (at least at the current state of corpus availability and tagging; such a comparison may be entirely possible and fairly easy to do in the not so distant future). The background information for the figures presented below is as follows.

For English, the frequency counts were performed on the British National Corpus (hereafter BNC) by Leech, Rayson and Wilson (2001). BNC covers a sample of some 100 million words. The texts come from a wide variety of genres; 90% of the data are written text, and 10% are spoken. The figures given below represent a normalized frequency score of occurrences (tokens) per million words. So if the normalized frequency for a given word, say, the word *go* is 2,078, the actual raw counts for the all the forms of *go* are in the range of 207,800.

For Spanish, Russian, Turkish and Chinese, the figures reflect the number of hits in the corpus, rather than normalized frequency scores. The counts for Spanish were obtained online by my own searches in the corpus. *Corpus del Español* consists of two parts, a historical one which includes texts from the 1200s until the 1800s, and a modern part which includes data from spoken Spanish, modern Spanish fiction and finally newspapers and encyclopedias. The data from modern Spanish cover some 20 million word tokens. The frequency scores presented in the comparative tables below reflect usage in Spanish of the 1900s.

The frequency counts for Russian, by Steinfeld (1965), are based on a corpus of 400,000 words which come from the following types of text: fiction for children (100,000 words), fiction for adults (50,000 words), plays (50,000 words), radio broadcasts for youth 1958–1960 (100,000 words), articles from periodicals 1958–1960 (100,000 words).

The frequency counts for Turkish, by Pierce (1963), are based on two samples of Turkish data: a spoken sample of 138,000 words, of which 47,000 unelicited data, and 91,000 elicited dialogue; a written sample of 2,000,000 words of running text, out of which a sub-sample of over 103,000 words was actually counted. The written materials were selected from the genres listed below; the figure in the brackets gives the number of words from that genre which were included in the count: short

(85) Comparison between high-token-frequency verbs in English, Spanish and Russian with suppletive verbs according to tense and aspect

Rank	BNC, (Leech et al., 2001) Word	Freq[a]	Corpus del Español (Davies 2004) Word	Gloss	Freq[a]	Russian Word Count (Steinfeldt 1965) Word	Gloss	Freq	Suppletive verbs according to tense and aspect (Ch 4:5.2) Verb meaning	Weight value	%
1	*be*	42277	**ser**	be	369063	*byt'*	be	4186	**be/exist**	12.035	23.55
2	*have*	13655	**haber**	have	191417	**skazat'**	say	1419	**come/go**	11.142	21.81
3	*do*	5594	estar	be	118188	moch'	can	1076	say/speak	5.565	10.89
4	*will*	3357	tener	have	108141	*govorit'*	speak	1012	give	3.53	6.91
5	*say*	3344	**hacer**	do	84220	Znat'	know	926	see/watch/look	2.752	5.39
6	*would*	2904	**decir**	say	80191	*stat'*	become	707	**do**	2.524	4.94
7	*can*	2672	**ir**	go	77269	**idti**	go	633	die	1.825	3.57
8	*get*	2210	poder	can	76273	xotet'	want	580	eat	1.675	3.28
9	*make*	2165	ver	see	42038	pojti	start	505	**have**	1.39	2.72
10	**go**	2078	**dar**	give	40353	rabótat'	work	473	**sit**/stand/stay	1.23	2.41
11	*see*	1920	saber	know	38816	vídet'	see.IPFV	457	drink	1	1.96
12	*know*	1882	querer	want	30729	*est'*	there is	445	think so, happen, guess	1	1.96
13	*take*	1797	pasar	happen	29299	dúmat'	think	423	bring/carry	0.58	1.14
14	*could*	1683	deber	must	22101	smotrét'	look.IPFV	380	**take**	0.568	1.11
15	*think*	1520	creer	believe	22066	stojat'	stand	373	become, happen, go	0.500	0.99
16	*come*	1512	llegar	arrive	21299	sprosit'	ask	364	fall	0.500	0.99
17	*give*	1284	parecer	seem	19724	délat'	make	354	wake up	0.500	0.99
18	*look*	1151	hablar	speak	19356	zhit'	live	343	walk	0.500	0.99
19	*may*	1135	poner	put	19155	sdélat'	do	337	become	0.46	0.9
20	*should*	1112	dejar	leave	17898	**prijtí**	come	329	get	0.188	0.36
21	*use*	1071	quedar	be at, stay	17424	*vzjat'*	take.PFV	311	**lay/put**	0.181	0.35
22	*find*	990	trabajar	work	16997	*davát'*	give.IPFV	289	hit	0.17	0.33
23	*want*	945	contar	tell	16605	net	there is not	288	kill	0.17	0.33
24	*tell*	775	seguir	follow	16004	*sidet'*	sit.IPFV	281	run	0.17	0.33

25	must	723	llevar	carry	15976	kazat'sja	seem	273	shoot	0.17	0.33
26	put	700	salir	depart	14365	dat'	give.PFV	263	strike, swear	0.17	0.33
27	mean	677	pensar	think	13760	nachat'	begin.PFV	256	become cold	0.165	0.33
28	become	675	vivir	live	12064	otvétit'	answer	254	hear	0.136	0.26
29	leave	647	mirar	look	11858	posmotrét'	look.PFV	246	cry	0.125	0.24
30	work	646	tratar	treat	11210	vyjti	go out	241	cry	0.125	0.25
31	need	627	llamar	call	10190	ponimat'	understand.IPFV	234	live	0.083	0.16
32	feel	624	tomar	take	9834	reshit'	decide	230	catch	0.028	0.05
33	seem	624	esperar	wait	8097	znachit'	mean	226	throw	0.025	0.05
34	might	614	caminar	walk	6950	projti	pass	211	aim	0.014	0.02
35	ask	610	convertir	turn	6021	uvidet'	see.PFV	209	beat	0.011	0.02
36	show	598	pesar	weigh	5982	slushat'	listen	195	move	0.007	0.01
37	try	552	correr	run	4765	ponjat'	understand.PFV	186	Total	51.089	100
84						brat'	take.IPFV	97			
141						polozhit'	put.IMPF	69			
381						klast'	put.PFV	29			

[a] The frequency scores for *ser* and *ir* differ from those obtained at an initial search of the corpus. This is because the corpus does not distinguish between the two senses 'was/were' and 'went' of the homonymous form indicative preterite and subjunctive imperfect of these verbs; so manual disambiguation as well as manual calculation of their frequency score was necessary for these two verbs. For the rest of the Spanish verbs above, the frequency scores are reported as calculated by the online corpus tools.

(86) Comparison between high-token-frequency verbs in Turkish and Mandarin Chinese with suppletive verbs according to tense–aspect

Rk	Turkish frequency counts: the spoken sample (Pierce 1963) Word	Gloss	Freq	Turkish frequency counts: the written sample (Pierce 1963) Word	Gloss	Freq	Most frequent Chinese words (Suen 1986) Word	Gloss	Freq	Suppletive verbs according to tense and aspect (Ch 4:5.2) Verb meaning	Weight value	%
1	*demek*	say (so), mean(s), so	8742	*olmak*	become	2053	*shi4*	be	16504	**be/exist**	12.035	23.55
2	*olmak*	become	2645	atmak	throw away	1944	*you3*	have	10685	**come/go**	11.142	21.81
3	*gelmek*	come	2372	*demek*	say (so), mean(s) so	946	*nung2*	can	9907	**say/speak**	5.565	10.89
4	*gitmek*	go	2372	*yapmak*	do, make	650	*lai2*	come	4930	give	3.53	6.91
5	*var*	there is	1801	*görmek*	see, notice	569	*shwo1*	speak	4452	see/watch/*look*	2.752	5.39
6	*almak*	take	1281	geçmek	Pass	559	yau4	want	3574	**do**	2.524	4.94
7	*yapmak*	do, make	1264	*gelmek*	Come	559	*chii4*	go	3136	die	1.825	3.57
8	*vermek*	give	1216	*vermek*	Give	546	dau4	arrive	2906	eat	1.675	3.28
9	*yok*	there isn't	1175	bulmak	Find	486	duh1	get	2519	**have**	1.39	2.72
10	etmek	AUX	1098	*almak*	Take	458	yüoong4	use	2146	**sit**/stand/stay	1.23	2.41
11	*bakmak*	look, see	1080	bilmek	know, learn	382	reu1	drink	1991		1	1.96
12	çikmak	go out	830	*gitmek*	Go	342	gwo4	pass by	1986	think so, happen, guess	1	1.96
13	söylemek	speak, tell	667	çikmak	go out	326	kuh3	can	1773	bring/carry	0.58	1.14
14	bilmek	know, learn	512	*bakmak*	look, see	305	jiang1	will	1694	**take**	0.568	1.11
15	*görmek*	see, notice	506	anlamak	Understand	282	*shi3*	make	1604	become, happen, go	0.500	0.99
16	*yemek*	eat	497	*durmak*	Stand	280	kuh2 yi3	can	1598	fall	0.500	0.99
17	değil	nom neg	429	istemek	Want	255	*kan4*	look	1320	wake up	0.500	0.99
18	varmak	arrive	426	değil	NOM NEG	250	dung3	wait	1314	walk	0.500	0.99
19			416	kapamak	Close	236	xiang3	want	1095	become	0.46	0.9
20	koymak	chase (away)	407	*söylemek*	speak, tell	227	*jien4*	see	1078	get	0.188	0.36
21	*kalmak*	stay (behind)	384	*düşmek*	Fall	210	hwei2	go home	1070	**lay/put**	0.181	0.35
22	anlamak	understand	379	dönmek	(re)turn	205	jin4	enter	1055	hit	0.17	0.33
23	*ölmek*	die	363	*kalmak*	stay (behind)	190				kill	0.17	0.33

24	*durmak*	stand	356	çalışmak	Work	188	run	0.17	0.33
25	kesmek	cut	356	Yok	There isn't	188	shoot	0.17	0.33
26	yatmak	lie (down)	334	yazmak	Write	177	strike, swear	0.17	0.33
27	açmak	open	328	Değişmek	Change	150	become cold	0.165	0.33
28	istemek	want	302	Sürmek	Paint, put through	149		0.136	0.26
29	atmak	throw away	297	girmek	Enter	148	*hear*	0.125	0.24
30	getirmek	?	292	Göstermek	Show	146	cry	0.125	0.25
31	bulmak	find	286	yatmak	lie (down)	146	cry	0.083	0.16
32	tutmak	hold, take	268	getirmek	?	140	live	0.028	0.05
33	I	copula root	267	Karışmak	Interfere	138	catch	0.025	0.05
34	vurmak	beat, knock	267	tutmak	hold, take	130	throw	0.014	0.02
35	oturmak	sit (down)	266	Kullanmak	Use	125	aim	0.011	0.02
36	girmek	enter	259	oturmak	sit (down)	124	beat	0.007	0.01
37	çekmek	pull	253	konuşmak	speak, talk	107	move		
40	kaçmak	run (away)	217	ölmek	Die	105	Total	51.089	100
41	düşmek	fall	205	atmak	throw away	103			
45	içmek	drink	190						

Note: The digit in the romanized version of the Chinese word indicates level tone.

stories (20,827 words), novels (21,014 words) newspaper articles from 1958 (24,641 words), military field manuals (18,905 words), public school textbooks (16,209 words), religious pamphlets (3,754 words), poetry (2,246 words).

The frequency counts for Mandarin Chinese present 6,321 of the most commonly used Chinese words. The words were extracted from a corpus study where the corpus covered texts from popular newspapers, magazines and periodicals, fiction and non-fiction, elementary and secondary school textbooks, children's extra-curricular reading materials, and reader's digests.

In (85) and (86) above, I present a comparison between the high token frequency verbs in the languages mentioned above and the verbs which tend to use suppletive forms for tense–aspect distinctions. Generally, most of the suppletive verbs are found in the top 100 high token frequency items in their respective languages. The only exception is the Russian aspectual pair *polozhit': klast'* 'put.IPVF: put.PFV'; *polozhit'* was found on position 141 in this frequency list whereas *klast'* was even lower, at position 381.

Bold italics is used to indicate the suppletive verbs according to tense and aspect in English, Spanish and Russian; the same style is also used to indicate the corresponding verb meaning in the list of suppletive verbs. In Turkish and Mandarin Chinese, bold italics are used to indicate the verb meanings identical with those of the common suppletive verbs. The abbreviation **freq** in (85) and (86) stands for FREQUENCY.

Not surprisingly, the suppletive verbs with highest weight value scores, 'be', 'come/go', 'say', 'do' tend to be amongst the top ranking high token frequency verbs in specific languages. However, if we look at languages where there is no tense–aspect suppletion, such as Turkish and Chinese in (86) above, we cannot help but notice that the same verbs top the high token frequency lists as well.

Thus it seems to hold that if a verb tends to show tense–aspect suppletion cross-linguistically, it will also tend to be amongst the highest ranking top frequency verbs. However, the opposite does not seem to be true: that is, if a verb shows a high token frequency, it does not have to suppletive or even irregular. So, on the synchronic level, high token frequency appears to be a necessary though not a sufficient condition for the occurrence of suppletion (Östen Dahl, p.c.).

As already stated in Chapter 1: 2.2.3.3, frequency is undoubtedly part of the story when we seek an account for suppletion. However, it cannot possibly be the main driving force for the emergence and maintenance of suppletion for the following reasons. First, as pointed out by Fertig (1998), if we are to accept an account based on frequency, we will have to account for the less than universal occurrence of suppletion as the same lexical items tend to be the most frequently used ones in languages across the world. This observation is fully corroborated by the frequency counts in (85) and (86) above.

Second, the distorting effect of frequency has to be considered as well. It is well known that high token frequency items tend to (i) be subject to phonological reduction; (ii) become predictable and thus tend to be avoided and (iii) become so void of expressive meaning that they start to be replaced by other lexical items. These observations are especially valid for grammaticalized or grammaticalizing lexical items, and, as is well known, suppletive verbs are often such items. The following frequency scores for the present tense forms of the verb *be* in BNC will be used to illustrate (i) above.

(87)   English (Indo-European, Germanic) (Leech et al. 2001: 144–7)
   Spoken English   **Written English**
   '*m*   2,512   *am*   264   '*m*   443   *am*   255
   '*re* 4,255   *are* 4,663   '*re* 439   *are* 4,713
   '*s*   17,677   *is*   10,164   '*s*   1,848   *is*   9,961

As we can see, the contracted form '*s* is more frequent than the full form *is* in the spoken part of BNC, while '*m* is more frequent than *am* in both the spoken and the written texts. So it is most probably likely that both the *am* and *is* forms will eventually become clitics only and maybe even fully bound forms and thus disappear from the current paradigm of *be*.

We can use English data as well for illustrating (ii) above. For instance, it is common to eliminate the copula in informal statements such as *You happy now?*, instead of *Are you happy now?* Finally, a brief illustration of (iii) can be given by Spanish. In Spanish the verb *quedar* 'stay, be at, be located' has not only started to replace the older copula verbs *ser* and *estar* in locative statements such as *queda a 6km de aquí* 'it's 6 kilometers from here' but has also taken over some other copula functions in constructions such as *el autobus quédo destrozado* 'the bus was wrecked', (cf. also Section 4 below for more data on this issue).

Thus high token frequency appears to provide for several different and maybe even contradictory factors as regards suppletion. On the one hand, high token frequency appears to help preserve suppletion and irregularity in general over a certain amount of time; however, since the frequent use of a form has apparent distorting effects as well, and suppletive forms are not immune to them, high token frequency probably plays a role for the elimination of suppletive forms too. At present, it is unclear what role high token frequency plays for the creation of suppletion. The line of thinking developed by Aski (1995), and followed by myself in a subsequent case study suggests that probably the main trigger for the introduction of suppletive forms in a paradigm is type frequency and analogical re-structuring of paradigms rather than token frequency as commonly thought (cf. section 3 below for further details and discussion of this issue). However, more studies are necessary for a stronger support of this hypothesis.

3. Suppletion and analogy

In this section I trace the origins of some well known suppletive paradigms, the verbs 'go' in Romance languages as well as for the verb 'go' in English. Using ideas presented in the work of Janice Aski (1995), I argue that the emergence of suppletive paradigms can be shown to follow analogical processes. This is contrary to the widespread view (cf. Chapter 1, section 2.2.3.1) that suppletive paradigms are resistant to analogy.

As is well known, the paradigms of the verbs 'go' in Romance languages consist of several stems which can be traced back to different verbs in Latin. For the French verb *aller* 'go', the Latin ancestors are *īre* 'go' > French *irai* 'go.1SG.FUT', *ambulāre* 'walk, stroll' > French forms using the stem *all-*, and *vadere* 'go rapidly, rush, advance' > French *vais* 'go.1SG.PRES' etc. It is a debated issue whether the Italian forms using the stem from *andare* as well as the Spanish *andar* are to be traced back to *ambulāre* or to another Latin verb *ambīre* 'go around', cf. (Buck 1949; Manczak 1966). In any case, there have been at least three, possibly more Latin verbs with a sense related to 'go' whose paradigms merged in different ways in the Modern Romance verbs 'go'. The interesting question is how and why this happened.

In Early and Classical Latin the verb *īre* 'go', see (88) below, was one of the most common and semantically unmarked verb. In the Modern Romance languages this erstwhile frequent verb survives only partially e.g. in citation forms cf. Spanish *ir* and for future tense forms as in French *irai*, etc. and similarly Spanish *iré*.

(88) Present tense of Latin *īre*, adapted from (Aski 1995: 409)[2]

		INDICATIVE	SUBJUNCTIVE
1	1SG	*ēo*	*eam*
2	2SG	*īs*	*eās*
3	3SG	*it*	*eat*
4	1PL	*īmus*	*eāmus*
5	2PL	*ītis*	*eātis*
6	3PL	*eunt*	*eant*

In most historical grammars of Modern Romance languages, the replacement of the present tense forms of Latin *īre* with forms of *ambulāre* and *vadere* is said to be motivated by the fact that the forms of *īre* had become highly eroded and irregular. A motivation along these lines is also proposed by Rudes (1980: 670). Aski (1995) cites two Italian historical grammars (Rolfs 1968; Tekavcic 1972) where a similar idea is articulated in somewhat more specific terms, namely that the present tense forms of *īre* were replaced by *vadere* since they were monosyllabic.

---

2. The numbering of the forms follows the presentation in Aski (1995).

Rosén (2000) examines the uses of the verbs *īre*, *ambulāre* and *vadere* in Early, Classical and Late Latin texts. She finds that the verb *vadere* was hardly used in written Early and Classical Latin. The complimentary distribution of *īre* and *ambulāre*, begins, according to her, already in Early and Classical Latin. Specifically, she observes that the imperative form of *īre*, *i,* was extremely frequent, to the point of becoming a pro-clitic word devoid of any lexical content. At the same time the verb *ambulāre*, originally used without any goal adverbials since its early sense was 'walk, stroll', was undergoing a semantic and syntactic change whereby it came to be more compatible with a goal adverbial. Thus the constructions where *ambulāre* came to be used were very similar to those where *īre* appeared. Rosén states that gradually the highly eroded forms of *īre* were replaced by *ambulāre* but this could only occur because the verbs had also become semantically and syntactically very similar. The merging of the two verbs, started in her view with the de-lexicalization of *īre* in its use in the imperative.

Rosén's comments that *vadere* is "definitely a latecomer" (Rosén 2000: 280) since there are only two occurrences of this verb in Catullus Attic poems and neither Petronius nor Pliny the Younger use it in their writing. The verb *vadere* is used very frequently and with a general meaning 'go' in Late Latin texts such as *Peregrinatio Aetheriae* ('Pilgrimage of Etheria') as well as the Vulgate.[3] Since this author restricts her investigation to written texts, she does not mention that *vadere* was very frequently used with the general sense 'go' in spoken registers as well as in Vulgar Latin. Otherwise, it is difficult to account for its frequent appearance in Late Latin texts. Rosén gives us a clear description of how the merging of *īre* and *ambulāre* may have started. However, she does not propose a motivation for the present day paradigms of the verbs 'go' in Romance languages where forms of the old verbs *īre*, *ambulāre* and *vadere* appear, in a seemingly haphazard fashion.

Gradual change of meaning along with change of syntactic frame and frequency of use definitely play a role for the restructuring of the expressions for 'go' in Latin and subsequently for the present day paradigms of the verb in Romance languages. There is also evidence that these paradigms were subject to general analogical processes in their respective languages. Such evidence is provided by Janice Aski (1995) for Italian, French and Spanish 'go'.

---

3. I am not sure if this clarification is necessary but since nowadays instruction in Latin literature is not part of the general curriculum, providing a few details on the sources mentioned probably wouldn't hurt. Catullus is a famous a Roman poet, *c.* 84–54 BC. Petronius, *c.* 22–67 AD, also known as *arbiter elengatiae* during Nero's time, is the author of *Satyricon*. Pliny the Younger, was a governor of Pontus/Bithynia from 111 to 113 AD; he wrote to emperor Trajan on a number of political and administrative matters. The *Pilgrimage of Etheria* describes the travels of a Western European nun in the Middle East; the account was most probably written in the fourth century. The Vulgate is the first Latin translation of the Bible, dated 405.

Aski suggests that the weak nature of the forms of Latin *īre* cannot be the only factor involved in the suppletive replacement. Specifically, she finds that this explanation runs into problems if one examines the suppletive replacements in both French and Spanish paradigms of 'go'. In both languages the Latin 1 and 2PL forms *īmus* and *ītis*, which are not monosyllabic, were nonetheless replaced by forms of *ambulāre* and *vadere* respectively. In her view a better understanding of the emergence of suppletive paradigms can be gained if we look beyond specific stem alternations and into the broader morphological patterns created by such alternations. Such broad patterns are referred to by Aski as **morpho-phonological templates** (the notion was originally introduced in morphological theory by Nigel Vincent).[4] An introductory illustration of a morpho-phonological template is provided in (89) by the alternations in infinitive and preterite verb forms in Spanish.

(89) Spanish, adapted from Aski (1995: 410) quoting Mel'čuk (1976)

INFINITIVE	PRETERITE	Alternation
quer-(er)	*quis-(e)*	/er/-/is/
ten-(er)	*tuv-(e)*	/en/-/ub/
pon-(er)	*pus-(e)*	/on/-/us/
dec-(ir)	*dij-(e)*	/eØ/-/ix/
sab-(er)	*sup-(e)*	/ab/-/up/

The alternations in (89) are different for each verb, but they occur in the same positions of the paradigm: infinitive and preterite. Therefore, in Aski's and Mel'čuk's (1976) view they cannot be considered entirely unique.

We can examine the paradigms of a few Italian verbs in (90).

(90) Italian, adapted from Aski (Aski 1995: 410–11)
   a. /e/-/o/: *dovere* 'to have to'

		INDICATIVE	SUBJUNCTIVE
1	1SG	*dévo*	*déva / debba*
2	2SG	*dévi*	*déva / debba*
3	3SG	*déve*	*déva / debba*
4	1PL	*dobbiámo*	*dobbiámo*
5	2PL	*dovéte*	*dobbiáte*
6	3PL	*dévono*	*dévano / debbano*

   b. /e/ /u/: *uscire* 'to exit'

		INDICATIVE	SUBJUNCTIVE
1	1SG	*ésco*	*ésca*

---

4. The notion of template is similar to Bybee's (1988) **representational patterns** or **schemas**, which are abstractions of lexical forms that share phonological or semantic properties. I concentrate on Aski's approach here since it deals directly with suppletion.

		2	2SG	ésci	ésca
		3	3SG	ésce	ésca
		4	1PL	usciámo	usciámo
		5	2PL	uscíte	usciáte
		6	3PL	éscono	éscano
c.	-isc-:	*finire* 'to finish'			
				INDICATIVE	SUBJUNCTIVE
		1	1SG	finísco	finísca
		2	2SG	finísci	finísca
		3	3SG	finísce	finísca
		4	1PL	finiámo	finiámo
		5	2PL	finíte	finíte
		6	3PL	finíscono	finíscano
d.	/wo/ /o/:	*suonare* 'to sound, play'			
				INDICATIVE	SUBJUNCTIVE
		1	1SG	suóno	suóni
		2	2SG	suóni	suóni
		3	3SG	suóno	suóni
		4	1PL	soniámo	soniámo
		5	2PL	sonáte	soniáte
		6	3PL	suónano	suónino

As the examples show, these four verbs have each a different alternation but these alternations occur in identical positions in the paradigm. Since they show this kind of symmetry these paradigms can be said to belong to one and the same template.

The template for the verbs above is shown in (91). In the suppletive conjugation of *andare* 'go', the diverse verb stems have the same distribution as the alternation found in *dovere, uscire, finire, suonare*.

(91) Template of *dovere*, etc. *-ire* inchoatives, *suonare* and *andare*

INDICATIVE	SUBJUNCTIVE	INDICATIVE	SUBJUNCTIVE
1	1	vado	vada
2	2	vai	vada
3	3	va	vada
4	4	andiamo	andiamo
5	5	andate	andiate
6	6	vanno	vadano

Thus in Aski's view, the stem alternation in the paradigm of *andare* cannot be considered as a completely isolated phenomenon since it is similar to the one found with several other verbs.[5]

In more general terms, Aski uses the notion of morphological template to model paradigmatic restructuring.

> Templates are language-specific conjugational frameworks that evolve over time. However, once established in a language system, they operate as guides for paradigm restructuring. Templates operate on both synchronic and diachronic level. They are stored in lexicon and create connections between items with identical templates. The strength of a connection depends on the number of verbs sharing a particular template such that more populated configurations attract new members. Moreover, when a verb shifts from one template to another, there is a strong tendency for it to shift from a less populated to a more populated template. (Aski 1995: 412–18)

Such a shift is illustrated by Aski by the evolution of the paradigm of Modern French 'go'. Its paradigm in Old French is presented in (92)

(92) Old French *aller*, adopted from (Aski 1995: 419), the bold styles are mine.

	INDICATIVE	SUBJUNCTIVE
1	**vois**	**voise**; aille, alge/auge
2	vas	**voises**; ailles, alge/auge
3	va(t) (vet, vait)	**voise** (**voist**); aille, alge
4	alon	**voisiens/voisions**; ailliens/aillions; algiens
5	alez	**voisiez**; ailliez; algiez
6	vont	**voisent**; aillent; algent/augent

As shown in (92), in Old French the present subjunctive of the verb 'go' had three different stems, *voise, aille, alge/auge*, the choice of which depended on the dialect. With the subjunctive forms built on *voise*, the verb shared a template with the Old French verbs *avoir* 'to have', *pooir* 'to be able to', *soloir* 'to have the habit', *doloir* 'to suffer', *trover* 'to find', *rover* 'to ask', and *prover* 'to prove'. This template is shown in (93).

(93) The Old French template for *pooir* 'be able to', etc., adopted from Aski (Aski 1995: 420) (the bold style is mine)

INDICATIVE	SUBJUNCTIVE	INDICATIVE	SUBJUNCTIVE
1	1	*puis*	*puisse*
2	2	*pues*	*puisses*
3	3	*puet*	*puisse*
4	4	poons	**poissiens/puissiens**
5	5	poez	**poissiez/puissiez**
6	6	pueent	**puissent**

---

[5]. A similar idea, though presented in less detail and without historical perspective is expressed by Carstairs-McCarthy (1990).

The Modern French template for *aller*, however, is different.

(94) Modern French template for *aller*, adopted from Aski (Aski 1995: 421) (the bold style is mine)

INDICATIVE	SUBJUNCTIVE	INDICATIVE	SUBJUNCTIVE
1	1	*je vais*	*aille*
2	2	*tu vas*	*ailles*
3	3	*il vas*	*aille*
4	4	***nous allons***	***allions***
5	5	***vous allez***	***alliez***
6	6	*ils vont*	*aillent*

Many Modern French verbs that have vowel alternation due to stress shift belong to this template. An example and a partial list are shown in (95).

(95) Modern French, partially adapted from (Aski 1995: 421)

a.

INDICATIVE	SUBJUNCTIVE	INDICATIVE	SUBJUNCTIVE
1	1	*je veux*	*veuille*
2	2	*tu veux*	*veuilles*
3	3	*il veut*	*veuille*
4	4	***nous voulons***	***voulions***
5	5	***vous voulez***	***vouliez***
6	6	*ils veulent*	*veuillent*

b. Other verbs which share this template
verbs ending in *-oir*   *ouir* 'to hear'
mourir 'to die'[6]   *conquerir* 'to conquer'
tenir 'to hold/possess'   *acquerir* 'to purchase'
traer 'to pull'   *requerir* 'to request/require'
payer 'to pay'   *venir* 'to come'
broyer 'to grind'   *envoyer* 'to send'

To summarize, the paradigm of *aller* from Old French to Modern French seems to have evolved as follows. The Old French subjunctive forms built on *voise* were dropped in Modern French. This way the verb dissociated from a template of about 8 verbs and joined a template shared by all verbs ending in *–oir* plus 11 other verbs. So viewed from this perspective, the verb *aller* actually came to fit a pattern shared by a substantial number of verbs. This in turn means that it is not just an odd idiosyncrasy. Diachronically, the verb shifted from a less populated to a more populated tem-

---

6. See *vouloir* 'want, wish', above.

plate which indicates that it has not been excluded from analogical leveling either.

The model suggested by Aski was presented in detail since in my view it is very instructive as to how linguistic patterns may evolve. Besides I use this line of thinking to account for the emergence of *went* as the past tense of 'go' in English.

(96) Old English verb(s) 'go' (Prokosch 1939: 223–4)

	INF	PST	PST PTCP
a.	*gangan*	*gēong*	*gangen*
b.	*gān/gōn*	*ēode*	*gegān*

As indicated in (96) above, it appears that in Old English there were two verbs which had essentially the same sense, and are also structurally very similar. Prokosch (1939: 223) describes them as 'long' and 'short' versions of the verb 'go'. Historically, however, *gangan* and *gān* are said to originate from different Indo-European words. For *gangan* the cognates are said to be Lithuanian *žengiu* 'I step' and Sanskrit *jáṅghā* 'lower leg' < Indo-European **ghə-ghōnā* 'crotch'. For the short version *gān* the reported cognates are Greek κίχημι /kixemi/ < Indo-European **ĝhi-ĝhē-mi* 'I reach'. I am not in a position in to evaluate these etymologies. However, even if the verbs were completely different words some 5000 years ago, at the stage of Germanic that is relevant to us (the Old English period, that is, *c.* tenth century and onwards), they had become very similar both formally and semantically. So chances are that their forms were easily confused and the distinction between them was gradually wiped out. In fact, this is what seems to have happened in Old and Middle English. In standard dictionaries such as the Oxford English Dictionary, and the Middle English Dictionary (Lewis et al. 1952–) it is stated that the verb *gān* uses two suppletive preterites *ēode* and also *gēong* (in Early Middle English *ging*). Besides, it is unclear how often the verb *gangan* was used. In the presentation below I concentrate on the verb *gān* since its forms are very frequently used judging by respective entries in the dictionaries cited above..

In Old English, the verb *gān/gōn* appears to have a conjugation similar to that of another highly irregular verb, namely, *dōn* 'do'. Partial paradigms of both verbs are shown in (97).

(97) Old English 'go' and 'do' (Quirk and Wrenn 1971: 55)

		gān 'go'	*dōn* 'do'
PRES INDIC	1SG	*gā*	*dō*
	2SG	*gǣst*	*dēst*
	3SG	*gǣð*	*dēð*
	1–3PL	*gāð*	*dōð*
PST INDIC	1SG, 3SG	*ēode*	*dyde*
	2SG	*ēodest*	*dydest*
	1–3PL	*ēodon*	*dydon*
	Participle	*gegān*	*gedōn*

Thus in Aski's terms, we can say that the two verbs form a template in Old English, albeit a very restricted one. During the Middle English period the two verbs remained paired together, at least to a certain extent cf. (98) below.

Before I proceed with the paradigms of 'go' and 'do', I would like to mention some general changes the verb system was undergoing at that time. One, due to changes in the vowel system, the distinction between the seven classes of strong verbs was becoming more and more blurred. Two, a substantial number of strong verbs from the seven ablaut classes developed alternative preterite forms by analogy with weak verbs. For instance the main forms of the verb 'help' are recorded both as *help-holp-holpen* and *help-helped-helped*. Third, as a consequence of the just mentioned analogical development, the number of weak verbs in Middle English was increasing rapidly. These new verbs seemed to fall into two classes:

(i) Those which formed their preterite by adding -vde to the stem as *fremman* 'perform, do' cf. *fremmede* (the epenthetic vowel was usually /e/ or /o/).
(ii) Those which formed their preterite by adding *-de* directly to the stem without an epenthetic vowel as *deman* 'deem, judge', cf. *demde*. In this group there is a sizable number of verbs where the dental suffix is realized as *-te* as in *brennen* 'burn', cf. *brunte*.

Finally, changes in the semantic field of motion verbs become apparent at the time roughly defined as Late Middle English (ca. 1350–1450). The verb *faran, fēran* 'a word expressing every kind of going from one place to another' (Bosworth and Toller 1882–1898: 469) was acquiring a somewhat different sense 'travel'. The verb ʒewitan 'start, pass over, go, depart' (Bosworth and Toller 1882–1898: 469) was gradually falling out of use. The verb *walke(n)* < Old English *wealcan* 'roll, toss' came to be used with the meaning 'go on foot'; the Old English sense of *gān* 'walk, to be able to walk' was shifting to a more general sense 'go'. The verb *wendan* 'turn' was changing into a more intransitive verb with a basic meaning 'direct oneself, go' with metaphorical meanings such as 'die'; 'vanish'; 'disappear'. Thus the verb system as whole was undergoing a great deal of restructuring.

As shown in (98) the Middle English *gān* had several forms for the past tense: *gaid*, a regular form; ʒede the Middle English descendant of *ēode*, and finally *wente*, the past tense form of the verb *wendan*.

(98) Middle English 'go' and 'do' (Roseborough 1938: 79)

		gon 'go'	don 'do'
PRES INDIC	1SG	go	do
	2SG	gost	dost
	3SG	goð	doð
	1–3PL	gon	don

PST INDIC	1SG, 3SG	ȝede, wente, gaid	dide
	2SG	wentest	didest, dides
	1–3PL	ȝeden, wenten	diden
	ptcp	gon	don, do

The regular form *gaid* shows several orthographic variants: *geid, gade, gaed, gede, geed*. These forms materialized in the dialects of Northern England as well as in Scottish English. Wełna (2001) quotes instantiations of these forms in documents from Northern England and Scotland dated as late as 1596 and states that they even survived in the nineteenth-century poetical language of the North. However, they remained geographically and functionally restricted and never really gained currency in other parts of the country.

The form *ȝede* /jede/ appears in Middle English sources in a great variety of spellings *ȝeode, (y)oede, yude, yo(o)de, oede* to list a few; its pronunciation showed likewise a great deal of variation. These forms result from mainly two modifications of the old preterite *ēode*: either from stress shift from the first to the second element of the diphthong which produced the *yode*-forms, or from insertion of initial *j*- or preservation of the transformed old perfective prefix *ge*- (cf. Wełna 2001[7] for details on the variety of pronunciations of *ȝede*).

Thus both the regular form *gaid* as well as the old suppletive *ȝede* can be described as unstable forms since they show numerous orthographic and most probably, also phonological variants.

The forms based on *went*, on the other hand, were very stable in the sense that their orthographic variants are substantially fewer than those of *ȝede*. I perused the data quoted in the *Linguistic Atlas of Late Mediaeval English* (McIntosh et al. 1986) and also did searches in the *Corpus of Middle English Prose and Verse* (http://www.hti.umich.edu/c/cme/).[8] In both sources I located only single occurrences of *wentte, whynt, wynt, whent,* and *wenth*.

Given that the regular *gaid* forms remained confined to the North, the two competing forms for the past tense of *go* were *ȝede* and *wente*. Wełna (2001) reports a declining frequency of use of the *ȝede* forms in Midland dialects already in the first half of the fourteenth century. My own searches in the Middle English corpus which covers works from the fourteenth and fifteenth century produce 3690 hits of *wente*, only 793 of *ȝede* and 0 for *gaid* (all figures include orthographic variants of these forms).

So it appears that the *wente*-forms were gaining ground while the use of *ȝede*-forms was declining. In my view these facts can be accounted for if we adopt Aski's

---

7. I was able to obtain only an rtf version of this article which is why I am omitting references to exact pages.

8. The URL valid as of November 2005.

line of thinking and look at the way(s) the paradigm of *gān* fit with the rest of the Middle English verbs. As indicated in (98) above, the present tense forms of the verb fit a restricted template shared with the verb 'do' only. As regards the past tense forms: neither the geographically restricted *gaid*, nor the variants of *ʒede* fit any significant pattern that I can think of. The form *went*, on the other hand, was part of a pattern shared by a number of other verbs, some of which are listed in (99).

(99) Verbs with a past tense similar to that of *went*
 menen, mente 'mean' *leven, lafte* 'depart, leave, stop'
 brennen, brente 'burn' *kissen, kiste* 'kiss'
 dwellen, dwelte 'dwell' *kēpen, kepte* 'keep'
 bilden, bilde/bilte, bilt 'build' *grētten, grette* 'cry'
 fēlen, felte 'feel' *girden, girt, girt* 'put on a belt or girdle,
 surround, encircle'

So it looks like that the form *went*, the only one that was kept as a past tense of *go* in Modern English, was also the one that fit better with a number of other verbs. A conclusion along these lines is also offered by Wełna (2001). Thus the process whereby a new suppletive form was selected was, in fact, part of an analogical process.

One might, of course, ask if we after all shouldn't fall back on the notion of blocking (cf. Chapter 1: 2.2.1.1), and say that *went* being so frequently used, ousted *ʒede* and simply blocked the further spread of the regular *gaid*-forms back in Chaucer's time and still does today (at least after the first stages of language acquisition have passed). One of the main problems with blocking, especially as understood in generative morphology, is that it is a static notion. It does not take into account that forms which supposedly act as 'blockers' are themselves subject to processes of change and moreover, that such 'blockers' evolve in a system of other forms. In the case of the evolution of *went* as the past tense of *go*, *went* existed in competition with two other forms and was consolidated because it was more congruent with the rest of the new past tense forms of numerous other English verbs. Thus similarly to the emergence of suppletion in the paradigms of Romance verbs 'go', the process here is part of a general system restructuring. As such this process is neither an isolated phenomenon, nor can it be described as accidental.

4. Emergence of suppletion and general grammaticalization processes

One of the main ways the emergence of suppletion is related to grammaticalization is the evolution of copula verbs. As indicated by the counts of the typological data in Chapter 4 above, it is cross-linguistically very common for verbs glossed 'be' to have suppletive paradigms. As the typological data also show, this kind of suppletion is not random in the sense that is can be correlated with particular language families and geographical areas. Suppletion in the paradigms of copula verbs can be also correlated with the ways they are used.

This section is organized as follows. In section 4.1, I present the typical contexts where copula verbs are used, and in connection with them a correlation between the occurrence of suppletive verbs and particular encoding strategy for non-verbal sentences. In section 4.2, I offer a brief survey of the known lexical sources for copula verbs. In 4.3, I discuss the grammaticalization of one dynamic verb 'become' as future copula based on the work of Dahl (2000). In 4.4, I present speculations on the possible paths for the development of position verbs into copulas. This section is closed by a summary in 4.5.

4.1 Suppletive copulas and the field of intransitive predication

Verbs glossed as 'be' and usually labeled copulas are typically used in non-verbal sentences that cover senses such as identity, assignment of permanent and/or temporary quality, location, existence and possession. Such clauses are illustrated in (100) below.

(100) Copula clauses

		Example	Meaning
a.	i.	*This is Mary.*	IDENTIFICATION
	ii.	*Mary is a teacher.*	CLASS INCLUSION
b.	i.	*Mary is tall.*	PROPERTY (PERMANENT)
	ii.	*Mary is sick.*	PROPERTY (TEMPORARY)
c.		*Mary is in the kitchen.*	LOCATION
d.		*To everything, there is a reason.*	EXISTENCE
e.		Russian: *U nego est' mašina*	POSSESSION
		to him is car	
		'He has a car.'	

A note on terminology is in order before I proceed with the presentation. The term **copula** has received different interpretations in the literature. For example, Stassen (1997), whose work I cite abundantly below, restricts copula to the lexical items used in identity, class inclusion and attributive statements (constructions (100a–b) above). Dixon (2002) extends the use of the term to items used in all constructions (100a–e) above. In the discussion below, I use "copula" in the Dixon sense, and specify if it is functionally restricted whenever relevant.

Languages code the above listed semantic domains differently. For a detailed and extensive documentation, consult Stassen (1997). Stassen's work on these issues is monumental and I cannot possibly do justice to all the richness of detail and sophisticated analysis in it. His findings relevant to our topic will be summarized in a very general way.

One of the main points in Stassen's description of the domain of intransitive predication is that languages may have separate strategies for the encoding of event predicates (in his study intransitive verbs) as in *he runs,* locational predicates (100c above) and predicate nominals (100a above). However, there is no language where a separate strategy for the encoding of predicate adjectives (100b above) is observed. Predicate adjectives "borrow" a strategy either from intransitive verbs (a verbal strategy), from predicate locationals (a locational strategy) or from predicate nominals (a nominal strategy). Furthermore, languages may employ more than one strategy for the encoding this domain. Finally, there are languages where full or partial switch from one strategy to another is observed. Strategy takeovers operate on synchronic level but it is conceivable that they occur as diachronic processes as well.

Stassen's work on the typology of intransitive predication is based on a very large sample of 410 languages. My own WALS sample of 193 languages is subset of his, with the exception of 40 languages. Those languages, however, are matched by genealogically related languages in Stassen's sample. So a correlation between his coding and mine is warranted. The question of greatest interest for my purposes was to check if the occurrence of tense suppletion with 'be' verbs can be correlated with Stassen's findings on the encoding of non-verbal sentences.

The languages with suppletive 'be' verbs which are both in Stassen's and in my sample are 49. Stassen codes 41 of these languages as using a nominal strategy for the encoding of predicative adjectives. In other words, in languages with suppletive 'be'-verbs, the predicate adjectives tend to be encoded in the same way as predicate nouns.

In Stassen's sample, there are 247 languages where the nominal strategy is used as one of the possible strategies for the encoding of predicative adjectives, cf. (Stassen 1997: 124). So such languages constitute more than half of the languages in his sample.

In my own sample there are 91 languages where the nominal strategy is one of the strategies for the encoding of predicative adjectives. While proportionally such languages are somewhat less than in Stassen sample, they are still close to half of the investigated languages. In this group, 47 languages have suppletive copulas (the total number of languages with suppletive copulas is 55 but in 8 of them do not employ the nominal strategy for the encoding of predicative adjectives). As the figures indicate, a correlation between the occurrence of suppletion with the verb 'be' and the use of nominal strategy for encoding of predicative adjectives is not perfect but rather outlines a tendency. Namely, suppletive 'be' verbs seem to be contingent on a particular strategy languages employ for encoding of concepts such as identity, class inclusion and property assignment. This in turn, means that suppletion is much more systematic than previously thought. This statement cannot be formulated as a bi-directional universal since it is not the case that if a language employs a nominal strategy for the encoding of predicative adjectives it will necessarily have a suppletive copula. What seems to hold is that, if a language has a suppletive copula, it will, more often than not, employ a nominal strategy for the encoding of its predicative adjectives.

Before I proceed with two other generalizations offered by Stassen which are relevant for our topic, a comment on general characteristics of copula verbs is in order. Regular copulas which are used in all or most of the constructions (100a–e) above are extremely rare. In my material, such instances amount to five languages: Imbabura Quechua, Warao, Ainu, Sango, and Kolyma Yukaghir, illustrated by Imbabura Quechua.

(101) Imbabura Quechua (Quechua) (Cole 1985: 67–8)
    a. *ɲuka ali jambii-mi ka-ni.*
       I good healer-VALIDATOR be-1
       'I am a good healer.'
    b. *Juan-ka mayistru-mi ka-rka.*
       Juan-TOP teacher-VALIDATOR be-PST
       'Juan was a good teacher.'
    c. *ɲuka wasi-ka yuraj-mi ka-rka.*
       my house-TOP white-VALIDATOR be-PST
       'My house was white.'
    d. *kan-paj chagra-ka San Pablu-pi-mi ka–nga.*
       you-of field-TOP San Pablo-in-VALIDATOR be-FUT
       'Your field will be in San Pablo.'

While regular copulas of the kind observed in Imbabura Quechua are encountered very seldom, examples of copula verbs showing some kind of irregularity can be found all over the world. Although these irregularities cannot be classified as suppletion by the definition adopted in this work, they still set copula verbs apart from all other verbs in a given language. For instance, in the description of Iraqw, a Southern Cushitic language from Tanzania, we read "There are two kinds of verbs: the verbs 'be' and other verbs" (Mous 1992: 123). Similarly, in Mongolian (Grønbech and Krueger 1955; Poppe 1964), the verbs *amui* 'be', *bui* 'there is' and *bol-* 'be, become' show highly defective paradigms. Whether they are in truly complimentary distribution and thereby suppletive or not is hard to determine based on the material in the descriptions I used. Dixon in his survey of copula clauses in Australian languages notes that there is a tendency for a copula verb to have irregular forms;

and there are a couple of examples of a copula verbs showing a defective paradigm (Dixon 2002: 29). So suppletive 'be' verbs appear as a part of a more general cross-linguistic phenomenon: copula verbs which are used in more than one semantic domain of non-verbal sentences show different degrees of irregularity, and suppletion is only one of them. From another perspective, we can say, that such copula verbs, having a different function than the rest of the verbs in a language are also encoded differently.

Stassen makes two other generalizations which need to be brought up in a discussion of suppletive copula verb a typological and diachronic perspective. One, he finds that if a language uses the same encoding strategy for both predicate nominals and predicate adjectives, it will also tend to have tense (Stassen 1997: 356). Two, as regards strategy switching he observes that strategy takeover (that is the encoding of adjectives may be taken over by the strategy used for encoding of intransitive verbs or locationals or nouns) occurs when a permanent and temporary property are encoded differently (Stassen 1997: 157–62). A few examples of such strategy takeovers are presented below.

In Latin the nominal strategy is replaced by a verbal one in property assignment statements when the intended reading is a temporary property. Thus (102b) where the predicative adjective is encoded as a verb, the redness of the rose is a momentary feature of the scenery.

(102) Latin, adapted from (Stassen 1997: 368)
　　a. *Rosa rubra　　　　est*
　　　 rose red.NOM.SG.FEM be.3SG.PRES
　　b. *Rosa rube-t.*
　　　 rose red-3SG.PRES
　　　 'The rose is red.'

In Mupun, a West Chadic language form Nigeria, the special identity copula *à* is used with a property word when the intended reading is a permanent one and in that case the property word is construed as a noun as in (103a) (see also Stassen on switching to nominal strategy (1997: 206). When the intended reading is a temporary property, the nominal copula is not used as in (103b).

(103) Mupun (Afro-Asiatic, West Chadic), (Frajzyngier 1986: 378)
　　a. *wùr à ráp.*
　　　 he is dirt
　　　 'He is garbage.' (an obvious insult)
　　b. *wùr ráp.*
　　　 he dirty
　　　 'He is dirty.'

A locational switch is illustrated by Amele, a language from the Madang Province of Papua New Guinea. In this language a copula is not used with nominal predicates and is normally omitted with adjectives too as in (104a). However, if the predicated quality is temporary in nature, a position verb is used as in (104b).

(104) Amele (Trans-New Guinea, Mabuso, Gum) (Roberts 1987: 66)
    a. *jo   i   nag*
       house this small
       'This house is small'
    b. *ugb me bil-i-a*
       3SG good sit-3SG-PRES
       'He is   well'

Since such strategy switches are observed in the modern languages, they most probably occur as diachronic processes as well. In fact the lexical sources for suppletive 'be' verbs provide grounds for such a hypothesis. It will be expanded further on below when I propose accounts for at least some stages of the development of copula verbs (see section 4.4 below).

4.2 Historical information on copula verbs

Historical sources for the roots used by suppletive copula verbs in familiar Indo-European languages are described briefly in (105) below (none of the lists of modern cognates of a particular root is exhaustive).

(105) Reconstructed roots for copula verbs in Indo-European languages (Buck 1949; Stassen 1997: 97–8)
    a. Indo-European **es* > Latin *sum* 'be.1SG.PRES', French *suis* 'be.1SG.PRES', Latvian *esmu* and similarly in present tenses of 'be' in Albanian, as well as in Slavic and Iranian languages, present tense forms of English 'be', Dutch and German *is* 'be.3SG.PRES'.
    b. Indo-European **bh(e)u* 'grow, become' > Latin *fui* 'be.1SG.PERF', Old Church Slavonic *byti* 'be.INF', English *be*, German *bin* 'be.1SG.PRES'
    c. Indo-European **wes* 'remain, dwell' > Gothic *wisan* 'be, remain, dwell', English/Dutch *was* 'be.1/3SG.PAST' (in Dutch the form is used for all forms in the singular), German *war* 'be.1/3SG.PAST', Swedish *var* 'be.PAST'.
    d. Indo-European **sta* 'stay' > Latin *stare* 'stay' > Spanish *estar* 'be', French *étais* 'be.1SG.IMPF'; Hindi *thā* 'be.SG.PAST', Irish *tá* 'be'.

Comparative and historical linguists generally agree on the reconstructed meanings of the roots listed in (105b–d). The root **es* in (105a) is subject to debate. Under one view (Buck 1949: 635) this root is said to originate from a "colorless" locative-existential item meaning 'be present, be alive, 'exist'. Another view advocated by Shields (1992), and also supported by Stassen (1997: 98–9), is that the root *es might have originated from a pronoun. I am not in a position to take a stance in this debate.[9] Regardless of what the original meaning of *es might have been, the noteworthy fact about the other roots is that two of them, *wes and *sta apparently originate from position verbs, and the root *bh(e)u is traced back to a dynamic verb 'grow, become'. Similar sources for copula verbs, both suppletive and non-suppletive have been identified in a wide range of languages around the globe, cf. general work on grammaticalization, (Heine et al. 1991; Bybee et al. 1994; Heine and Kuteva 2002). So as regards their historical origins, suppletive 'be'-verbs do not appear as an isolated phenomenon but rather result from processes which are cross-linguistically very common and produce similar outcomes.

Identifying the lexical sources is, however, only the initial step of tracing the development of verbal copulas. The really interesting issue is documenting the stages of this development. I do not hope to arrive at any definite answers here. In sections 4.3 and 4.4 below I present work on this topic together with some speculations.

4.3 Grammaticalization of become as future copula

Dahl (2000) discusses the development of future copulas out of verbs meaning 'become' in the languages of Northern Europe. He argues that although the semantic potential of a word such as 'become' makes it look natural for the expression of states in the future, its evolution as a future copula stems from some quite special uses. In particular, he observes that the process of desemanticization seems to start from contexts where the distinction stative: dynamic is easily neutralized. For instance in the sentence below the use of the Swedish verb *bli* 'become' does not imply any change, only a particular characteristic of an event that will take place in the future.

(106) Swedish (Indo-European, North Germanic) adapted from Dahl (Dahl 2000: 2)[10]
Den här festen blir   nog   trevlig.
this here party become:PRES surely pleasant
'This party will turn out nice.'

---

[9]. There is relatively recent article on this topic (Tanaka 2002) which I have not been able to obtain.

[10]. The page numbers follow the printout of the article I received from Dahl. Thus they are different in the published version.

The 'turn out' sense in (106) which makes *bli* look close to copula represents a special use of this verb in Swedish. In a variety of other contexts the sense of 'change of state' is still present as for instance in (107) below.

(107) Swedish (Indo-European, North Germanic) interpreted from (Dahl 2000: 2)
Barnen   blir   mycket sömniga när   pappa kommer.
child:PL become:PRES very   sleepy   when Father comes
'The children will become/get very sleepy when Father arrives.'

Generally the implication in (107) is that Father's arrival will make the children sleepy. According to Dahl, predications about entities that can be said to acquire a given property X as they develop (cf. (106) above) are among the most felicitous contexts where the inchoative meaning of *bli* 'become' is easily lost and the verb acquires a copula-like function there. Thus in this case we are dealing with an incipient, context dependent grammaticalization.

The use of verbs meaning 'become' as future copulas is commonly reported in grammars. In my own sample I have unearthed it in more than 30 languages a few of which are listed here: Burushaski *maiyam,* Turkish *olmak,* Japanese *nan/natte,* Wolaytta *han,* Supyire *m-pyi* 'make, do, become, call', Chukchi *nʔəl.* Heine and Kuteva (2002: 64) as well as Östen Dahl (p.c.) observe that although such statements are frequently found in grammars it is unclear if in these cases we are dealing with true copulas or some extended uses of the verbs glossed as 'become'.[11]

4.4 Grammaticalization of position verbs to copulas

As stated above verbs of position are commonly reported as lexical sources for copula verbs. The stages of their semantic bleaching are by and large unclear cf. Heine and Kuteva (2002: 278) who comment "Not infrequently, verbs meaning 'sit' have some copula-like uses in certain contexts… This pathway appears to be primarily an instance of desemanticization, but more information is required on the conceptual nature of the process".

---

11. Dahl notes the use of Gothic *wairþái* 'become' as future copula and a similar use for Old Church Slavonic *bǫdetŭ* 'becomes' and comments that if we are to accept the etymology proposed for *bǫdetŭ* < Indo-European **bhu,* then we would have an instantiation of a complete development from 'become' to 'will be'. The Old English *bið* 'be.3SG.PRES' (as well as the rest of the finite forms on this stem) can be added to his list. In Old English the verb *bēon, wesan* 'be' has two present tense paradigms *eom, eart, is* etc. and *bēo, bist, bið.* The *bið-*forms are regularly used in the sense 'will be'. It is commonly noted in Old English grammars that the verb *bēon, wesan* is the only verb in the language with a special future form. The rest of the Old English verbs use present tense forms for future time reference. Since *bið* is said to originate from Indo-European **bhu,* its usage would again confirm the possiblity of the path 'become' > 'will be'.

As shown in section 4.1, predicate adjectives may "borrow" a locative strategy when a temporary property is predicated. Such a takeover is illustrated here in (108) from Martuthunira, a Pama-Nyungan language, once spoken in Western Australia. In this language there is normally no copula in statements of identity in the present tense if the reading of the sentence is generic as in (108a). Whenever the situation is seen as temporary, a position verb must be used as in (108b).

(108) Martuthunira (Australian, Pama-Nyugan) (Dench 1995: 209–10)
    a. *Ngunhaa jami   panyu ngurntura-a.*
       that.NOM medicine good cold-ACC
       'That medicine is good for colds.'
    b. *Pukarti-ngara nyina-marri-nguru jalya-rru.*
       snakewood-PL be-COLL-PRES   rubbish-now
       'The snakewood trees are all rubbish now.' (they weren't always)

The verb *nyina-* used in (108b) means 'sit, stay' in other contexts. When used as a copula, it completely loses its lexical meaning. While other position verbs such as *karri-* 'stand' and *wanti-* 'lie' may also be used as copulas, they never really lose their lexical content. Generally, the use of *nyina-* not only allows the ascription of a property to the subject of the clause but it also makes to it possible to relate this property to a particular time frame or mood as in (109).

(109) Martuthunira (Australian, Pama-Nyugan) (Dench 1995: 209–10)
    Ngaliwa mirntiwul nyina-marni nhuura!
    1PL.INCL all   be-CONTR knowing
    'We should all know [that]!'

So the initial stage of the grammaticalization path for locative verbs may be their use in statements denoting a temporary quality. As this use is extended to property predicates of a more permanent nature the position verb comes closer to the status of copula verb. In some cases the most grammaticalized position verb may start to oust other position verbs from their copula-like functions. For instance, Dixon (2002: 22) reports data from Guugu Yimidhirr, a Pama-Nyungan language from Hopevale, Queensland. In this language younger speakers use the verb *wu-* 'lie, exist' as a copula without any sense of 'lying' as in (110).

(110) Guugu Yimidhirr (Australian, Pama-Nyungan) adapted from Dixon (2002: 22)
    gana-aygu   ngayu yinil   wu-nay.
    before-EMPHATIC 1SG frightened be-PST
    'Before, I used to be frightened.'

Dixon quotes a comment from the language description "older speakers criticize younger speakers for indiscriminately using *wu-* ... as a tense-carrying dummy verb, when the subjects...involved do not actually *lie* but rather stand or sit" (Haviland 1979: 118).

It appears, however, that the grammaticalization of position verbs as copulas does not have to always originate from their use in property statements. For example, in Mundari, a language spoken in the Ranchi District, State of Assam, India, there is a special copula of identity *tan*, adjectives are encoded as verbs, and a special copula *menaʔ* is used in locative-existential statements. In statements with non-present time reference *tan* and *menaʔ* are replaced by the position verb *tai* 'stay'.

(111) Mundari (Austro-Asiatic, Munda) (Osada 1992: 119–20)
    a. *Soma tan-iʔ.*
       Soma be-3SG
       'This is Soma.'
    b. *Soma-eʔ tai-ke-n-a.*
       Soma-3SG stay-AP-ITM-PREDICATOR[12]
       'It was Soma.' or 'Soma was there.'
    c. *Soma oɟaʔ-re menaʔ-i-a.*
       Soma house-in exist-3SG-PREDICATOR
       'Soma is in the house.'
    d. *Soma oɟa-re-ʔ tai-ke-n-a.*
       Soma house-in-3SG stay-AP-ITM-PREDICATOR
       'Soma was in the house.'

Position verbs are used in a similar way in Lango, a Nilo-Saharan language from Uganda. In this language locative-existential and possessive statements require the verb *tíe* 'be present' in statements with present time reference. However, *tíe* cannot be used in sentences with future or past time reference. Instead, a position verb must be used or the verb *ònwòŋò* 'find'; the latter seems especially common in sentences with past time reference.

(112) Lango (Nilo-Saharan, West Nilotic) (Michael Noonan, p.c.)
    a. *tíê kân.*
       3SG.be present here
       'It's here.'
    b. *bèdɔ kân.*
       3SG.sit here
       'It will be here.'
    c. *ònwòŋɔ kân.*
       3SG.find here
       'It was here.'

---

12. AP = Aspect marker; ITM = Intransitive marker.

So in such cases, a general metaphorical transfer may be at work. Specifically, we may think of a metaphor of the kind 'if X stood/will stand somewhere, then X has been/will be there' cf. (111b) from Mundari above. A lot more data are necessary to truly substantiate such a claim.

The data I have at present seem to confirm it. Thus in Greek, the perfect participle of *īmai* 'be' is borrowed from the verb *staθō* 'stand'. The verb *staθō* exists as a full lexical verb; it is only when used in the perfect construction as a copula that its lexical meaning is lost.

In Gothic, the verb *wisan*, usually glossed as 'be, remain, dwell' preserves its lexical meaning only with two present tense forms of the indicative: *wisa* 'abide.1SG.PRES' and *wisiþ* 'dwell.3SG.PRES' plus a few forms of the present subjunctive. No other present tense forms of *wisan* occur in the four Gospels.

(113) Gothic (Indo-European, East Germanic), (Wulfila's Gospel texts, John 6:56)
saei matjiþ   mein leik jah driggkiþ   mein bloþ,
who eat.3SG.PRES my   flesh and drink.3SG.PRES my   blood
in mis wisiþ   jah ik in imma
in me dwell.3SG.PRES and I   in him
'He that eateth my flesh and drinketh my blood, dwelleth in me and I him'
(the idiomatic translation follows the King James Version)

No lexical meaning can be traced in the past tense forms of the verb *wisan: was* etc which also supply the past tense of *im, is, ist*, etc. 'be.PRES'. Thus the verb *wisan* appears fully grammaticalized in the past tense while traces of its lexical sense can be observed in the present tense. This suggests that the bleaching process must have started in contexts associated with a past, or in any case, a non-present time reference.

The uses of position verbs outlined above suggest that there is more than one path whereby they evolve into copula verbs. One starts with their use in property statements typically predicating a temporary property or state. Another seems to originate from their use in non-present tense contexts as replacements for identity and existential predicates which are incompatible with non-present time reference.

Since suppletive copula verbs typically consist of several roots, it is conceivable that several processes of the kind outlined above are involved in the creation of such paradigms. Moreover, such processes need not occur at the same time. Besides, whether the copula verbs come to stand in relation of suppletion according to tense depends very much on whether a particular language has tense or not. For instance, the replacement described above for Lango above, would have been classified as suppletion in a language that has tense coded on the rest of its verbs. However, verbs in Lango do not make tense distinctions. So postulating suppletion is not justified in a strictly formal sense but functionally the verbs *bèdò* 'sit, stay' and ònwòŋò 'find' when used in locative-existential and possessive statements in effect "supply" each other in different time-frames.

4.5 Conclusion

In this section I demonstrated that the occurrence of suppletive copula verbs can be correlated with a particular strategy for the encoding of semantic domains such as identity, property assignment, location, existence and possession. Specifically, in a substantial part of the languages where suppletive 'be' verbs are observed predicate nominals and predicate adjectives use one and the same encoding strategy.

Historically, both suppletive and non-suppletive copulas appear to originate from the same lexical sources: verbs of position, dynamic verbs such as 'do', 'become', 'happen', 'go', erstwhile pronouns or focus markers. The exact stages of these grammaticalization processes still require documentation. Whether a suppletive paradigm according to tense evolves out of these sources or not depends also on whether a language has tense or not.

Generally copula verbs are used in a domain that is semantically and functionally different from that of full lexical verbs. This, in turn, motivates their special formal encoding.

5. Suppletion and lexicalization

In this section I explore the relationship between suppletion and lexicalization. In particular, I look at two factors that seem to trigger lexical renewal: one is frequency of use in word formation processes; the other is pragmatically conditioned. Historical-comparative data from Slavic languages are used as a basis for the discussion.

I have concentrated on imperfective: perfective verb pairs in 11 modern Slavic languages and Old Church Slavonic (hereafter OCS). The presentation is organized as follows. All the pairs collected from language descriptions are listed in Table A5 in Appendix 3.[13] The infinitive forms of the verbs are used for all the languages that have infinitives; for those without infinitives, I used the standard citation forms: 1SG.PRES for Bulgarian, and 3SG.PRES for Macedonian. In the text below I quote only the pairs that I discuss in detail: the imperfective: perfective expressions of three senses 'take', 'lay, put' and 'say/speak'.

The Modern Slavic verbs for 'take' are listed in (114).

---

13. The verbs of motion are excluded from the table as in most of these languages they are so complex that they require a separate table.

(114) Slavic verbs 'take'

Group	Language	IPFV	PFV
EAST	Russian	*brat'*	*vzjat'*
	Belorussian	*brats'*	*uzjats'*
	Ukrainian	*brati*	*uzjati*
WEST	Polish	*brać*	*wziąć*
	Upper Sorbian	*brać*	*wzać*
	Czech	*bráti*	*vzíti*
	Slovak	*brat'*	*vzjat'*
SOUTH	Slovene	*jemati*	*vzeti*
	Serbo-Croatian	*uzimati*	*uzeti*
	Macedonian	*zema*	*zeme*
	Bulgarian	*vzemam*	*vzema*
	OCS	*vъz-jьmati*	*vъz-ęti*

As shown above, East and West Slavic languages use different verbs for the expression of the imperfective: perfective distinction of the sense 'take', which have the same historical source. The imperfective member of the pair, *brat'* (the Russian variant is used in the text) in the East and West Slavic languages historically related to the OCS verb *bərati* 'pick, collect, take' which in turn is cognate with Latin *ferre*, Greek φέρω /fero/, Sanskrit bhṛ- 'carry' (Buck 1949). The perfective *vzjat'* is historically related to the OCS verb *vъz-ęti*. As it will become clear from the presentation below the Slovene verbs *jemati: vzeti* represent the oldest aspectual pair of verbs meaning 'take' and the pair *brat': vzjat'* found in the East and West languages is a newer creation.

The Common Slavic verbs for 'take' are related to the words which mean 'have' and also 'grasp, seize'. Townsend and Janda (1996) reconstruct the paradigms of three verbs in Late Common Slavic shown in (115) below.

(115) Late Common Slavic, ca. 4th–5th C. AD (Townsend and Janda 1996: 216)[14]

	jьměti 'have' IPFV	*ęti* 'take' PFV	*jьmati* 'grasp, seize' IPFV
1SG	*jьmamь*	*jьmǫ*	*emjǫ*
2SG	*jьmaši*	*jьmeši*	*emješi*
3SG	*jьmatъ*	*jьmetъ*	*emjetъ*
1PL	*jьmamъ*	*jьmemъ*	*emjemъ*
2PL	*jьmate*	*jьmete*	*emjete*
3PL	*jьmǫtъ/jьmějǫtъ*	*jьmǫtъ*	*emjǫtъ*

Indo-European cognates: Latin *ěmo, emere* 'buy'

---

14. No dual forms are cited in the reconstructed paradigms.

These authors describe the difference between the three verbs as one of stative vs. dynamic action: *jьměti* (stative) vs. *ęti* and *jьmati* (dynamic). The verb *jьměti* which expresses a state, rather than an action is construed as imperfective. The verbs *ęti* and *jьmati* are further differentiated by their aspectual values, *ęti* is perfective, while *jьmati* is imperfective.

In the modern Slavic languages, there are no reflexes of the simpex verb *ęti*. The verb *jьmati* survives only in Slovene *jemati* with the general simplex sense 'take.IPFV'. It is also found in Serbo-Croatian *jemati* but with a very specific sense, 'pick grapes'. In Polish sources its cognate *imać* is listed as an archaic verb meaning 'grasp'.

The important fact about *ęti* and *jьmati* is that both verbs are very commonly used as bases for derivation for new verbs, with senses related to 'take' but very often also substantially altered. This process must have been very active already at time of the dialect split because we find numerous instances of such derivations in OCS. A handful of them are listed in (116).[15]

(116) OCS derivative of *ęti* and *jьmati*

PFV	IPFV
vъz-ęti 'take'	*vъz–jьmati* 'take'
ot-ęti 'take away'	*ot-jьmati* 'take away'
pri-ęti 'receive'	*pri-jьmati* 'receive'
iz-ęti 'take out'	
ob-ęti 'take, receive, comprehend, apprehend'	*po-jьmati* 'pick'

There are numerous examples of prefixed cognates of the pair *ęti: jьmati* in the modern Slavic languages too. The prefixes have merged with the stems so that they are no longer recognizable as such as for instance in the Russian verbs *prinjat': prinimat'* 'take, accept, receive [guests]', *pronjat': pronimat'* 'seize [with fear], pierce, penetrate with cold', *ponjat: ponimat'* 'understand'. Herman (1975: 160–9) provides extensive lists of such verb pairs in Russian, Czech, Polish and Serbo-Croatian. So what seems to have happened is that the simplex verbs were used so often as bases for derivation of new verbs with new lexical meanings that they lost their status of free words. For the expression of the general sense 'take' the West and East dialects retorted to the semantically close imperfective verb *bərati* 'pick, collect, take' and the perfective prefixed variant of *ęti*, *vъz-ęti* where the prefix and the stem were gradually fused together into a new stem, as in modern Russian *vzjat'*.

---

15. It is unclear whether the simplex verbs *ęti* and *jьmati* were very common even in OCS. My searches of OCS texts yield only sporadic occurrences. The situation is similar for Old Russian: the simplex verb does not seem to be very common, and in Russian historical dictionaries its latest occurrence is quoted from the First Novgorod Chronicle dated *c*.1215.

The exact process of the semantic change of the old verb *bərati* 'pick, collect, take' > modern Russian *brat'* 'take' is hard to pinpoint with certainty as in the West and East languages it must have started already in preliterate times. However, the shift from the sense 'pick, collect [usually fruit or many scattered things]' to a more general verb that denotes the process of taking is rather natural.[16] Given that the original Slavic verb *jьmati* was apparently lost to derivational processes, the verb *bərati* was the next best choice for the unmarked imperfective expression of the sense 'take'.

One may of course ask how come *brat'* never formed a regular perfective. In fact, prefixed perfectives of *brat'* are numerous but usually the derived verbs have a slightly different, and in many cases, less general lexical meaning: *vy-brat'* 'choose, select, pick out, elect', *vo-brat'* 'absorb, drink in, soak in, inhale', *za-brat'* 'take (in one's hand), take (away), take over, appropriate', *na-brat'* 'gather, collect, assemble, take on', *so-brat'* 'gather (together) [thing, people], collect, pick, accumulate, invite'. Compared with these verbs the verb *vzjat'* both in Old and present day Russian has a much broader lexical content and a much wider range of contexts where it can be used.

What we observe with the evolution of the pair *brat':vzjat'* in West and East Slavic languages is a restructuring of the expressions for closely related concepts as a consequence of a very productive derivational process whereby the older expressions for the sense 'take' lose their free lexical status. Subsequently they are replaced by other lexical items with the broadest possible semantic potential and contextual applicability.

A similar story can be told about the pair *klast': položit'* 'lay, put' observed again in the languages from the West group as well as in Russian. All the verbs are shown in (117).

(117) Basic Slavic verbs 'lay, put'

Group	Language	IPFV	PFV
EAST	Russian	*klast'*	*položit'*
	Belorussian	*klas'tsy*	*paklas'tsy*
	Ukrainian	*klasti*	*poklasti*
WEST	Polish	*kłaść*	*położyć*
	Upper Sorbian	*kłac*	*položyć*
	Czech	*klasti*	*položiti*
	Slovak	*klast'*	*položit*
SOUTH	Slovene	*postavljati*	*postaviti*
			položiti
	Serbo-Croatian	*stavljati*	*staviti*

---

16. The verb *bərati* is used even in OCS with the sense 'take' but such uses are not very common.

	Macedonian	klava	klade
			položi
	Bulgarian	slagam	složa
	OCS	polagati	
		klasti	položiti

In historical grammars of East and West Slavic languages it is common to find a statement to the effect that the old simplex verb of position *ložiti* 'lay, put' became obsolete rather early in the history of language X. However, such a statement does not explain what happened to this verb. It did not simply vanish into thin air. In fact it is still very much around but is no longer a root that can be used without a prefix. It was, and still is used as a basis for derivation of other verbs so often that it has completely lost its status of a free word. So the next best, semantically closely related verb *klast'* < OCS *klasti* 'store, put something inside [a container], lay'[17] was reanalyzed as the neutral imperfective expression of the sense 'lay, put'. As I already pointed out in section Chapter 4: 2.2 above (Suppletion according to aspectual distinctions), *klast'* in Russian (joint with derivations) is the imperfective correspondent of *položit'* in more literal uses. For the abstract senses the perfective *položit'* pairs up with the regular (though secondarily derived) imperfective *polagat'*. So in this case we observe an instantiation of lexical split.

With the pairs above, I argued that one of the primary reasons for lexical renewal is the fact that the older basic words lost their free lexical status as a consequence of being commonly used as bases for the derivation of new words. Lexical renewal, and thereby the emergence of suppletion, can be driven by other reasons, which are essentially pragmatic in nature. The semantic field of verbs of 'saying' and 'speaking', especially in historical perspective provides an excellent illustration of such replacements. The basic verbs of 'saying' and 'speaking in Slavic languages are listed in (118).

(118) Basic Slavic verbs for 'say'/'speak'

Group	Language	IPFV	PFV
EAST	Russian	*govorit'*	*skazat'*
	Belorussian	*kazats'*	*skazats'*
		gavaryt	
	Ukrainian	*kazati*	*skazati*
		govorit	

---

17. Cognate with the Gothic verb *hladan* 'load', English *lade,* German *laden* 'load'; in Lithuanian the cognate is *kloti* 'spread out' (Vasmer 1964–1973; Buck 1949).

Chapter 5. Tense–aspect suppletion II: synchronic and usage-based perspective   131

WEST	Polish	*mówić*	*powiedzieć*
	Upper Sorbian	*prajić*	*prajić*
			rieść/powěsć
	Czech	*říkati*	
		mluviti	*říci*
	Slovak	*vraviet'*	
		hovorit'	*povedat'*
SOUTH	Slovene	*praviti* 'say'	*reč I* 'say'
		govoríti 'say, tell'	*povédati* 'tell'
	Serbo-Croatian	*reći*	
		govoriti	*izgovoriti*
	Macedonian	*zboruva*	
		veli	
		kažuva	*kaže*
			reče
	Bulgarian	*govorja*	
		(pri)kazvam	*kaža (reka)*[18]
	OCS	*(rečti)*	
		glagolati	*rečti*

An aspectual pair for the general sense 'say/speak' is observed in 5 of the 11 surveyed modern Slavic languages as well as in OCS. It should be noted that in the languages where such a clear cut pair is missing, a cluster of verbs is observed. That is that there exists more than one verb to express a given aspect, and typically it is hard to establish which one is more common or marked in any sense (semantic or pragmatic/stylistic).

In the discussion below I present the historical sources for the verbs listed above. I also point out some general characteristics of the semantic field of words denoting speaking and saying, and the relevance of a grammatical category such as aspect to these words.

If we take a look at the imperfective column in (118) above, we can see that no clear generalization can be made as regards a uniform historical source for the expression of the imperfective 'speak'. There is an obvious presence of *govorit'* < OCS *govor* 'noise, uproar', cognates of which are encountered in seven out of the eleven modern languages. However, several other historical sources gave rise to general imperfective 'speak' verbs in the different languages. The Czech *mluviti* and Polish *mówić* can be traced back to OCS *mləva* 'noise, tumult' and the verb derived from it

---

18. This latter verb is very rarely used, and stylistically marked.

mluviti 'make a noise, a tumult'. The Macedonian verbs are traced back as follows: *zboruva* comes from OCS *səborə* 'assembly', also used in the sense of 'conversation', and *veli* from OCS *(po)velěti* 'command, give an order'.

The historical sources for perfective verbs 'say' are equally diverse. In the South and East languages the old Common Slavic verb *rečti*, also the most common verb of 'saying' in OCS, is replaced by cognates of the OCS verb *kazati* 'explain, show' or its prefixed variants. Other sources for the modern Slavic 'say' are verbs which such as the old verb *praviti* 'make straight, set right' or prefixed derivatives of *věděti* 'know'. The derived verb *poveděti* meant once 'make known, inform, relate' and was subsequently reinterpreted as 'say' in the West Slavic languages.

So it looks like that just about anything from words referring to 'noise' to words denoting 'order' may in the course of time become reanalyzed as a general verb denoting an ordinary speech act. A plausible explanation for this is suggested by Buck (1915: 5–6). This author points out that a factor of "first importance in changes of vocabulary, …is the fondness for new and picturesque expressions, and the tendency to replace familiar and common-place words by such, until they in turn lose all special coloring and are ready to be displaced by others". This idea is articulated again at the end of the twentieth century by Keller (1994: 101–5), in somewhat different terms. He enumerates a set of maxims which he calls **static** and another set which he calls **dynamic**. Those maxims are seen are primary factors in shaping language use, and subsequently change. The static maxims are those which drive our behavior when we aim mainly to be understood. The dynamic maxims are the ones which we follow when we want to stand out, be noticed as unusual. Keller (1994: 105) notes that

> Under normal circumstances, we do not choose out linguistic means according to exactly one maxim. When we are talking, we try to kill several birds with one stone: we try to conform, attract attention, be understood, save energy. It is extremely rare that someone wants nothing but to be understood.

The historical sources for words expressing senses such as 'say/speak', appear to be a good example for such pragmatically driven replacements. As the common words become so common to the point of being void of any expressive value, in marked or informal registers they start to be replaced by less conventional expressions. As these new expressions become more frequently used, they gradually oust the original word but also in course of time lose a lot of their stylistic coloring. So they in turn become very common and subject to new replacements.

Another reason why verbs such as 'say' are frequently replaced by new expressions is that they are very prone to evolve into grammatical markers of various kinds. For instance, the Common Slavic verb *rečti* 'say' was grammaticalized into a quotative marker in various degrees in the different languages. In some this occurred relatively early in their history. Zaliznjak (1995: 124) states that in Old Russian there was only one form of this verb, *reče* which was used with just as a quotative marker, without any lexical function whatsoever.

Finally, as we recall from the survey of the typological data, the verbs 'say/speak' are among of the most frequent suppletive verbs, especially according to aspect. This is no accident. The senses 'speak' and 'say' are commonly expressed by separate lexical items in many languages, and the only essential difference between such lexemes is their Aktionsart. The English verbs *speak* and *say* illustrate this very well. The verb *speak* is durative or imperfective; it describes the act of speaking as a process and naturally combines with a durative adverbial as in *he spoke for two hours*. A verb such as *say* is inherently perfective in nature. It describes the act of speaking with an emphasis on its result. Its use with a durative adverbial is ungrammatical e.g. the sentence **he said it for two hours* is incorrect except maybe when used in some pejorative sense. In languages where the distinction imperfective: perfective coded on all or nearly all verbs, the most general words for 'speak' and 'say' are reinterpreted as the sole expressions for a particular aspect and thereby as a suppletive pair.

The emergence of suppletive verbs according to aspect as traced in the Slavic data seems to originate from the restructuring of the expressions for a particular concept. As such it is similar to lexicalization. It instantiates lexical renewal which can be motivated by different factors in individual cases: in some the introduction of a suppletive form is driven by paradigm restructuring, in others, it appears to be pragmatically motivated.

6. Summary and conclusions

In Chapter 4 and in this chapter I presented suppletion in tense–aspect categories from a synchronic and diachronic perspective.

Synchronically this kind of stem change shows an obvious areal concentration in Europe and the western parts of Asia. Other hotbeds are Meso-America and Papua New Guinea.

In terms of cross-linguistic frequency tense–aspect suppletion is observed in about one third of the sampled languages. This in turn shows that it is far from a marginal phenomenon. It is clearly favored by certain linguistic phyla such as Indo-European, North and South Caucasian, Oto-Manguean, Carib and Sepik-Ramu. This is not to say that it is not observed in other phyla, only that it is most prominent in those just mentioned.

Two kinds of stem change are distinguished: non-categorial and categorial suppletion. Non-categorial suppletion covers cases of complex paradigms where a single stem per category is not present, but rather the paradigm consists of several portmanteau morphs. Such paradigms are particularly common with grammaticalized or grammaticalizing items such as copula verbs or auxiliaries of different kinds. Categorial suppletion is a term reserved for paradigms where there exists one stem for a particular tense–aspect category. Tense-aspect categories typically distinguished by stem change are general semantic distinctions such as present: past: future or perfective: imperfective. It is less common to use different stems for remoteness distinctions in the past or to make the distinction imperfect: preterite or perfect vs. other tense–aspect categories.

The lexemic groups which show tense–aspect suppletion are numerous but their quantitative distribution is not evenly distributed. Specifically, more than half of the verbs which show this kind of stem change express senses such as 'be', 'come' and 'go'. This is not accidental. As suggested in section 4 above (Emergence of suppletion and grammaticalization processes), suppletive copula verbs most probably result from several different grammaticalization processes. This in turn would account for the presence of several roots in their paradigms. Besides, such verbs are typically used within a domain that is semantically and functionally different from the domain of lexical verbs which motivates their special encoding. The motion verbs with suppletive paradigms are about as numerous as the 'be' verbs. Suppletion in the paradigms of motion verbs is motivated by several factors. Similarly to verbs glossed 'be', words such as 'come' and 'go' are commonly used with grammatical functions as well. In the group of verbs with non-categorial suppletion, the verbs of motion are the next large group following the group of 'be'-verbs. The verbs of motion with suppletive paradigms that are not in the non-categorial suppletion group fall for the most part in the group of verbs with aspect suppletion or very complex paradigms with stem changes in both tense and aspect. Aspect is highly relevant to an action such as motion which is why it is not surprising to find lexical expressions that are highly compatible with one specific aspectual category but incompatible with others. As discussed above, the relevance of a particular grammatical category to the meaning of a lexical item which uses suppletive forms can be demonstrated for other lexemic groups too.

Diachronically, suppletive forms according to tense and aspect result from several distinct processes. In some cases, such as the development of copula verbs, emergence of suppletion shares similarities with grammaticalization. In others, it comes close to lexicalization in that such processes involve either specification of meaning or general restructuring of the expressions for a given concept. Frequency is part of the story behind the evolution of suppletive forms, but it can be shown to provide several different motivations for their development. Finally, there is evidence that historically, the emerging suppletive forms are subject to the same system pressure and analogical processes that operate on all other verbs. In this sense suppletive verbs appear a lot less idiosyncratic and haphazard than previously thought.

CHAPTER 6

Suppletive imperatives

The subject matter of this chapter are paradigms where there is a special form for imperative as illustrated by the Lezgian verb 'go' in (119).

(119) Lezgian (Haspelmath 1993: 135)
'go'
fi-(a)-na   go-(THEMATIC VOWEL)-AOR
fi-zwa   go-IPFV
alad   go.IMP

Section 1 of this chapter offers an introductory discussion of the functions and morphological marking of the imperative category in general. Issues pertinent to suppletion in the imperative are discussed in the subsequent sections as follows. The synchronic distribution of suppletive imperatives is discussed in section 2. Specifically, the semantic distinctions outlined by suppletive imperatives are presented in 2.1. Types of stem change (e.g. alternation of regular and suppletive forms) as well as the form of suppletive imperatives are discussed in section 2.2. The lexemic groups observed with this kind of suppletion are presented in section 2.3; estimates of its cross-linguistic frequency can be found in section 2.4. Comparative-historical data on this phenomenon as well as hypotheses for the development of suppletive forms in the imperative are presented in section 3. A summary and discussion in section 4 conclude the chapter.

1. A brief note on the functions and the marking of imperative

The prototypical function of the imperative is to express direct commands, e.g. *Come!* Other uses are possible as well, such as request, advice, suggestion, permission, depending on the context and speech situation (Birjulin and Xrakovskij 2001: 41). Bybee et al. (1994: 210) note that within a language, imperatives may be distinguished by features such as polite, emphatic, immediate or delayed.

The imperative is thus to used to express a particular speech act, commands with varying degrees of politeness. It is also a category mainly relevant for dynamic verbs, for obvious reasons. While not completely ruled out in stative contexts, e.g. sentences such as *Stay put/Be calm* are perfectly acceptable, the use of the imperative with other stative vebs such as *Know it!* is clearly odd, if not downright ungrammatical.

Grammatical expression of imperative is very frequent across languages. Van der Auwera, Lejeune, Umarani and Goussev (2005) find that among the 549 languages they investigated as regards their imperative morphology, 289 of them (a little more than half) show dedicated markers for the second singular and second plural imperatives. Van der Auwera and his colleagues consider zero as a marker when opposed to other forms and I follow them in this respect. In their sample the imperative is coded as having special marking if any of the following alternatives is true (a) imperative (especially 2SG) is marked by zero as opposed to other moods; (b) there is a special morphological marker for the imperative. An illustration of special imperative marking is provided by Standard Arabic in (120).

(120) Standard Arabic (Afro-Asiatic, Semitic) (Benmamoun 1996: 156–7)
'study' (partial paradigm)

	INDICATIVE IMPEFECTIVE	IMPERATIVE
2SGM	ta-drus-u	ʔu-drus
2PLM	ta-drus-uu-na	ʔu-drus-uu

My own WALS sample is a subset of the one used by van der Auwera and his colleagues with the exception of 10 languages. As regards marking of imperative in the second-person singular and plural, a similar proportion holds, that is 100 out of 193 languages show dedicated marking for these forms in the senses defined above. In the subsequent sections I will discuss exceptions to these morphological patterns. Such exceptions are observed in 41 languages (see section 2.4 for details on areal and genetic distribution); in 29 of them, regular imperatives have morphological markers for both second-person singular and plural.

2. Suppletive imperatives from a synchronic perspective

2.1 Semantic distinctions indicated by suppletive imperatives

The use of a special form in the imperative, singles out this mood against all other moods. In the examples below, the imperative is shown in contrast with indicative forms, as illustrated by Egyptian Arabic in (121), Modern Greek in (122) and Jakaltek, a Mayan language from Guatemala, in (123).

(121) Egyptian Arabic (Afro-Asiatic, Semitic) (Mitchell 1962: 152)
'come'

ana geet	I come.PRV.M.SG
ana aagi	I come.IMPF.M.SG
taʔaala	come.IPFV.M.SG
taʔaali	come.IMP.F.SG
taʔaalu	come.IMP.PL

(122) Modern Greek (Indo-European, Hellenic), (Christiades 1980: 76)
'come'
erx-ese   come-PRES.IND.2SG
erx-ste   come-PRES.IND.2PL
Ela   come.IMP.2SG
Ela-te   come.IMP-IMP.2PL

(123) Jakaltek, (Mayan, Kanjobalan), (Day 1973: 61)
'come'
chach titoj   you come.2SG.IND.FUT
cata   come.2SG.IMP

Van de Auwera et al. (2005) observe that languages may have more than one imperative paradigm, distinguished along parameters like tense (most typically present vs. future), aspect (e.g. perfective vs. imperfective), politeness, movement towards or away from speaker, voice or transitivity. Such distinctions do not appear to be relevant for suppletive imperatives. In my database, there is, however, one language, Ingush, where the imperative of the verb 'come' has two separate suppletive forms that differ with regard to time reference as shown in (124).

(124) Ingush (North Caucasian, Central) (Johanna Nichols, p.c.)
'come'
	INDICATIVE	IMPERATIVE
PRES	*d-oagha*	*d-iel* (right now, specific time)
FUT	*d-oaghaddy*	*d-oula* (future or unspecified time)

A grammatical meaning closely related to imperative is the **hortative**. It is defined by Bybee et al. (Bybee et al. 1994: 179) as follows "the speaker is encouraging or inciting someone to action". Suppletion that singles out hortative only is encountered, but it is less common than suppletion according to imperative. Here it is exemplified in (125) from Krongo, a Kordofanian language from the Niger-Congo phylum, spoken in Sudan.

(125) Krongo (Reh 1985: 198)
'go'
càáw   go.INF
yàáw   go.IMP.2SG
t-ín-tí INF-go-HORTATIVE.1SG

Most of the imperative suppletives express direct positive commands. This, however, might reflect a shortcoming in the data collection rather than the actual situation. Lexical/suppletive expressions are probably more common for this function than my data currently suggest. Among languages that use an inflected auxiliary to negate sentences (declarative as well as imperative), there are two examples in my database of suppletion in the imperative, both from the Uralic family: Nenets, and Finnish, as illustrated by the following paradigm:

(126) Finnish (Uralic, Finno-Ugric) (Päivi Juvonen, p.c.)
'negative verb'
et   negative verb. IND.2SG
ei   negative verb. IND.3SG
älä   negative verb. IMP.2SG
äläköön negative verb. IMP.3SG

2.2 Types of stem change and form of suppletive imperatives

The discussion on this issue is rather short as there aren't too many noteworthy facts to be brought to light. First, unlike tense–aspect or other kinds of suppletion, alternation of regular and alternative forms appears common with suppletive imperatives. Typically, it is very hard or downright impossible to determine if use of the regular or the suppletive form is conditioned by any semantic or pragmatic factors. Likewise, it is not possible to say which one of the forms is more common than the other. A case of such alternation is illustrated by Iraqw, a Southern Cushitic language, spoken in Tanzania.

(127) Iraqw (Afro-Asiatic, Cushitic), (Mous 1992)
'come'
xawn   come here.2SG.IND
xawé' come here.2SG.IMP
qwaláɲ come here.2SG.IMP

Second, as regards the morphological structure of suppletive imperatives, inasmuch as there is morphological marking on regular imperatives in the language in question, suppletive forms tend to have it too. So in this sense, they are verbs. As we shall see in the section on diachrony, verbs restricted to the imperative function seem to be common sources for suppletive imperatives along with particles or lexical items of unclear word class status which in the course of time acquire pertinent morphological markers.

2.3 Lexemic groups that occur with suppletive imperatives

The number of suppletive imperatives per language is very restricted, usually one or two verbs at the most. Consult Table A6 in Appendix 3 for more detailed data on suppletive imperatives.

Table 21. Lexemic groups

Meaning	No.[a]	%	Weighed value sum	%
come/go	47	70	10.911	72.9
give	6	9	0.960	6.41
do	2	3	0.330	2.20
negative verbs	2	3	0.750	5.00
be	3	5	1.253	8.36
say	2	3	0.415	2.77
eat	1	2	0.165	1.10
take	2	3	0.021	0.14
sit (down)	1	2	0.167	1.12
Total	66	100	14.972	100.00

[a] Number of occurrences: this figure reflects the number of verbs with suppletive imperatives rather than the number of languages where this phenomenon is observed (for the latter, consult Tables A4 and A6 in Appendix 3). For instance, in Swahili, both verbs *kuja* 'come' and *kwenda* 'go' have suppletive imperatives; they are counted as two verbs in the table but in the verb meaning index (Table A3) in Appendix 3, Swahili is reflected just once.

The verbs with suppletive imperatives in the current database fall into nine semantic groups. Table 21 presents the frequency of their distribution. It is easy to see that the predominant group of verbs which use suppletive forms in imperative and hortative are basic motion verbs such as 'come' and 'go'. This can hardly be an accident as one of the most common ways to use the imperative is with motion verbs. Hence separate expressions for this function are motivated. The imperative as category is likewise highly relevant for the other verbs with suppletive imperative which show a somewhat lower cross-linguistic frequency of occurrence: 'give' in the sense 'give me', 'say', in the sense 'tell me', 'sit down' as an invitation or 'take' in the sense 'help yourself' (see Comrie 2003 for a discussion on recipient person suppletion with this verb).

2.4 Frequency of distribution in the samples

The quantitative distribution of suppletion in the imperative is shown in Tables 2 and 3 as well as Map 5 in Appendix 3. A word of caution is in order here: I am simply not convinced that I have all the pertinent data. Not all grammars care to mention suppletive imperatives. It is my impression that they are best elicited. If one is to fully trust the figures below, based on both absolute number of languages where the phenomenon is attested as well as on the weight values count, suppletive imperatives do not show a very high cross-linguistic frequency. The four counting procedures show essentially two proportions, 15 and 20 percent. The lower proportion is shown by the language count for the small sample as well as by the weight values count. According to count of languages in the WALS sample, and likewise, the count of genera (the Dryer Distribution) suppletive imperatives appear to occur in one fifth of the genera.

Table 22. Language count

Small sample		WALS sample			
No	%	No	%	W	% of 70
15	15.96	41	21.24	10.449	14.92

Note: No. = Number of languages; W = Weight values sum; the total of weight values for the WALS sample is 70

Table 23. The Dryer Distribution

	Africa	Eurasia	SEA and Oceania	A-NG	N Am	S Am	Total
Yes	11	11	0	1	5	4	32
No	16	24	18	23	24	23	128

Note: Yes = presence of categorial tense suppletion; No = absence of categorial tense suppletion; Total number of genera = 150

Suppletive imperatives show a clear concentration in Africa, in the Arabic-speaking Middle East as well as in the Caucasus. This areal distribution is very different from the one shown for the more 'established' (better known) kinds of suppletion such as tense–aspect suppletion. While it does not form as coherent an area as tense–aspect suppletion does in Europe and Western Asia, still an areal patterning

Table 24. Linguistic phyla with suppletive imperatives

Phylum	No. \ Total
Afro-Asiatic	9 \ 13
Carib	1 \ 3
Chibchan	1 \ 2
Indo-European	8 \ 25
Keres	1 \ 1
Khoisan	1 \ 2
Mataco-Guaicuru	1 \ 1
Mayan	1 \ 1
Niger-Congo	3 \ 12
Nilo-Saharan	4 \ 8
North Caucasian	2 \ 4
Oto-Manguean	1 \ 3
South Caucasian	1 \ 1
Trans-New Guinea	1 \ 9
Tupi	1 \ 1
Uralic	3 \ 3
Uto-Aztecan	2 \ 9

Note: No. = number of languages; '\' stands for 'out of'; Total = number of investigated languages from that phylum

is present, and it is worth noting that it includes areas and families which are usually said not to have any suppletion at all.

As regards the distribution in linguistic phyla, the phenomenon is very stable in the whole of the Afro-Asiatic phylum (see for elaboration on this below). Other phyla in which it appears common are Uralic, North Caucasian and Nilo-Saharan.

3. Suppletive imperatives from a historical perspective

In this section I present the currently available historical–comparative evidence for the development of suppletive imperatives. Three main paths for their evolution are suggested:

(i) Incursion of "imperative-only" verbs into paradigms of verbs with a similar meaning.
(ii) Incursion of "imperative particles" into the paradigms of basic motion verbs.
(iii) Direct borrowing of imperative forms in a situation of intensive language contact.

We shall start the discussion with the presentation of defective verbs restricted to the imperative function. As stated in (i) above, they appear to be one possible source for suppletive imperatives. A few descriptions report verbs such as 'go', 'come' and 'watch out' to occur in the imperative or hortative only. The data on this phenomenon are not abundant but they come from very diverse languages: Acoma, a Keresan language from New Mexico (North America), Chalcatongo Mixtec, an Otomanguean language from Central America, Macushi, a Carib language from Guyana (South America), Taba, an Austronesian language, spoken in Maluku, Indonesia, Nunggubuyu, a Non-Pama-Nyunga language from Australia, Alagwa, a Cushitic language from Tanzania and Algerian Arabic in Africa.

(128) Acoma (Keres) (Maring 1967: 101–2)
 ʔiima   go.2SG.HORTATIVE

(129) Chalcatongo Mixtec (Otomanguean, Mixtecan) (Macaulay 1982: 417)
 Čóʔò   go.HORTATIVE

(130) Macushi (North Carib) (Abott 1991: 51)
 asi'-tî   come.IMP-2.COLL

(131) Taba (Austronesian, Central Eastern Malayo-Polynesian, South Halmanera) (Bowden 1997: 425)
 Mo!   come here!

(132) Nunggubuyu (Australian, Gunwingguan) (Heath 1984: 343)
 Aɲi-ɲ   come.IMP-2SG
 Aɲi-ɲa come.IMP-2PL

(133) Alagwa (Afro-Asiatic, Southern Cushitic) (Mous In Preparation)
 'go'
 xáa   go.IMP
 kway go.HORT.2SG

(134) Algerian Arabic (Afro-Asiatic, Semitic) (Lameen Souag, p.c.)
 beʀka   watch out!

There are two issues that remain unclear as regards these data. First, for Taba, it is not clear if the form quoted above is morphologically a verb. The author classifies it as such but since morphological marking is minimal (if any), it is unclear whether such a description is based on morphological or semantic criteria. Second, again, for Taba, and likewise Nunggubuyu, it is difficult to judge whether this verb is an alternative form of a regular imperative of a full-fledged verb with a corresponding sense, or it is the only form used in the imperative for that sense. The grammars of these languages do not cite the paradigms of a regular motion verb and the verbs quoted above are described as defective, occurring in imperative only. In Macushi the *asi'-tî* appears to be an alternative form of a regular imperative for 'come', *m-aipî-i* 'FUT.IMP-come-IMP', but again, one would wish for more data.

While I cannot fully assess the cross-linguistic frequency of verbs restricted to the imperative function, the fact that they are observed in so diverse languages, scattered all around the globe suggests that they are probably more common than it is previously acknowledged[1].

Scarce as it are they are, the synchronic data quoted above link very well the diachronic and comparative data that I have been able to obtain on suppletive imperatives. For example the Modern Greek suppletive imperative *ela* (see example (122) above) is reported to originate from the Classical Greek verb *elaon* 'drive, set in motion', used in imperative only, cf. (Lidell and Scott 1871; Dvoreckij 1958). Similarly, the suppletive form of the Chalcatongo Mixtec verb 'come' *naʔà* is said to be a defective verb restricted the imperative function only. This verb does not seem to have a cognate in a closely related dialect Diuxi (cf. Macaulay 1982: 420–1).

The evidence from Arabic varieties as regards the origins of their suppletive imperatives brings up an "imperative-only" verb as well. As it was already mentioned, suppletion in the imperative of basic motion verbs 'come' and 'go' is widespread in

---

1. Most probably there is work done on this issue. I have done my share of searching various databases but so far haven't been able to locate any pertinent references.

Table 25. Suppletive imperatives in Afro-Asiatic (a partial survey)

Family	Language	INDIC	IMP	Gloss
Berber	Tamazight (Central Atlas)	la ytaddu	adud	'come'
			awra	
Semitic	Moroccan Arabic	ghadi	sir	'go'
	Algerian Arabic*	yji	ayya	'come'
	Tunisian Arabic	yji	i:ja	'come'
			ayya (i:ja)	
			taʔaala[a]	
	Maltese	jigi	ejja	'come'
	Egyptian Arabic	aagi	taʔaala	'come'
	Lebanese Arabic*	jit 3SG.M.PFV	taʔa	'come'
	Syrian Arabic*	iji	taʔaa	'come'
	Iraqi Arabic*	izhi	taʔaala	'come'
	Modern Standrad Arabic*	yji	taʔaal	'come'
	Geez*	masʼa 3SG.M.PFV	naʔa	'come'
	Amharic*	matʼatʼa 3SG.M.PFV	na	'come'
Cushitic	Oromo (Boraana)	d'ufa	koti	'come'
		deema	beeni	'go'
	Oromo (Harar)	d'ufa	xootuu	'come'
	Somali*	yimi/ yimid	kaalay	'come'
	Iraqw	xawn	xawé'	'come'
			qwaláɲ	

[a] This form is restricted to rural areas.

the Afro-Asiatic phylum, specifically in the Berber, Semitic and Cushitic families. Here I gratefully acknowledge the help all the respondents[2] to my query posted on the LINGUIST List who provided me with additional data from languages not included in my sample. In Table 25. such languages are indicated by a star (*) following the language name.

Table 25 presents the comparative data from Afro-Asiatic languages. My primary purpose was to check whether suppletive imperatives are a stable phenomenon or not, specifically in the Semitic family, so there is no claim that whole Afro-Asiatic phylum is covered. Unless otherwise indicated, in the column entitled INDIC (Indicative) the imperfective (present) forms for 3 singular masculine are listed. The column labeled IMP (Imperative) lists the imperative forms for the second-person singular masculine imperative.

As we can see the use of suppletive imperatives is common in a number of different varieties of Arabic. However, North African Arabic dialects show some fluctuation as to which motion verb uses a suppletive form: in Moroccan Arabic it is

---

[2]. Nisrine Al-Zahre, Lina Choueiri, Bernard Comrie, Mika Hoffman, Zouhair Maalej, Baruch Podolsky, Lameen Souag, Peter Unseth.

the verb 'go', in the other North African dialects it is 'come'. Moreover, the suppletive forms for 'come' differ in these dialects. Some of them are obviously cognates: *ayya* in Algerian Arabic, *ejja* in Maltese, and likewise the imperative particle *ayya* in Tunisian Arabic (see discussion below for its use). However, in Tunisian Arabic there are several alternating expressions for the imperative of 'come', one of which is regular *i:ja*, another possibility is to use the imperative particle *ayya* and a third one is to use *taʕaala*. The latter form is used in rural areas only. In Egyptian Arabic *taʕaala* is the standard form for the imperative of 'come' and is suppletive with regard to the indicative. Arabic dialects in the Middle East as well as Modern Standard Arabic use *taʕaala* or variants thereof as suppletive imperatives of 'come'. The verb *taʕaala* 'come here' existed in Classical Arabic and was even then a verb, in the sense that it took verb morphological markers but it was restricted to the imperative function (Zouhair Maalej, p.c.).

Given the synchronic evidence, e.g. existence of imperative-only verbs and the diachronic evidence from Classical Greek and Classical Arabic as well as the Mixtec data, it is not too farfetched to make a hypothesis about one possible path of development for suppletive imperatives. They seem to originate from imperative-only verbs which are incorporated into the paradigms of verbs with similar meanings. In the typical case imperative-only verbs express a command to move and are associated with a richer paradigm of a semantically related general verb of motion.

Exhortative particles appear to be another source for suppletive imperatives. While it remains unclear how common imperative-only verbs really are, it is most probably very common for all languages to have particles or words of uncertain word-class status (not necessarily interjections) used only in direct commands or invitations. Such particles seem very prone to "invade" paradigms of verbs such as 'come', 'give' and 'look' which are frequently used in the imperative. This phenomenon will be illustrated first by Tunisian and Algerian Arabic and then by Turkish and Serbo-Croatian.

In Tunisian Arabic the imperative particle *ayya* cannot be used alone in the sense of 'Come!', but it can be used in an elliptical fashion to stand for many different types of verbs (and not only motion verbs) in context as in the examples shown in (135) (Zouhair Maalej, p.c.).

(135) Tunisian Arabic (Zouhair Maalej, p.c.)
    a. *ayya* (*i:ja*)   come on, (come here)
    b. *ayya* (*kul*)   come on, (eat)
    c. *ayya* (*ʕiqra*)   come on, (read)

Thus, when used to address a second person, *ayya* is used in the sense of "come on" or "hurry up". When it is used with inclusive "we" it means 'let's' as illustrated in (136).

(136) Tunisian Arabic (Zouhair Maalej, p.c.)
    a. *ayya* (*nimshi:w*)   let's go
    b. *ayya* (*naaklu*)   let's eat
    c. *ayya* (*niqraaw*)   let's read

In Algerian Arabic however, the word *ayya* appears to have gained independence in the sense that it can be used alone and not just in an elliptical fashion as in Tunisian Arabic. According to native speakers is the sole imperative form of the verb 'come'. A similar development is observed with the Turkish particle *hajde*[3] in some of the Balkan languages. It figures as a borrowing in Bulgarian, Rumanian and Serbo-Croatian. In the latter language, however, this word has also acquired the morphological markers that make it look like a verb. Thus it has become an alternative suppletive form of the verb 'go' and 'come', illustrated in (137) below by the verb *itči* 'go'.

(137) Serbo-Croatian (Elvira Veselinovic, Vladan Boskovic, p.c.)
    ide-m   go-PRES.1SG
    Id–i   go-IMP.2SG
    Id–i-te   go-IMP-2PL
    (h)ajde   go/come.IMP.2SG
    (h)ajde-te   go/come.IMP-2PL

Whether one labels developments as those in Algerian Arabic and Serbo-Croatian as cases of lexicalization or something else is, of course, a matter of how one defines the latter notion. Here I have adopted the perspective proposed by Moreno-Cabrera (1998: 214–18). This author defines lexicalization as "the process creating lexical items out of syntactic units"; in his view idioms constitute the best known cases of this process as they are syntactic constructions that have lost their compositionality and have acquired a new idiosyncratic content. Essentially, lexicalization involves a great deal of specification of meaning. If we accept particles such as the Arabic *ayya* or Turkish *hajde* to be items with a very general content that have scope over the entire proposition, then when they become restricted to the sense invitation/command to motion only, they become more limited and acquire a more specific use. In that sense they have become lexical expressions for that notion. It should be noted that in Serbo-Croatian, *hajde* can still be used in an elliptical fashion similar to the Tunisian usage in (135) and (136) above so this word has not "walked" the whole lexicalization path.

---

3. I am not sure about the correct lexico-syntactic status of this word. It is anything between a hortative/imperative particle and an interjection. In any case, it is completely isolated as a word; does not inflect for anything and is used in direct speech acts only such as invitations, commands and similar.

A third source for suppletive imperatives is direct borrowing of foreign imperative forms. This is the case in Bulgarian where the alternative suppletive form of 'come' was borrowed from (Modern) Greek and is nowadays equally common, if not even more frequent than the native regular imperative of 'come'.

(138) Modern Greek and Bulgarian imperative for 'come'
'come'
a. Modern Greek (Indo-European, Hellenic) (Christiades 1980: 76)

erx-ese	come-PRES.IND.2SG
erx-ste	come-PRES.IND.2PL
Ela	come.IMP.2SG
Ela-te	come.IMP-IMP.2PL

b. Bulgarian (Indo-European, South Slavic) (own data)

idva-š	come-2IND.SG
idva-te	come-2IND.PL
idva-j	come-IMP.2SG
idva-j-te	come-IMP-2PL
Ela	come.IMP.2SG
Ela-te	come.IMP-IMP.2PL

Cases such as (137) and (138) above come to challenge the original understanding of suppletion as coming to fill in a gap in a paradigm or a weakened form. As the examples above demonstrate, suppletion can arise even when there are no missing or eroding forms in a paradigm (cf. also Chapter 5: 3).

The data on the diachronic development of suppletive imperatives are not abundant, but they come from very diverse languages and share several characteristics. Specifically, the sources and development of suppletive imperatives show a striking cross-linguistic similarity. They appear to be directly amenable to verbs restricted to the imperative function, exhortative particles and direct borrowings. While in languages such as Modern Greek and Arabic such suppletive imperatives are apparently very old, they can hardly be described only as non-functional historical residues. On the contrary, they are lexical expressions for a category that is highly relevant to the sense of verbs which express motion, and are obviously very often used in the imperative. As such suppletive imperatives can be rightly considered as semantically and functionally motivated.

4. Summary and conclusions

In this chapter I presented suppletion in imperative as it is found in the languages of the current sample. It shows a clear concentration in Africa and the Middle East, where it is very common in three families of the Afro-Asiatic phylum but it is also present in all other African phyla. This areal distribution sets suppletive imperatives apart from suppletion according to other grammatical categories which are observed in completely different geographical areas.

Suppletion in imperative is largely restricted to the basic verbs of motion 'come' and 'go' as well as to verbs such as 'give', 'do', and to verbs used as negative auxiliaries. The synchronic and diachronic evidence highlight the existence of "imperative-only" verbs which typically express a command to move towards or away from the speaker. Suppletive imperatives may also result from the process whereby imperative particles acquire verb morphology and this way get incorporated into the richer paradigms of motion verbs.

While relatively restricted (which may reflect shortcomings in the data collection and grammatical descriptions rather than the actual situation), suppletion in imperative can hardly be described as an accidental or unnatural phenomenon. Command and motion (or incentive to motion) form a coherent semantic whole which is why it is not strange to find unified lexical expressions where they are fused together. Verbs restricted to the imperative function as well as particles which acquire regular verb morphology represent such expressions. It was also observed that suppletive imperatives originate from borrowing in a situation of intensive language contact. It is not surprising that exactly commands for simple motion are passed on from a language with greater prestige and whose speakers have more power to the speakers who have less. Thus suppletive imperatives appear both semantically and pragmatically motivated, which in turn should preclude describing the phenomenon as haphazard or unsystematic.

CHAPTER 7

Verbal number and suppletion

Before we embark on describing suppletion according to **verbal number**, a note of clarification is in order since the metalanguage used to describe this category is often a source of confusion. Number as a verbal category can reflect the number of times an action is done or the number of participants in the action. Corbett (2000: 246) makes a distinction between **event number** and **participant number**.

When we say that a verb or verb phrase in an Indo-European language, say French, is in **plural**, as in *ils étaient fatigués*, what we mean is that the verb phrase *étaient fatigués* agrees with the subject *ils* in number. The term **plural verbs** or **verbs in plural** in many of the languages to be discussed below, on the other hand, refers to all or anyone of the following senses: the action is performed several times (**iterative**) or at several places (**distributive**); or the action affects or involves several participants. For example, Mupun, a West Chadic language from Nigeria, uses derivational means such as infixation in (139a), suffixation in (139b) or completely different verbs in (139c) to express plural action or plural participants.

(139) Mupun (Afro-Asiatic, West Chadic), (Frajzyngier 1993)
    a. *pūt*   go out.SG.ACTION
       pú-a-t   go out-**pl.action**-go out
    b. *yà*   catch.SG.ACTION
       yà-k   catch-**pl.action**
    c. *cīt*   beat.SG.ACTION
       nás   beat.PL.ACTION

Some uses of these verbs are illustrated in (140).

(140) Mupun (Afro-Asiatic, West Chadic), (Frajzyngier 1993)
    a. *yit n-an*   *pūt*   vs.   *mun*   *púat*.
       let 1SG-PREP go out.SG   1PL.OPT go out.PL
       'Let me go out.'   'Let's go out.'
    b. *mo ya*   *joos*   vs.   *mo yak*   *joos mo*
       3PL catch.SG rat   3PL catch.PL rat 3PL
       'They caught a rat.'   'They caught rats.'

Thus the derived verbs *pú-a-t* 'go out.PL' and *yà-k* 'catch PL' can be used to indicate that several people went out/someone caught many things. It should be stressed that the use of the plural verbs in (140) is not a matter of syntactic agreement. For one, the plural marker on the noun that would trigger agreement is optional; see (141).

(141) Mupun (Afro-Asiatic, West Chadic) (Frajzyngier 1993)
      n-tu   *joos*   vs.   *n-tue*   *joos.*
      1SG-kill.SG rat   1SG-kill.PL rat
      'I killed a rat.'   'I killed rats.'

Secondly, while a singular form of a verb is generally ruled out with a plural object cf. (142a), a plural verb may be used with a singular object to indicate an action performed with some intensity, or many times as in (142b).

(142) Mupun (Afro-Asiatic, West Chadic) (Frajzyngier 1993)
    a. **wu   cit   mo*
       3SG.M hit 3PL
       *he hit.SG them
    b. *wu   nás   war*
       3SG hit.PL 3SG.F
       'He hit her many times.'

Thus while a separate grammatical category, verbal number, in many instances, comes very close to and at times becomes inseparable from other categories. In particular, event number is akin to aspect in a number of cases; participant number is not always very easy to distinguish from nominal number as reflected in agreement; there are also cases where verbal number evolves into nominal number (Corbett 2000: 256).

As discussed in Chapter 1, it is a controversial issue whether verb pairs such as the Mupun ones *cit* vs. *nás* 'hit.SG.ACTION vs. hit.PL.ACTION' are to be considered cases of suppletion according to verbal number or simply different words. There exists a discrepancy between grammars on the one hand, and theoretical work in morphology and suppletion on the other. While grammars usually treat pairs such as *cit* vs. *nás* as cases of suppletion, authors of theoretical work (Mithun 1988; Mel'čuk 1994; Corbett 2000) argue that such cases are to be considered separate lexical items which are related semantically but not paradigmatically.

Due to this conflict in views, the status of these verbal pairs needs serious consideration in a study devoted to suppletion. In this chapter, I will present the data as they are collected from language descriptions. Throughout the presentation I use the phrases 'verbal number pairs' and 'suppletive verbs according to verbal number' interchangeably. The organization of this chapter is similar to that of the preceding ones. The semantic distinctions and the verbal meanings expressed by such pairs are presented in section 1, and section 2, respectively. Section 3 outlines the genetic and areal distribution of this phenomenon. In section 4, I discuss the controversy on whether such verbal number pairs are suppletive or not and argue that a simple yes–no solution is problematic in several respects. A summary and conclusions are presented in section 5.

1. Presentation of the data

1.1 Semantic distinctions indicated by verbal number suppletives

The verbal number distinctions indicated by separate verb stems are either singular vs. dual vs. plural or singular vs. plural. This is illustrated in (143) by Koasati, a Muskogean language from Louisiana, USA.

(143) Koasati (Muskogean) (Kimball 1991: 323–4)
    a. 'dwell'
        ătal   dwell.1SG
        alísw   dwell.1DU
        ís-tílk dwell-1PL
    b. 'run'
        walíka-l run-1SG
        tół-hílk   run-1PL

In the languages where triples indicating singular vs. dual vs. plural shown in (143a), pairs that indicate singular vs. plural as in (143b), are also found (as in Koasati above). There are languages where only singular vs. plural pairs are observed. This latter group is illustrated in (144) Krongo, a Kordofanian language from the Niger-Congo phylum, spoken in Sudan, and in (145) by Ute, spoken in the Ute Reservation, Colorado, USA. Maricopa, a Yuman language from the Hokan phylum, is the only language I am aware of where only triples exist.

(144) Krongo (Reh 1985: 198)
        'call'
        ò-cóonì-ící VERB.MARKER-call.SG.ACTION-SUFF
        ò-múnó-óní VERB.MARKER-call.PL.ACTION-SUFF

(145) Ute (Uto-Aztecan, Northern, Numic) (Givón and Southern Ute Tribe 1980: 40)
    a. 'stand'
        wɨn(ɨ)y stand.SG
        yuʔwiy stand.PL
    b. 'kill'
        paqχai kill.SG.OBJ
        qoʔaj   kill.PL.OBJ

The stem alternation reflects either the number of times the action is performed (event number) as in Krongo above or number of participants most strongly affected by the event (participant number), as in Ute. Thus the selection of verbs follows an ergative-absolutive pattern: for intransitive verbs, the stems reflect the number of the only argument whereas with transitive verbs the stems reflect the number of the participant typically, though not necessarily, realized as direct object.

As already indicated the labels 'singular', 'dual' and 'plural' refer to quantification of the verbal action rather than the nominal arguments of the verb. It should be noted also that, in some languages, such as Ainu, their content differs in yet another way from what is traditionally meant by 'singular' and 'plural'. Traditionally, 'singular' refers to 'one' and 'plural' to 'more than one'. In Ainu, however, if quantity is specified by a numeral and it is small such as 'one', 'two', 'three' and sometimes 'four', the singular form of the verb is used. For larger numbers, normally, the plural form is used. This applies to both regular and suppletive verbs and is illustrated by the verb 'come' in (146) below.

(146) Ainu (Tamura 1988)
   a. *tu okkaypo* **ek.**
      two youth come.SG
      'Two youths came.'
   b. *tupesaniw ka* **arki** *ruwe ne.*
      eight   even come.PL NMLZ COP
      'Eight people came.'

Apart from Ainu, there are five other languages in this group which behave in a similar way, in that they group 'two' or 'dual' together with 'singular' and not with 'plural'. They are Eastern Pomo (Hokan), Navajo (Na-Dene, Athapaskan), Ute (Uto-Aztecan), Wichita (Caddoan) and Kiowa (Kiowa-Tanoan), all in North America.

1.2 Form of verbal number suppletives

The verb number pairs are usually cases of prototypical suppletion as regards their form. That is, the verb pairs or triples of the kind illustrated above tend to be completely different, without any segments, syllables or morphemes shared between them. There are a few cases, however, which can be described as just unique, but not formally completely different. For example, in Barasano, a Tucanoan language from Columbia, the singular and plural forms of the verb 'move down/away' are *roka* vs. *rea*, respectively. Similarly, in Murle, we find that the stems of the verb 'go' are -*kɔ* in the singular, and -*vɔ* in the plural. It could be argued that one segment is not a substantial difference to go by in the first place but since it is the only verb which does this according to the number of its subject, this makes it special among all the other verbs.

2. Lexemic groups that with verbal number suppletion

The number of such verbs per language shows greater variation when compared with the number of suppletive verbs according to tense–aspect or imperative. In approximately half of the languages such verb pairs/triples are between 1 and 4; in another group of 7 languages the number of such verbs ranges between 5 and 7; finally, 9 languages show 10 and more such verbs. For the exact number of in specific languages, consult Appendix 3, Table A7.

The verb meanings in this group are more diverse and more numerous than the verb meanings encountered with other types of suppletion. This is also the only group of verbs covered in this study which includes verbs with very specific lexical meaning such as Hopi verbs *-toni* 'go around something out of sight SG' vs. *-kya* 'go around something out of sight PL', together with semantically general verbs such as 'go' and 'sit' and finally grammaticalized or grammaticalizing lexical items as for instance the !Xu auxiliaries *n!hún* (SG) vs. *cóá* 'walk, do while walking'. As we recall, in the other groups, (see Chapter 4, section 5 and Chapter 6, section 2.3, for instance) the recurrent observation is that the verbs "suppleting" in tense–aspect or imperative are few, high-frequency verbs, with a very general meaning; a substantial part of them also function as grammatical items. With tense–aspect and imperative suppletion, lexical items with a very specific semantic content are generally missing, but such words are present in the group of verbs which use separate stems for verbal number distinctions. Since the table of frequencies of specific verb meanings is very long and would make the section rather cumbersome, it is placed in Appendix 3 (Table A8).

A generalization of the kind that was done with meanings observed in tense–aspect and imperative suppletion is not justified here because, as I already pointed out, some of these verbs are listed in grammars with a specific meaning such as 'grasp', 'land', 'fall in water'. This is different from the situation found in tense–aspect or imperative suppletion where the grammar usually states explicitly that a suppletive verb such as 'say' is a very common verb and it is glossed as 'say, speak'. In the latter case, I considered it acceptable to include the verb in a larger group of verbs meaning 'say' and report frequency of occurrence of that meaning. However, including a verb such as 'land' in the group of verbs meaning 'fall' here appears to me somewhat misleading. Such a generalization would conceal the fact that this group of verbs is different from the other groups of tense–aspect and imperative suppletion in that here verbs with specific lexical meaning are observed. So instead of generalizing, I chose to classify the verbs into the broad lexemic groups where they seem to belong.

The verbs pertinent here were thus classified into several broad lexemic groups. Some of them are clearly associated with concepts such as 'motion', 'position', 'die/

Table 26. Lexemic groups with verbal number suppletion

Lexemic group	Number of verb meanings[a]	No.[b]	%	W[c]	%
MOTION (intransitive)	22	56	32	25.85	30
MOTION (transitive)	13	26	15	15.26	12
POSITION	6	38	22	18.24	27
DIE/INJURE	8	29	17	12.33	14
STATIVE VERBS	7	16	9	10.02	12
Others	8	10	6	3.87	5
Total	54	174	100	85.58	100

[a] Number of verb meanings   [b] Number of verb meanings in a group   [c] Weight values sum

injure'.[1] One can isolate a group of stative verbs such as 'sleep' together with some verbs which express notions of dimension such as 'big', 'small', 'long' and 'short'. Finally, there is a group of very different verbs such as 'say', 'make netbag', 'make noise' where no single concept can be detected and they are thus called here 'Other' verbs. As it will be shown below, these groups show differences both in the number of verb meanings included in them as well as in their frequency of occurrence as verbal number suppletives.

Table 26 presents the broad lexemic groups, the number of meanings included in each group as well the frequency of occurrence of these meanings with verbal number pairs.

The two methods of calculating frequencies of occurrence yield somewhat different results but the difference lies between 1 and 3 percent for all groups except position verbs. The most frequent group according to both counting methods is the one of intransitive motion verbs.

For the group of position verbs the difference between the count based on absolute number of occurrence and that based on weight values is 5%. Thus these verbs appear cross-linguistically more common according to the weight values counting method but less common if one just looks at the absolute number of their occurrences as verbal number suppletives.

The counts on stative and transitive motion verbs show a similar tendency but with a lesser difference (3%). That is, stative and motion verbs appear cross-linguistically more common by the count of their weight values (this means they occur in more diverse languages) but are less common according to the frequency of their number of occurrences. Conversely, verbs in the 'die/injure' group appear more fre-

---

1. The word 'injure' is used here as a cover term only. It is to be understood very generally to mean 'affect an object X in a way that destroys it'. It covers verbs such as 'kill', 'hit', 'break', 'cut', 'bite off', 'injure' etc.

quent based on the number of their occurrences but less frequent based on the sum of their weight values.

A closer look at the verb frequencies within the lexemic groups reveals that the most frequent verbs in each group are the ones which can be described as the most general in meaning. Thus in the group of intransitive motion verbs, the most frequent one is 'go', for transitive motion verbs, the most frequent ones are 'put' and 'throw'. In the group of position verbs, the most frequent ones are 'sit' and 'lie'. Within the 'die/injure' group the most common ones are 'die' and 'kill'. From the stative verbs, the most common one is 'sleep'. In the group labeled 'Others', all verbs except 'eat', show one single occurrence in the sample; 'eat' appears twice. The verbs in this latter group can be described as rather unusual for this kind of suppletion.

The frequencies of verbal meaning reported here suggest that a hierarchy for the lexicalization/suppletion of such pairs may be established the way that was done with tense–aspect suppletion. The suggested hierarchy is presented in (147) below.

(147)   Verbal number lexicalization /suppletion hierarchy

> Intransitive motion verbs   > 'die/injure' >   Transitive motion verbs   > Others
> Position verbs   Stative verbs

The hierarchy thus states that if a language has verbal number pairs at all, they will most probably be verbs such as 'go', 'sit' and 'die' (the lexemic groups on the left end of the hierarchy) rather than transitive verbs of motions such as 'give' and 'take' or verbs from other semantic fields. Corbett (2000: 258) makes a similar observation based on data from North American languages analyzed by Karen Booker. All languages pertinent corroborate this generalization here except Ket (see data from Ket below).

Thus the examination of the verbal meanings which occur with verbal number suppletion shows the following characteristics:

(i) It is by far the most numerous group when compared to the groups of verbs with other kinds of suppletion. Highly specific lexical meanings are commonly encountered here whereas such meanings are absent from the verbs observed in other kinds of suppletion.
(ii) Two lexemic groups appear to be especially frequent with verbal number pairs: intransitive verbs of motion and position verbs. The most frequent verbs within these groups are 'go' and 'fall' and 'sit' and 'lie' respectively.
(iii) Other lexemic groups that are common but not as frequent as the ones in (ii) cover verbs of transitive motion such as 'put' and 'throw', as well as verbs which center around notions of 'die' and 'kill', and finally stative verbs such as 'sleep'.
(iv) Verbs from other semantic fields such as 'say', 'eat', 'make noise', 'bet' are highly unusual in this group.

3. Frequency of distribution in the samples

The cross-linguistic distribution of verbal number pairs in the current sample is presented in the tables. Table 27 gives the language count in the samples, the weight values sum and pertinent proportions. Table 28 outlines the areal distribution and the count based on genera. Finally, the distribution of languages according to larger linguistic phyla is presented in Table 29. A complete list of the languages together with their corresponding weight values and number of suppletive verbs per language is given in Appendix 3. As we can see, counting the absolute number languages where verbal number pairs are found yields practically the same proportion in both the sample which consists of genetically independent languages and the WALS sample where some phyla are represented by a greater number of languages than others. Calculating the frequency of this phenomenon by using the weight values procedure results in a substantially greater frequency.

The occurrence of verbal number pairs shows a clear areal patterning, presented in Table 28 and also on the accompanying Map 6 in Appendix 3. As can be seen from Table 28, verbal number pairs are particularly common in the native languages of North America but they can be found. in every other area as well, the lowest concentration being in Australia and Papua New Guinea.

The distribution of languages in larger linguistic phyla is set out in Table 29. It is worth noting that families usually cited in studies of suppletion are not present here. Verbal number pairs appear as a steady phenomenon in Uto-Aztecan and as well as in a number of smaller linguistic stocks, most of them located in North America.

In Europe and Asia (Eurasia in Table 28), verbal number pairs are found in two

Table 27. Language count

Small sample		WALS sample			
No	%	No	%	W	% of 70
16	17.02	33	17.09	17.461	24.94

Note: No. =Number of languages; W = Weight values sum; the total of weight values for the WALS sample is 70

Table 28. The Dryer Distribution

	Africa	Eurasia	SEA and Oceania	A-NG	N Am	S Am	Total
Yes	5	5	1	3	13	4	31
No	21	29	18	21	14	20	122

Note: Yes = presence of categorial tense suppletion; No = absence of categorial tense suppletion; Total number of genera = 150

Table 29. Linguistic phyla with verbal number pairs/triples

Phylum	No \ To
Afro-Asiatic	1 \ 13
Ainu	1 \ 1
Algic	1 \ 2
Austronesian	1 \ 12
Burushaski	1 \ 1
Caddoan	1 \ 1
Chapacura-Wanham	1 \ 1
Hokan	2 \ 2
Khoisan	1 \ 2
Kiowa-Tanoan	1 \ 1
Macro-Ge	1 \ 1
Muskogean	1 \ 1
Na-Dene	2 \ 2
Niger-Congo	1 \ 12
Nilo-Saharan	2 \ 8
North Caucasian	2 \ 4
Panoan	1 \ 1
South Caucasian	1 \ 1
Trans-New Guinea	3 \ 9
Tucanoan	1 \ 1
Uto-Aztecan	6 \ 9
Yenisei-Ostyak	1 \ 1
Zuni	1 \ 1

Note: No. = Number of languages where verbal number pairs are found; '\' stands for 'out of'; To = Total number of languages from that phylum which are included in the sample

genera of the Caucasus and the rest are either language isolates or nowadays minor families of Asia. The only major linguistic phylum represented here is Austronesian; the genus from it is Oceanic represented by Samoan. Interestingly, the Austronesian languages cited by Durie (1986) to have similar verbal number pairs are Kapingamarangi and Tongan, both closely related to Samoan.

The various counting methods tested here provide somewhat different results for frequency of occurrence of verbal number pairs in this sample. Based on absolute number of languages where such pairs are observed, they appear fairly uncommon (*c.* 17 %). Their proportion based on the sum of weight values of these languages is close to 25% of the total weight value of the sample which presents them as a substantially more common phenomenon. The count of genera rather than languages yields a proportion that falls in between the previous ones: around 20% of the genera in this sample have verbal number pairs. While the phenomenon cannot be described as a very frequent one, there is enough evidence for describing it as a linguistic feature which occurs regularly in particular areas and language families, and specific genera within these families. So it is not an exotic feature of extreme rarity either.

4. Verbal number pairs: suppletive forms of the same word or separate words

As already mentioned, there is a mismatch between grammatical descriptions and theoretical work as regards the status of verbal number pairs in the grammar of the languages where they occur. Mithun (1988) as well as Corbett (2000) argue that such verb pairs are separate lexical items which are related semantically but not paradigmatically. Mel'čuk, however, (1994: 371) recognizes suppletion according to verbal number inasmuch as there is some kind of morphological expression for it. This latter author rejects suppletion according to this category in languages where morphological expression for it is not present and the selection of a singular or plural verb is conditioned by semantic factors, not by syntactic agreement. Thus the discrepancy between grammatical descriptions and theoretical work as to whether the verbal number pairs are in relation of suppletion or simply different lexical items, appears to stem from the following issues:

(a) The difference between verbal number and syntactic agreement.
(b) The way one defines paradigmatic relations and thereby suppletion. Although it is never made explicit, the term suppletion is, more often not, restricted to describe exceptions to inflectional patterns only (cf. quote from Corbett 2000 below.)

In this section I discuss these issues. Specifically, in section 4.1, I present more details on the distinction between verbal number and syntactic agreement already introduced in the initial paragraphs of this chapter. In section 4.2, I discuss concepts such as lexicalization, derivation and suppletion in connection with verbal number. Furthermore, it can be demonstrated that the criteria used by Mel'čuk and Corbett as regards suppletion are not entirely watertight, nor is their application free of contradictions. Finally,[2] I argue that the typology of suppletion should allow for intermediate cases which are on the borderline between different lexical items and paradigmatically related forms.

4.1 Verbal number and syntactic agreement

As already mentioned, verbal number often comes very close to other categories relevant for verbs such as aspect and syntactic agreement. A great part of the literature where suppletion according to verbal number is discussed, puts an emphasis on the differences between verbal number and syntactic agreement, often using them as a reason to see the verbal number pairs discussed here as separate

---

2. Many thanks to Martin Haspelmath for his lengthy, detailed and patient discussion on the corresponding chapter on verbal number in WALS.

lexical items rather paradigmatically related forms of one and the same word.

For instance, Durie (1986) argues that in a lot the languages in his sample such verb number pairs "select rather than agree" with their arguments in number. Some of the examples cited by him, as well as by Mel'čuk (1994: 384–6) are shown in (148)–(149); example (148) is from Georgian, and (149) from Navajo, an Athapaskan language, currently spoken in the Navajo Reservation in Arizona/New Mexico, USA.

(148) Georgian (South Caucasian), adopted from Mel'čuk (Mel'čuk 1994)
   a. *tkven da-Ø-   žek-i-t.*
      you.PL down-2SG- **sit.sg-AOR-PL**
      'You [one person; plural of politeness] sat down.'
   b. *sami megobar-Ø-i   da*-sxd-*a.*
      three friend-SG-NOM down-**sit.PL**-AOR.3SG
      'Three friends sat down.'

The examples in (148) demonstrate that the selection of singular or plural stem is determined by the actual number of the subject and not by syntactic marking of agreement. As we can see the stem -*sxd*- 'sit.PL' admits of a singular agreement marker. A true suppletive form for plural agreement should not do that.

(149) Navajo (Durie 1986: 358), quoting Jeanne, Hale and Pranka (1984).
   a. *shí ashkii bi-ł   yi-sh-'ash.*
      I boy   him-with PROG-1SG-walk:DUAL
      'I am walking with the boy.'
   b. *nihí ła'   di–iid-áál.*
      we subset FUT-1NON:SG-walk:SG
      'One of us will go.'

The agreement affixes -*sh*- '1SG' in (149a) and -*iid*- '1NON-SG' in (149b) follow the number of subject, the selection of stems follows the number of participants. What is usually not pointed out, however, is that the situation described for Navajo is not the only possibility for the languages with verbal number pairs. For instance, in Slave, (see (150) below) a language closely related to Navajo, the facts of agreement and stem selection are different. The alternation of stems not only reflects the number of participants but also agrees in number with the agreement affixes.

(150) Slave (Na-Dene, Athapaskan) (Keren Rice, p.c.)
   a. *ʔehts'é   thí-ke.*
      RECIPROCAL TO ASPECT/1DU-**sit:DU**
      'We two are facing each other.'
   b. *kó gá   de-í-kw'i.*
      fire near ASPECT-1PL-**sit:PL**
      'We (plural) sat near the fire.'

Generally, in Slave, it is important that the verb stem agree in number with the overt subject marker. Combining a non-singular subject marker with a singular stem as in Navajo, (cf. (149) above) is impossible in Slave for first- and second-person subjects (Keren Rice, p.c.). The constructions in (149) from Navajo and in (150) from Slave are not exactly parallel in that Navajo uses comitative constructions which are not present in the Slave examples. Keren Rice (p.c.) states that she tested for such constructions in Slave but speakers simply would not produce them. However, the noteworthy fact, relevant for our topic, is that in Slave, "clashes" between syntactic agreement and semantic selection do not occur with first- and second-person subjects. For such subjects, the selection of the verb stem appears conditioned solely by syntactic agreement.

It is often pointed out that the verbal number pairs show an ergative pattern of stem selection that is independent of general agreement rules in the languages where they occur. Thus in Ute, there is a suffix -*qa* (with various phonologically conditioned allomorphs) that is obligatorily used to indicate number of subject for all verbs that take animate arguments.

(151) Ute (Uto-Aztecan, Northern, Numic) (Givón and Southern Ute Tribe 1980: 41)
    a. *mama-ci   ka:-y.*
       woman-NOM:SUFF sing-IMM
       'The woman is singing.'
    b. *ma:ma-ci-u   ka:-qa-y.*
       RDP-woman-NOM:SUFF-PL sing-PL-IMM
       'The women are singing.'

The intransitive verbal number pairs change their stem according to the number of their subject as in (152). However the transitive verb pairs select the stem according to the number of their object as in (153).

(152) Ute (Givón and Southern Ute Tribe 1980: 42)
    a. *Taʔwa-ci   ʔu pʉi–pʉga.*
       man-NOM-SUFF he sleep.SG-REM
       'The man slept.'
    b. *ta:taʔwa-ci-u ʔumʉ kway-pʉga.*
       RDP-man-NOM:SUFF-PL they sleep.PL-REM
       'The men slept.'

(153) Ute (Givón and Southern Ute Tribe 1980: 122)
    a. *siva:tu-ci ʔuru paχa-gu:-pu̧.*
       goat-NOM be   kill.SG-MOD-NOM
       'I wish s/he would kill the goat.'

b. *siva:tu-ci ʔuru paχa-qa-gu-pu̯.*
   goat-NOM be   kill.SG-PL-MOD-NOM
   'I wish they would kill the goat.'

The plural verb *qoʔaj* 'kill.PL.OBJ' is impossible in (153b) because the object is in the singular. Since there is no object pluralization affix in Ute, the two verbs *paχa* 'kill.SG.OBJ' and *qoʔaj* 'kill.PL.OBJ' are said not to be paradigmatically related but rather different words.

The above facts of agreement have been taken as a reason for wiping out all cases of verbal number cf. (Mel'čuk 1994: 386–7) "... the Georgian examples ... and Uto-Aztecan ... and Athabaskan ... must be removed from the list of stock examples of verbal root suppletion according to the grammatical number of subject/object". I think such a generalization is not warranted because (a) there is variation between the facts for agreement even for closely related languages (see Navajo (149) and Slave (150) above), and (b) as it will become clear from the presentation below, there are languages where the verbal number pairs do belong to the agreement system. In these languages, when a stem changes according to a particular number category, this change appears as a genuine exception to established agreement patterns. Describing them as different words only would be simply misleading.

In the languages presented below, regular verbs generally agree with their arguments. Verbal number suppletion is restricted to one and maximum two verbs. Typically, though not in all cases, these verbs are intransitive verbs of motion.

In Murle, a Nilo-Saharan language from the Sudanic group, spoken in Sudan and Ethiopia, the inflection of regular verbs involves a prefix or circumfix (for first and second person) which indicate person and number of the subject. According to the description (Arensen 1982), there is only one verb which changes its stem according to number of the subject; the person–number affixes remain the same even for this irregular verb.

(154) Murle (Nilo-Saharan, East Sudanic, Surmic) (Arensen 1982: 60, 72)

	a. 'climb'	b. 'go'
1SG IMPERFECT	ka-tood-i	ka-kɔ
2SG IMPERFECT	a-tood-i	a-kɔy-i[3]
3SG IMPERFECT	a-toɔt	a-kɔ
1PL EXCL IMPERFECT	ka-toɔt	ka-vɔ
1PL INCL IMPERFECT	ka-toodd-a	ka-vɔy-a
2PL IMPERFECT	a-toodd-u	a-vɔy-u
3PL IMPERFECT	a-toɔt	a-vɔ

---

3. The final person suffix may be preceded by an epenthetic consonant whose quality is partially phonologically conditioned. If the stem ends in a vowel, then /n/ or /y/ is inserted before the final person suffix.

It is, of course, unclear whether the stems -*kɔ* and -*vɔ* of the verb 'go' in Murle originate from two different words or result from a phonological process that is no longer productive. However, synchronically it is the only verb in Murle that uses different stems according to number of its only argument and as such it should be described as a suppletive verb.

In Shipibo-Konibo, a Panoan language from Peru, almost all verbs have a single root and establish the singular–plural distinction only in the third person, by suffixing the plural marker -*kan* as illustrated in (155). The verbs *jo*-'come' and *ka*-'go' are the only two verbs that make the number distinction with all persons by using different singular/plural roots (Valenzuela 1997: 49) as shown in (156) and (157).

(155)   Shipibo-Konibo (Panoan) (Valenzuela 1997: 48)
    a.   *jaskat-ax rama-kama-bi chii **ja**-ke.*
        so-INTR now-until-EMP fire exist-CMPL
        'And it so that even until now there is fire.'
    b.   *ani jema-nko icka joni-**bo** **ja-kan**-ke.*
        big village-LOC many person-PL exist-PL-CMPL
        'There are many people in the city.'

(156)   Shipibo-Konibo (Valenzuela 1997: 49)
        'come'   'go'
  SG   *jo-*   *ka-*
  PL   *be-*   *bo-*

Like all other verbs, these two verbs take the third-person plural suffix.

(157)   Shipibo-Konibo
    a.   *Ja-Ø-ra   Kako-nkoniax   **jo**-ke.*
        3-ABS-AS[4] Caco-from:INTR come:SG-COMPL
        '(S)he came from Caco.'
    b.   *Ja-bo-Ø-ra   Kako-nkoniax   **be-kan**-ke.*
        3-PL-ABS-AS Caco-from:INTR come:PL-PL-COMPL
        'They came from Caco.'

Thus in Shipibo-Konibo the two verbs 'come' and 'go' appear as true exceptions to established agreement patterns. Similarly to Murle above, we do not have any diachronic data on these verbs. In view of the agreement patterns of the modern language, they appear as deviations and are as such suppletive according to number of subject.

In Ket, the only remaining language from the Yenisei-Ostyak family of Siberia,

---

4.   AS = ASEVERATIVE or DIRECT EVIDENTIAL, first-hand information (Pilar 1997)

Russia, there is one verb 'drowse' where change of stem is observed according to number of its subject.[5]

(158) Ket (Yenisei-Ostyak) (Vall and Kanakin 1988: 24)

	'throw up and down'	'drowse'
1SG	d-sitayit	d-iskayut
2SG	k-sitayit	k-iskayut
3SG M	d-sitayit	d-iskayut
3SG F	da-sitayit	da-iskayut
1PL	d-sitayit-n	d-es'kis'damin
2PL	k-sitayit-n	k-es'ki's'damin
3PL	d-sitayit-n	d-es'ki's'damin

As demonstrated above the singular/plural pairs in Murle, Shipibo-Konibo and Ket appear integrated in the agreement systems of their respective languages. Thus they must be described as suppletive even from a very restrictive point of view. However, if verbal number suppletion is apriori rejected as a possibility, these data have to be excluded from the discussion. Which in turn would make for an, at best, incomplete description of the cross-linguistic variety of verbal suppletion.

4.2 Lexicalization, derivation and the concept of suppletion

Mithun (1988) and later Corbett (2000) correlate the existence of verbal number pairs or triples with the so-called **classificatory verbs** in a number of North American Indian languages.[6] The term classificatory is typically used to refer to verbs which express concepts such as 'lie', 'give', 'fall' and have different stems depending on the shape, animacy, and/or physical consistency of the thing being located or handled.[7] Such verbs are illustrated below in (159) and (160).

(159) Cherokee (Iroquoi, Southern), (Haas 1948: 244)
    a. či-ʔahsĭ   I gave [a round object]
    b. čii-tîisĭ   I gave [a long object]
    c. čii-nąhsĭ   I gave [flexible object]
    d. čii-neʔáhsĭ I gave [container with liquid contents]
    e. čii-yáàk'áàsĭ I gave [living being-non-human]

---

5. Krejnovich (1968: 79, 174), passim] lists about more than a dozen suppletive verbs which express single vs. one time action.

6. Such verbs exist also elsewhere in the world but the term is not always used to describe them.

7. For a detailed treatment of classificatory verbs, consult (Newman 1997) generally and (Hoijer 1945) for Apache.

(22) Comanche (Robinson and Armagost 1990: 197, passim)
*ut*u̱*katu̱*   'give in a hanging container'
tsaʔuru̱   'give something' (=give SG.OBJ)
himiitu̱   'give several things' (=give PL.OBJ)

Both Mithun and Corbett focus on the fact that there are languages which lexicalize notions for position, motion and a few other concepts differently. The verbal number pairs discussed here are part of such larger lexicalization pattern(s) in the languages where they are found. Such verbs are not related paradigmatically, cf. Mithun (1988); rather for certain actions or states such as giving, going, running, falling, sitting, standing, dying the languages in question also lexicalize physical characteristics or the number of the participants most directly involved or affected by them. Describing the verbal number pairs discussed here as separate words is, thus, useful in that it allows us to see them as a part of broader lexicalization processes in the languages where they occur.

Another argument for describing verbal number pairs as different words rather than paradigmatically related forms refers to the expression of verbal number: it is derivational and rarely applies to all verbs in a language. Thus in *Number* Corbett states:

> Turning to the means for marking verbal number cross-linguistically, we find stem modification (frequently reduplication) used commonly, sometimes with a high degree of complexity, as for instance in Yuman languages (Langdon 1992), and also numerous instances of quite separate verbs being used. In the latter case the relation between the forms is often said to be one of suppletion (as though the opposition were similar to English *go ~ went*) but this usage is misleading. We are not dealing with suppletion. Rather we have two different verbs…When the two verbal number forms are related in form, then we have a derivational relationship. There can be various degrees of productivity.   (Corbett 2000: 258–9)

The implication here seems to be that the term suppletion should be generally reserved for exceptions to inflectional patterns. As we saw in chapter 1, section 2.1.2.2 (Derivational vs. Inflectional suppletion), the issue is far from settled. On the contrary, even Mel'čuk's study which claims to present a rigorous definition of suppletion, states overtly that for suppletion to be postulated, it would suffice with the presence of "ANY patterns" that express a grammatical meaning (Mel'čuk 1994: 344). For him grammatical meaning is either inflectional or derivational; it is as anything that is regularly expressed by an affix or an alternation is grammatical (as for instance -*er* for agent nouns or -*ness* for abstract nouns in English). Finally, there is a requirement that two linguistic signs which stand in relation of suppletion may differ only by their grammatical meaning. Exceptions to both inflectional and derivational patterns as accepted as cases of suppletion in Mel'čuk's theory. This author mentions productivity of a derivational pattern as something of importance for the derivation of gender forms in Russian, and subsequently for postulating suppletion according to gender in this language. However, he does not seem to apply the productivity criterion to other derivational patterns when defining exceptions to those as suppletive or not (see discussion of data from Krongo below as well as Chapter 1, section 2.1.2.2). Moreover, Mel'čuk allows suppletion to apply to verbal nouns which are completely unrelated to corresponding idioms as in (161c) and (161d) (the example was already cited in Chapter 1 but I repeat it here for the sake of convenience)

(161) Russian (adopted from (Mel'čuk 1994: 363))
    a. *govorit' krasno*   'talk magniloquently, to blarney'
    b. *krasnobaj*   'one who talks magniloquently, who blarneys'
    c. *molot' jazykom*   lit. 'to thrash with one's tongue' = 'to talk nonsense'
    d. *pustozvon*   'one who talks nonsense'

It is unclear if (161a) and (161b) are supposed to illustrate a derivational pattern, and how widespread such a pattern is.

I already pointed out in Chapter 1, section 2.1.2.2, that Mel'čuk presents the words *korova* 'cow.FEM' and *byk* 'bull' as an example of suppletion according to gender in Russian. He does show some hesitation about this issue but never comes to any solution except offering a short discussion in an endnote. For him *korova* 'cow.FEM' vs. *byk* 'bull' as well as similar nouns are suppletive, although probably not the most prototypical cases of suppletion since gender is not an inflectional category for Russian nouns but a lexico-derivational one.

For the sake of consistency, if we allow the term suppletion to describe exceptions to one derivational pattern such as the one whereby gender forms are derived, we should allow suppletion to cover exceptions to other derivational patterns as well. Or, we do not, we should state why. Mel'čuk never does that. Thus excluding verbal number pairs from the stock of suppletive verbs, but allowing pairs such as *bull* vs. *cow* to be considered suppletive is not entirely correct even by his own criteria.

In the languages discussed here, the scope of the derivation of verbal number pairs varies from language to language. For example in Burushaski, an isolate language of Asia, such a derivation (see (162a) and (162b) for an illustration) is limited to some thirty verbs (Tiffou and Patry 1995).

(162) Burushaski (Tiffou and Patry 1995)
       SG   PL   Gloss
    a. *gárk-* *gárča* 'catch, grasp, carry (fruit /wood)'
    b. *girát* *girača* 'dance, play'
    c. *-wál-* *gía-* 'fall' (for class x nouns)[8]

---

8. In Burushaski, the nouns are divided into the following classes: human males (class m), human females (class f), other nouns denoting animates and most concrete specific count nouns (class x); abstract, non-count/mass nouns and only a few count nouns (class y) (Tiffou 1995: 417).

Lorimer (1935) reports the pertinent verbal number pairs as the one shown in (162c) as different words. Tiffou and Patry (1995) support this view based on evidence which shows that syntactic agreement shows an ergative pattern and the different stems above are selected on a semantic rather than lexical basis. The main point here is that the derivation of pluractional verbs is very limited in Burushaski. Thus Lorimer does not see the singular: plural pairs of the kind illustrated in (162c) as paradigmatically related.

In Ainu, a language where both event number and participant number are represented, verbs expressing multiple action are regularly derived from verbs expressing single/one time action by suffixation as illustrated below.

(163) Ainu (Tamura 1988)

SG	PL	Gloss
maka	makpa	'open'
osura	osurpa	'throw away'
yasa	yaspa	'tear, split'

In Ainu, this kind of derivation covers about a hundred verbs, depending on the dialect. While the grammar author is very explicit on both the values of labels such as 'singular', and 'plural' and the status of this process as derivational rather than inflectional, he still refers to pairs such as the ones below as suppletive.

(164) Ainu (Tamura 1988)
    a. 'stand'
        as   stand.SG
        roski stand.PL
    b. 'kill'
        rayke kill.SG.OBJ
        ronnu kill.PL.OBJ

Deriving pluractional verbs by morphological processes such as prefixation, suffixation or reduplication is very restricted in some languages but quite pervasive in others. For example, in Krongo, pluractional verbs (usually expressing iterative and habitual meaning) are derived by means of prefixes or tone or reduplication, illustrated in (165a, b, c). These processes apply to a great number of verbs. There are fifteen verbs which do not use any of these morphological means but rather express iterative and habitual meaning by completely unrelated stems; one of them is shown in (165d).

(165) Krongo (Reh 1985, passim)
    a.   PREFIX
        SG   *à-mà*   VERB.MARKER-answer
        PL   *t-èe–mà*   VERB.MARKER-PL-answer
    b.   TONE
        SG   *ò-kídò-ònò*   VERB.MARKER-cut off-SUFF
        PL   *ò-kìdò-onò*   VERB.MARKER-cut off.PL-SUFF
    c.   REDUPLICATION
        SG   *t-áa-ṭà*   VERB.MARKER-PREF-go out
        PL   *à-ṭàa-ṭá*   VERB.MARKER-RDP-go out
    d.   SUPPLETION
        SG   *à-pá-ánà*   VERB.MARKER-hit.SG-SUFF
        PL   *à-rwà-ànà*   VERB.MARKER-hit.PL-SUFF

As the examples above show, verbal number in Krongo is clearly derivational in that it does not have a unified expression. Its functions, however, are very close to functions of verbal aspect, such as iterative (repeated action) and habitual. The singular counterparts of the derived verbs usually express punctual action. The derivational devices illustrated above are, according to the grammatical description, lexically conditioned; however, the derivation as a whole is a very wide-spread one and the suppletive verbs illustrated in (165d) are easily perceived as exceptions to a pattern rather than simply different words.

Languages where the derivation of verbal number is somewhat similar to that of Krongo are the following: Samoan (Austronesian), Wari' (Chapacura-Wahnam language from Brazil), Canela-Kraho (a Macro-Gê language from Brazil), Koasati, Kunama (a Nilo-Saharan language spoken in Eritrea), and Northern Tepehuan (a Southern Uto-Aztecan language spoken in the state of Chihuahua, Mexico). Thus in these languages, postulating suppletion according to verbal number is justified inasmuch as the verb pairs which differ solely on the basis of number appear as exceptions to a fairly widespread derivational pattern.

Generally, what seems to matter for many authors of grammars, is the existence of regular morphological patterns of some kind and subsequently deviations from them are described as suppletive. Authors such as Mithun (1988) and Corbett (2000) appear to object to such an understanding although the view is never made entirely explicit. Mel'čuk (1994) is very generous with the concept of suppletion since he appears to take anything that would break a pattern of whatever kind as a case of suppletion. What he objects to in the case of verbal number pairs is their description as conditioned by syntactic agreement, an issue, which I discussed in section 4.1.

As already stated, describing the verbal number pairs discussed here as separate words is useful in that it allows us to see them as a part of broader lexicalization processes in the languages where they occur. Such a description, however, conceals the fact that these words are also related by derivational processes which in some languages are very productive. The more general the derivational pattern is, the easier it is to see words which incorporate its grammatical sense in their lexical meaning as exceptions to it rather than independent lexical items.

The controversy outlined here can be used in a constructive way when we seek to understand the nature of suppletion and furthermore its diachronic development. Prototypical suppletive verbs often originate from separate lexical items which in the course of time get closely associated with a given category because their lexical meaning is highly compatible with it. The perfective: imperfective verb pairs in Slavic languages presented in Chapter 4 are in fact very similar to the verbal number pairs discussed here in that in both cases we deal with lexical expressions which are highly compatible with or even accommodate a grammatical meaning. The difference is that the perfective: imperfective opposition is typically applicable to a great number verbs in language (though far from all), whereas the number of times an action is performed or the number of people/objects it affects is relevant for a more restricted number of verbs. Thus expression of imperfective or perfective aspect tends to become widespread and in many cases close to inflection (Bybee 1985; Dahl 1985). Lexical expressions for such general aspectual meanings are described as suppletive since they appear as exceptions to broadly applied patterns. Lexical expressions of verbal number, on the other hand, are often exceptions to more restricted derivational patterns and as such maintain a "freer" lexical status. While a typology of suppletion should distinguish the most prototypical instances of this phenomenon from less prototypical ones, it should also accommodate cases which have an intermediate status between independent lexical items and paradigmatically related forms. The verbal number pairs discussed in this section exemplify the latter in many languages and as should be described as such.

In addition, the following needs to be said as regards the nature of suppletion and verbal number pairs. The typical take on suppletion is that it is a yes–no phenomenon, that is, a form is a clear exception to a well-established pattern or it is not. However, morphological theory does allow for degrees of suppletion in terms of form: some cases are less prototypical than others e.g. *see*: *saw* is a weak case whereas *go*: *went* is a strong one. Degrees of suppletion according to the derivational: inflectional status of a category seem to be at least implicitly banned (in any case the issue is never very much discussed which is examples such as *bull* vs. *cow* pop up here and there as an illustration of suppletion according to gender but without any further comment). In a lot of languages the verbal number pairs/triples represent ambiguous cases between separate lexical items and paradigmatically related forms. Besides, it is exactly such pairs (I don't know of any triples) that evolve into number markers for stative verbs in the languages where they occur (see 4.3 below). While the latter does not make them suppletive per se, it does demonstrate their special status in the languages where they are found. An analysis of this phenomenon should acknowledge these facts rather than conceal them.

4.3 Emergence of agreement markers out of verbal number pairs

The data presented below illustrate the use of verbal number as evolving agreement markers. While such use does not make them suppletive it does demonstrate their special status in the languages where they are found.

Durie (1986: 361) highlights the fact that singular–plural pairs are commonly used in compounds, often to indicate number.[9]

(166) Kapingamarangi (Austronesian, Oceanic) (adapted from Durie (1986: 361)
    a. *damana*   big.SG
        llauehe   big.PL
    b. *haga-damana* enlarge one thing
        hada-llauehe enlarge more than one thing

(167) Moses-Columbian[10] (Salishan), adapted from Durie (1986: 362)
    a. *ɫáq-lx*   sit.SG
        yər-íx   sit.NON-SG
    b. *k-ɫqlx-áwsn*   chair
        (n)l–yərx-áwsn chairs:NON-SG

In a similar fashion, in Barasano, a Tucanoan language from Columbia, the verb *roka* 'move down/away' has two roots, one for singular, the other for plural. Those are productively used in compounds to indicate number.

(168) Barasano (Tucanoan) (Jones and Jones 1991: 24)
    a. *roka*   move down/away.SG
        rea   move down/away.PL
    b. *bahi roka*   die.SG
        bahi rea   die.PL

Stative verb compounds which involve members of singular plural pairs appear very common in Uto-Aztecan languages. For example in Kawaiisu, an extinct lan-

---

9. See also Langdon (1992) for an account of a similar grammaticalization process in the Pai subgroup of the Yuman family.

10. An alternative name for this language is Wenachi-Columbia. It is spoken by 75 people (1990 census) in the Colville Reservation, North Central Washington, USA. The morpheme-to-morpheme translation is not perfect, however, this is all the data provided in the quoted source.

guage, formerly spoken in the Mojave desert, USA, stative verbs compounds use as their second element a verb which is sometimes glossed as 'sick', and sometimes as 'suffer'.

(169) Kawaiisu (Uto-Aztecan, Northern, Numic) (Zigmond et al. 1990: 81)

	FORM	MORPHEMIC ANALYSIS	TRANSLATION
a.	yeʔe	sick.SG	sick (one)
	cowiki	sick.PL	sick (many)
b.	ʔoho-yeʔe	bone-suffer	be thin
c.	pɨɨ-yeʔe	blood-suffer	menstruate
d.	suvi-yeʔe	[NO GLOSS]-suffer	be happy

The verb *cowiki* 'sick.PL', the plural counterpart of *jeʔe* 'sick.SG', is used when the compounds in (169b, c and d) describe the state of more than one person (cf. Zigmond et al. 1990: 296).

In other Uto-Aztecan languages, the verbs 'die/kill' are used to form stative verb compounds, in particular stative verb compounds that take an animate subject, that is characterize how an individual feels.

(170) Comanche (Uto-Aztecan, Northern, Numic) (Todd McDaniels, p.c.)

a.	tɨyai	die.SG
	koi	kill.PL
b.	tsiha-tɨyai-humia	hunger-die.SG-about to
	tsiha-koi-humia	hunger-die.PL-about to
c.	taku-tɨyai-humia	thirst-die.SG-about to
	taku-koi-humia	thirst-die.PL-about to
d.	sɨ-tɨyai-humia	feel cold-die.SG-about to
	sɨ-koi-humia	feel cold-die.PL-about to

(171) Northern Paiute (Uto-Aztecan, Northern, Numic) (Snapp et al. 1984: 53)

a.	yai	die.SG
	koi	kill.PL
b.	tɪo-yai	be sick-SG
	tɪoi-koi	be sick-PL
c.	paa-yai	be drunk-SG
	paa-koi	be drunk-PL
d.	pɪɪjai	be thirsty.SG
	pɪɪ-koi	be thirsty-PL
e.	cɪa-yai	hungry-SG
	cɪa-koi	hungry-PL

(172) Cora (Uto-Aztecan, Southern, Sonoran, Corachol) (Casad 1984)
    a. *Miʔi*   die.SG
       Kuʔi   die.PL
    b. *i-miʔi*   be hungry-SG
       i-kuʔi   be hungry-PL

In the Uto-Aztecan languages above the form of the verbs 'die/kill' is kept more or less intact; however, their meaning is generally reduced to the number component, either singular or plural. This development is not equally advanced in all languages. For example the Comanche examples may be used either in the literal sense 'about to starve/die of thirst/freeze to death' or as conventionalized hyperbolas that would parallel English expressions such as *famished, parched, chilled to the bone* (Todd McDaniels, p.c.). The descriptions of Northern Païute and Cora do not specify if the literal sense of the 'die/kill' verbs surfaces at all; they only list the compounds in (171) and (172) as singular: plural forms for the respective senses.

In other languages, not only the meaning but also the form is substantially reduced. This is illustrated by data from Northern Tepehuan in (173).

(173) Northern Tepehuan (Uto-Aztecan, Southern, Sonoran, Tepiman) (Bascom 1982: 352)
    a. *múúkui*   die.SG
       kóóyi   die.PL
    b. *bíúgu-mu*   hungry-SG
       bíúgu-koi   hungry-PL
    c. *kooshi-mu*   sleepy-SG
       kooshi-koi   sleepy-PL
    d. *ibí-mu*   tired-SG
       ibí-koi   tired-PL
    e. *uvá-mu*   cold-SG
       uvá-koi   cold-PL
    f. *baá-mu*   angry-SG
       baá-koi   angry-PL

To my knowledge such grammaticalization of the verbs 'die' is not yet discussed in the literature (Heine et al. 1991; Hopper and Traugott 1993; Bybee et al. 1994; Heine and Kuteva 2002). While it may be typologically unusual,[11] it might turn out that it is recurring in Meso-American languages. Søren Wichmann (p.c.) reports data

---

11. This is probably an issue that requires further investigation. For instance Östen Dahl (p.c.) reports a case from Maybrat (West Papuan) where the sense 'be hungry' is expressed by 'die (for) taro'. So such extended uses of the verb 'die' may be cross-linguistically more common than is currently acknowledged.

from Texistepec Popoluca, a Mixe-Zoquean language, where the verb *kaʔ* 'die' is homophonous with the part of a complex plural suffix for a small group of verbs that mostly refer to sounds and are reduplicated in the singular as illustrated in (174) below.

(174) Texistepec Popoluca (Mixe-Zoquean, Zoquean) (Søren Wichmann, p.c.)
        ker-kerdeʔ   RDP-croak.SG
        ker-tiŋ-kaʔ   croak-PL-PL

Again, in Mixe-Zoquean languages, Wichmann finds that the verb *yah* 'finish' is homophonous with the third-person plural suffix for stative verbs *yah*.

Wichmann proposes the following hypothesis for the development of 'die' as plural marker: 'die' > 'finish' > 'all' > 'plural'. Such a development is conceivable but the stages are yet to be documented and a lot more data are necessary.

At this point I can only speculate about the development of the 'die/kill' verbs in Uto-Aztecan as plural markers. On the whole, I think that a reanalysis of a verb such as 'die' to a general state verb such as 'suffer' and afterwards as a marker of general state is plausible. Another reason could be hyperbolas or ironic uses that become conventionalized (Todd McDaniels and Jennifer Spenader, p.c.). Regardless of the driving force for such a development (and its stages would still need further specification), the persistent semantic element, least prone to change appears to be that of the number of participants included in the lexical meaning of the verb(s). At the stage when all other content seems to have "bleached" the semantic component of number is the only one left and this way a verb that originally meant 'die' or 'cause to die' has become a number marker. Thus the verbal number pair has effectively contributed to the evolution of a paradigm. Once the paradigm of several verbs marking singular: plural is established the verbal number pair which started as separate lexical items is reinterpreted as a suppletive pair, which involves two forms of one and the same word.

5. Summary and conclusions

In this chapter I presented data on the lexical and derivational expression of verbal number as category. Since this study is focused on suppletion as a grammatical phenomenon, I explored the controversy whether lexical expressions of verbal number should be regarded as independent lexical items or derivationally related forms.

From a diachronic point of view, there is no doubt that the verbal number pairs discussed in this chapter are separate lexical expressions which include in their lexical meaning the number of times an action is done or the number of participants most strongly affected by the action or state. As Bybee (1985) and Mithun

(1988) point out, languages tend to combine notions which form coherent semantic wholes or are relevant to each other. The number of times an action of hitting is performed or the number of people moving or dying are highly relevant to these concepts which is why we find separate words for them. However, the fact that such words incorporate number in their meaning makes them also prone to become associated with derivational or inflectional processes where verbs are involved such as derivation for plural action and agreement.

The productivity of the derivation of verbal number as well as the facts for syntactic agreement show a great deal of variation even in closely related languages. This variation is relevant when we consider suppletion. The verbal number pairs discussed here are only semantically related in languages where the derivation of verbal number is very restricted or the stem selection comes in marked contrast with the rules of syntactic agreement as in Navajo above. However, in languages where the derivation is very wide spread and is used for more general aspectual meanings, these pairs appear also paradigmatically related as in Krongo and languages similar to it. Finally, there are languages such as Shipibo-Konibo above where the verbal number pairs are clear exceptions to general patterns of syntactic agreement. Thus synchronically we can see a scale where lexical expressions for verbal number are only semantically related on the one end and paradigmatically related on the other with a lot of cases in between. So as regards the typology of suppletion, they should be described as intermediate cases between prototypical suppletives and different lexical items. The use of singular/plural verbs in compounds and their subsequent development into sole markers of number for stative verbs demonstrates their special status in the languages where they are found. They are not just semantically related lexical items but words which easily evolve into grammatical markers and thus build paradigmatic relations.

Concluding remarks

1. Summary of the results and implications of the preceding chapters

The main claim put forth in this study has been that there is a system to suppletive verbs, a phenomenon that is seemingly random and unpredictable, and typically described as such too. Below I summarize the aspects that highlight the systematic nature of suppletion as manifested in verb paradigms.

Various types of suppletion according to grammatical category were presented in Chapter 3, Section 2. Depending on the number of languages where they are observed, a distinction was made between those which occur in a large amount of languages and those which occur, in the current sample, in less than ten languages. The first group was labeled major types and the second minor types. The major types include suppletion according to tense–aspect, mood, imperative in particular, verbal number and negation. The second group includes a few languages with suppletion to person–number of subject or object, form of object (definite or indefinite, or bound vs. non-bound), mood, specifically subjunctive, passive voice, and finally honorific levels in languages where degrees of politeness are grammaticalized. Within the limits of this project I was able to concentrate on three of the major types listed. Even if there is still work to be done, the picture presented by the data which were investigated in depth allows for several generalizations.

The suppletion types examined in detail show different cross-linguistic frequency, genetic affiliation and areal distribution. Suppletion according to tense–aspect categories is cross-linguistically the most widespread kind of stem change. I will elaborate below on the different counting methods, but for now, suffice it to say that I consider the results of the Dryer Distribution as well as the proportion offered by the language count in the small sample as the most reliable results for the evaluation of the cross-linguistic frequency of the examined suppletion types. According to these counting methods, tense–aspect suppletion occurs in more than one third of the examined languages. Areally, this kind shows a clear concentration in Europe and West Asia. Other hotbeds appear to be Meso-America and Papua New Guinea. It is favored in phyla such as Indo-European, North and South Caucasian, as well as Oto-Manguean, Carib and Sepik-Ramu.

Suppletive imperatives show a lower cross-linguistic frequency: about 15 percent in the small sample, and 20 percent according to the Dryer Distribution. As already pointed out (Chapter 6, Section 4) this may reflect a shortcoming in the data collection and grammatical descriptions rather than the actual situation. While the cross-linguistic frequency of this kind of suppletion may need to be re-considered in a future study, one of the most interesting facts about it is its concentration in Africa, according to the available data. Thus its geographic distribution is completely different from the one shown by tense–aspect suppletion. Suppletive imperatives are most clearly associated with two linguistic phyla: Afro-Asiatic, the Semitic and Cushitic branches in particular, as well as the Uralic phylum. This kind of suppletion is observed in other families as well but its presence there is not as obvious as in the two just mentioned.

Similarly to imperative suppletives, verbal number pairs are observed in about one fifth of the examined languages according to the Dryer Distribution, and a little less than that according to the proportion in the small sample. While the phenomenon is clearly not very frequent, it shows an obvious concentration in North America but it is not absent from any other geographical area either.

In addition to the areal and genetic distribution, the phenomena examined here show clear ordering in other respects too. For instance, it was shown in Chapter 4, section 5 that suppletion according to tense–aspect is not haphazard but rather predictable as regards the lexemic groups that show it. In fact, we can state with a certain amount of confidence that if a language has tense–aspect suppletion with full lexical verbs such as 'say' or 'do' it will, more often than not, also have tense–aspect suppletion with verbs such as 'be', 'come' or 'go'. Essentially, what this hierarchy states is that the first items to show suppletion in a language are the ones most prone to evolve as auxiliaries with various grammatical functions. As demonstrated in Chapter 5, section 4, suppletion in the paradigms of copula verbs can be correlated with a particular strategy languages employ for the encoding of semantic domains such as identity, class inclusion, and property assignment. In fact regular copula verbs, which are used in more than one of these domains, seem to be extremely rare. Given that both verbs glossed 'be' as well as the general verbs of motion 'come' and 'go' are typically used with a rich array of functions which set them apart form all other verbs in a language, it shouldn't be surprising that they are also encoded in a special way. Besides, aspect is highly relevant as a category both to an action such as motion as well as to actions denoted by other verbs such as 'say', 'do' or 'see' which commonly show aspect suppletion. Thus lexical expressions for these notions that are highly compatible with one specific aspectual category but incompatible with others are to be expected, if one adopts the line of thinking suggested by Bybee (1985).

In a similar vein, the relevance of the imperative and verbal number to the meaning of the verbs that show special forms for these categories can be demonstrated as well.

Diachronically, suppletion appears to result from a variety of processes that have different motivations. However, it should be emphasized that contrary to the widespread view, emergence of suppletion is not an isolated phenomenon, and there are diachronic processes which lead to suppletive forms in paradigms. Thus suppletion is not a byproduct of one historical process or another, but is, in fact a well motivated result of various directions of language change. In some cases suppletive forms evolve as part of general grammaticalization processes. In others, emergence of suppletion is closer to lexicalization. There is also evidence that suppletive evolve as a result of system pressure, in that their development is part of an overall system restructuring. In these cases, the development of suppletion follows analogical processes instead of resisting them. Finally, given that there are different diachronic processes that can be demonstrated to produce suppletive forms, it is not surprising that on the synchronic level, in a single language system, such forms appear rather unsystematic. However, if we adopt a cross-linguistic view, we can see that what appears as an idiosyncrasy on a language specific level, is in fact something that is cross-linguistically recurrent, and as such not idiosyncratic at all.

The suppletive forms according to the grammatical categories investigated here can be placed differently on the lexical-grammatical scale. The verbal number pairs discussed in Chapter 7 are in various degrees closer to the lexical end. Likewise, the suppletive aspectual pairs in Slavic languages where aspect is essentially a derivational category represent an intermediate case between semantically and grammatically related words. Given that imperative has a special status as a mood, and suppletive imperatives are often verbs restricted to that function, they should probably also be considered as an essentially lexical phenomenon. Suppletive forms which alternate according to tense distinctions come closer to the grammatical end of the scale. Finally, with the cases of non-categorial suppletion we are for the most part dealing with auxiliaries of different kinds, and thus essentially come to components of grammar rather than lexicon.

2. Directions for future research

For the assessment of the cross-linguistic frequency of the suppletive types examined in detail here I used four counting methods. Essentially, this was an experiment, and some of the detailed counts might appear as overkill. However, given that a truly reliable language sample is most probably quite unattainable goal, I do think that if we are to gain a realistic picture of the spread of a particular linguistic feature, at least two counting methods should be employed in a typological study. The procedure whereby weight values are assigned to a larger language sample has a future if it is further elaborated. In particular, there should be a limit to how high or low a language value may be. Admittedly, this would entail a certain amount of arbitrariness. However, the current system whereby language isolates and languages from very small families get very high values whereas closely related languages get very low values is not very good either. Thus it is necessary to achieve more balance in the weight values assignment. An appropriate system of how to achieve such a balance can be worked out after probably more experiments with several different samples, and several different systems of weight values assignment (Östen Dahl, p.c.).

Detailed discussion of syntactic suppletion had to be left out of this project. However, it is a phenomenon that should be investigated in depth. In particular suppletion according to polarity requires future research since even according the preliminary data I have it appears to be frequent. Unlike the other main kinds of suppletion I have not noticed any areal patterning but this is subject to future examination.

As regards the diachronic development of suppletive forms, more studies are needed to elucidate the nature of the processes whereby dynamic and position verbs evolve into copula verbs. Likewise, more studies are necessary to test the impact of type frequency on the evolution of suppletion in paradigms.

Finally, psycholinguistic aspects of acquisition and regression of suppletive forms were not discussed in this study. This does not mean that I consider them unimportant and future work should concentrate on these issues as well.

APPENDIX 1

The small sample

Genetic phyla as listed in the Ethnologue (February 1998)

The listing below presents the genetic phyla together with the number of languages they include in brackets. The listing reflects the Ethnologue as of February 1998. The phyla are listed in decreasing number of languages included in them. The lower level subgroupings that are relevant for sampling can are presented in Table A1 together with selection procedure applied to them.

Niger-Congo (1436)
Austronesian (1236)
Trans-New Guinea (539)
Indo-European (425)
Afro-Asiatic (371)
Sino-Tibetan (360)
Australian (257)
Nilo-Saharan (194)
Austro-Asiatic (180)
Oto-Manguean (173)
Sepik-Ramu (105)
Dravidian (78)
Arawakan (74)
Tupi (70)
Mayan (68)
Daic (68)
Creole (66)
Altaic (65)
Uto-Aztecan (60)
Torricelli (48)
Quechuan (47)
Na-Dene (42)
East Papuan (36)
Khoisan (35)
Uralic (34)
North Caucasian (34)
Geelvink Bay (34)
Algic (33)
Macro-Ge (32)
Hmong-Mien (32)
Panoan (29)
Carib (29)

West Papuan (27)
Salishan (27)
Penutian (27)
Hokan (27)
Tucanoan (26)
Chibchan (22)
Siouan (17)
Mixe-Zoque (16)
Andamanese (13)
Japanese (12)
Totonacan (11)
Mataco-Guaicuru (11)
Eskimo-Aleut (11)
Choco (10)
Iroquoian (9)
Sko (8)
Zaparoan (7)
Left May (7)
Barbacoan-Paezan (7)
Witotoan (6)
Tacanan (6)
Muskogean (6)
Mascoian (6)
Kwomtari-Baibai (6)
Wakashan (5)
South Caucasian (5)
Nambiquaran (5)
Maku (5)
Kiowa Tanoan (5)
Jivaroan (5)
Chukotko-Kamchatkan (5)
Chapacura-Wanham (5)

Caddoan (5)
Yanomam (4)
Subtiaba-Tlapanec (4)
Misumalpan (4)
Huavean (4)
Gulf (4)
Katukinan (3)
East Bird's Head (3)
Basque (3)
Aymaran (3)
Zamucoan (2)
Yuki (2)
Yukaghir (2)
Yenisei Ostyak (2)
Uru-Chipaya (2)
Salivan (2)
Peba-Yaguan (2)
Keres (2)
Chon (2)
Cahuapanan (2)
Arutani-Sape (2)
Araucanian (2)
Amto-Musan (2)
Alacalufan (2)
Mura (1)
Mosetenan (1)
Lule-Vilela (1)
English-Tahitian Cant (1)
Coahuiltecan (1)
Chimakuan (1)
Unclassified (114)
Language Isolate (31)

Selection procedure

I. Phyla consisting of fewer than 22 languages:
   A. Include all of the minimal groups (1 to 6) languages in a set, together with the language isolates.
   B. Calculate the total number of languages in the set and what proportion it represents in the universe of all 6703 languages. Include the number of languages corresponding to that proportion.
   Repeat IA and IB for the phyla consisting of 7 to 17 languages.

The first set consisted of 172 languages, that is, 2.5 percent of all languages, thus three languages were chosen:

Basque (Isolate)
Koasati (Muskoguean)
Ket (Yenisei-Ostyak)

The second set consisted of 139 languages, that is, 2.07 percent of all languages, so two languages were chosen from it:

Central Yup'ik (Eskimo-Aleut)
Oneida (Iroquoian)

II. Phyla consisting of more than 22 but fewer than 42 languages:
One language was chosen from each such phylum, provided there were sufficient reference sources, e.g. at least one good reference grammar. There are 16 such groups in the Ethnologue and each contributed one lg.

III A. n= (equals the number primary subgroups consisting of 20 or more languages) + number of languages in the residue subgroup divided by 30 rounded to the nearest number.

III B. m = (1+) the number of secondary subgroups of 20 or more languages with a residue of 20 or more. Add 1 if the residue in the primary subgroup covers a set of 20 or more languages.
r = number of primary subgroups of 20 or more languages from which no lg has been chosen after calculating and applying m + number of languages in the primary residue group divided by 30 rounded to the nearest integer.

The total number of languages sampled this way was 111, which is 1.6 percent of the languages listed in the Ethnologue. After the bibliographic search, the number of languages was reduced to 102. The number of languages that were eventually investigated from this planned sample came to be 94.

In Table A1, the heading N indicates the number of languages selected from a phylum or a corresponding subgrouping.

Table A1. The small sample

Phylum	Procedure	N	Language
AFRO-ASIATIC (371)	IIIB	6	
Chadic (192)		2	
West (72)			Mupun
			Hausa
Other Afro-Asiatic		4	Tamazight (Central Atlas)
			Oromo (Boraana)
			Wolaytta
			Hebrew
ALGIC (33)	II	1	Cree
ALTAIC (65)	IIIA	2	
Mongolian (13)		1	Mongolian
Tungus (12)			
Turkic (40)		1	Turkish
ARAWAKAN (74)	IIIB	1	Apurinã
Maipuran (53)		1	Garífuna
AUSTRALIAN (257)	IIIB	6	
Pama-Nyungan (176)		3	Martuthunira
			Kayardild
			Arabana
Other Australian (81)		3	Goonyandi [Bunaba]
			Mara [Maran]
			Nunggubuyu [Gunwingguan]
AUSTRO-ASIATIC (180)	IIIB	4	
Mon-Khmer (156)		3	
Eastern Mon-Khmer (69)		1	Khmer
Northern Mon-Khmer (38)		1	Khasi
Other Mon-Khmer		1	Vietnamese
Munda (24)		1	Mundari
AUSTRONESIAN (1236)	IIIB	7	
Malayo-Polynesian (1213)			
Central-Eastern (683)		3	
Central Malayo-Polynesian (149)		1	Mokilese
Eastern Malayo-Polynesian (532)			
South Halmanera West New Guinea (39)		1	Taba East Makian
Oceanic (493)		1	Samoan
Western Malayo-Polynesian (528)		6	
Borneo (137)		1	Malagasy
Meso Philippine (60)		1	Tagalog
Sulawesi (112)		1	Tukang Besi
Sundic (109)		1	Indonesian
CARIB (29)	II	1	Macushi
Chibchan (22)	II	1	Ika
Creole (66)	IIIA	1	Ndyuka

Table A1. (cont.)

Phylum	Procedure	N	Language
DRAVIDIAN (78)	IIIA	2	
Southern (28)			Kannada
Other Dravidian			Brahui [North]
EAST PAPUAN (36)	II	1	Kuot
ESKIMO-ALEUT (11)	I	1	Central Yup'ik
HOKAN (27)	II	1	Maricopa
INDO-EUROPEAN (425)	IIIB	6	
Indo-Iranian (302)			
Indo-Aryan (219)		1	Bengali
Iranian		1	Persian
Other Indo-European (133)		4	Ukrainian [Slavic]
			French [Romance]
			Greek (Modern) [Hellenic]
			Swedish [Germanic]
IROQUOIAN (9)	I	1	Oneida
ISOLATES (31)	I	1	Basque
KHOISAN (35)	II	1	!Xu
MACRO-GE (32)	II	1	Canela-Kraho
MAYAN (68)	IIIA	1	
Other Mayan (29)			Jakaltek
MUSKOGUEAN (6)	I	1	Koasati
NA-DENE (42)	IIIA	1	
Nuclear Na-Dene (41)		1	Navajo
NIGER-CONGO (1436)	IIIB	7	
Atlantic-Congo (1347)			
Atlantic (65)		1	Diola-Fogny
Volta-Congo (1272)			
Benue-Congo (895)		1	Luvale
Kru (41)		1	Grebo
Kwa (78)		1	Ewe
North (257)		1	Supyire
Kordofanian (31)		1	Krongo
Mande (58)		1	Maninka
NILO-SAHARAN (194)	IIIB	5	
Central Sudanic (64)		1	
West (41)			Bagirmi
Eastern Sudanic (96)		1	Murle
Nilotic		1	Turkana
Other Nilo-Saharan (34)		2	Songhai
			Kanuri
NORTH CAUCASIAN (34)	II	1	Lezgian

OTO-MANGUEAN (173)	IIIA	3	
Mixtecan (57)		1	Chalcatongo Mixtec
Otopamean (17)		1	Otomí (Ixtenco)
Other Oto-Manguean (99)		1	Lealao (Chinantec)
PANOAN (29)	II	1	Shipibo-Konibo
PENUTIAN (27)	II	1	Southern Sierrra Miwok
QUECHUA (47)	IIIA	1	
Quechua I		1	Imbabura
SALISHAN (27)	II	1	Squamish
SEPIK-RAMU (105)	IIIB	2	
Sepik (53)			
Sepik Hill (14)		1	Alamblak
Other Sepik Ramu		1	Yimas [Nor-Pondo]
SINO-TIBETAN (360)	IIIB	5	
Tibeto-Burman (345)		4	
Baric (102)		1	Garo
Himalayish (134)		1	Ladakhi
Burmese-Lolo (56)		1	Burmese
Other Tibeto-Burman (53)		1	Meithei [Meithei]
Other Sino-Tibetan		1	Mandarin [Chinese]
TAI-KADAI (70)	IIIA	1	Thai
TORRICELLI (48)	IIIA	1	
Kombio Arapesh (9)		1	Bukiyip
TRANS-NEW GUINEA (539)	IIIB	9	
Main Section (300)			
Central and Western (254)		5	Dani
			Kewa
			Sentani
			Daga
			Asmat
Eastern (46)		1	Suena
Madang-Adelbert Range (102)		2	
Adelbert Range (44)		1	Amele
Madang (58)		1	Usan
Other Trans-New Guinea		1	Imonda [Northern]
TUPI (70)	IIIA	1	
Tupi-Guarani (49)		1	Guarani
TUCANOAN (26)	II	1	Barasano
URALIC (34)	II	1	Hungarian
UTO-AZTECAN (60)	IIIA	2	
Southern Uto-Aztecan (48)		1	Pipil
Northern Uto-Aztecan (12)			Ute
WEST PAPUAN	II	1	Maybrat
YENISEI OSTAYK (2)	I	1	Ket

Map 1.

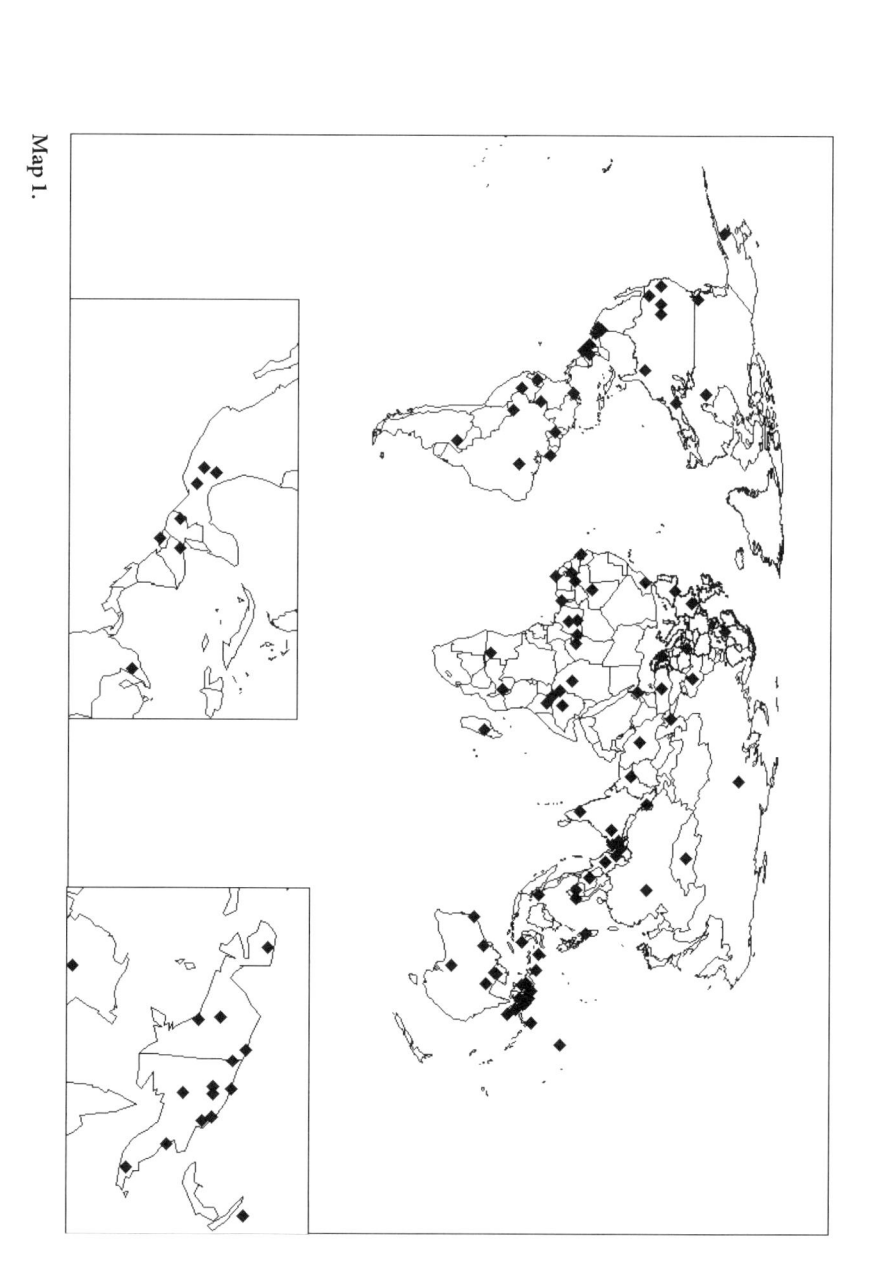

APPENDIX 2

Languages in the WALS sample

Table A2 lists the languages included in the WALS sample, together with pertinent phyla, genera, weight values, linguistic areas, countries where they are spoken, and reference sources I used.

As I stated in Chapter 2, section 5.1, the languages are grouped into **genera** of size and diversity roughly corresponding to Germanic or Romance families in the Indo-European phylum. This is the most difficult and certainly the most controversial issue in the method proposed by Dryer. I have tried to follow his guidelines as closely as possible.

Dryer (1992) defines the following areas: Africa, Eurasia, South-East Asia and Oceania, Australia-New Guinea, North America, and South America. The divisions between these areas are defined physically but in a few cases Dryer allows genetic groupings to define the actual boundary. Thus Semitic languages are treated as part of Africa (because their genetic relationships go in that direction). For similar reasons, Chibchan languages (occurring both in Central America and in South America) are treated as part of South America. The Austronesian languages are all considered part of South-East Asia and Oceania since they exhibit some typological similarities with the languages of South-East Asia. I follow Dryer in all of these respects. Additionally, all Arawakan languages are counted in South America; all Creoles in Africa. For instance, the reader shouldn't be shocked to see Maltese and Hebrew, being Semitic languages to be counted in Africa. Kilivila, Maori and Rapanoui, all Austronesian, are seen to belong to one and the same genus, Oceanic and counted all in South-East Asia and Oceania; likewise, Malagasy being Austronesian is counted in this area too.

Unlike Dryer, I use the Ethnologue classification whereas he appears to use one of his own. In case of discrepancies, I have tried to find out what exactly is included in a genus assigned by Dryer and then find a roughly corresponding grouping in the Ethnologue. The label from the Ethnologue was then used in order not to mix classifications. Below I present a list of discrepancies between classification in Dryer and in the Ethnologue together with ensuing differences in genus assignment.

South-East Asia and Oceania
AUSTRONESIAN
As Dryer points out, the genera assigned to some Austronesian languages are subject to great debate and on the whole very controversial. He uses a genus called Austronesian Philippine to cover Tukang Besi, Malagasy as well as Tagalog. In the Ethnologue, these languages are said to belong to three different branches, Sulawesi, Borneo and Meso-Philippine. The genus proposed by Dryer is not used here; I used the Ethnologue classification instead.

SINO-TIBETAN
Dryer includes Meithei a genus called. Kuki-Chin-Naga. The Ethnologue presents Meithei as a separate group, not inlcuded in Kuki-Chin-Naga but rather on the same level with it. Meithei is considered here, in accordance with the Ethnologue, a separate genus.

North America
Chibchan
Dryer includes Rama in a genus called Misumalpan. The Ethnologue lists Rama as a separate branch. The term Rama, rather than Misumalpan is used.

Salishan
Dryer uses the genus Coast Salish that corresponds, as far as I can see to the Ethnologue Central Salish. The Ethnologue term is used.

Uto-Aztecan
Dryer uses the genus Taracahitic, correponding to the Ethnologue grouping Cahita. The Ethnologue genus is used.

South America
Alacalufan
Alacalufan consists of two languages in the Ethnologue, Kawasqar (alternative name Kawesqar) and Kakauhua. Both in Dryer's and my sample it is represented by Qawesqar. Dryer uses Qawesqar as a genus. The Ethnologue term Alacalufan is used here.

Araucanian
Similarly to Alacalufan above, this family consists of two languages in the Ethnologue: Mapudungun (alternative name, Mapuche) and Huilliche. Both in Dryer's and in my sample the family is represented by Mapuche. Dryer uses Mapudungu as a genus name. The Ethnologue Araucanian is used here.

Chon
Chon consists of two languages in the Ethnologue: Selknam (alternative name, Ona) and Tehuelche. Both in Dryer's and in my sample the family is represented by Selknam. Dryer uses the term Patagonian to refer to its genus. The Ethnologue term Chon is used here.

Appendix 2. Languages in the WALS sample 187

Table A2.

Language	Phylum	Genus	Weight value	Linguistic area, country	Sources
!Xu	Khoisan	North Southern African Khoisan	0.5	Africa, Namibia	König and Heine 2001a
Abkhaz	North Caucasian	Northwest Caucasian	0.34	Eurasia, Georgia	Hewitt 1989, George Hewitt, p.c.
Acoma	Keres	Keres	1.000	N. America, USA	Miller 1965, Maring 1967
Ainu	Ainu	Ainu	1.000	Eurasia, Japan	Tamura 1988
Alagwa	Afro-Asiatic	Cushitic, Southern	0.05	Africa, Tanzania	Mous In Preparation
Alamblak	Sepik-Ramu	Sepik	0.5	A-NG, Papua New Guinea	Bruce 1984
Amele	Trans-New Guinea	Madang	0.170	A-NG, Papua New Guinea	Roberts 1987
Apurina	Arawakan	Maipuran	0.5	S. America, Brazil	Facundes 2000
Arabana	Australian	Pama-Nyungan	0.035	A-NG, Australia	Hercus 1994
Arabic (Egyptian)	Afro-Asiatic	Semitic	0.04	Africa, Egypt	Mitchell 1962
Arabic (Moroccan)	Afro-Asiatic	Semitic	0.04	Africa, Morocco	Hamid Ouali, p.c.
Arabic (Tunisian)	Afro-Asiatic	Semitic	0.04	Africa, Tunis	Zouhair Maalej, p.c.
Araona	Tacanan	Tacanan	1.000	S. America, Bolivia	Pitman 1980
Armenian (Eastern)	Indo-European	Armenian	0.125	Eurasia, Armenia	Kozintseva 1995, Jasmine Dum-Traugut, p.c.
Asmat	Trans-New Guinea	Central and South New Guinea	0.042	A-NG, Irian Jaya	Voorhoeve 1965
Awa Pit	Barbacoan	Barbacoan	1.000	S. America, Colombia	Curnow 1997
Aymara	Aymaran	Aymaran	1.000	S. America, Bolivia	Hardman 2001
Bagirmi	Nilo-Saharan	Bongo-Bagirmi	0.17	Africa, Chad Republic	Stevenson 1969
Barasano	Tucanoan	Tucanoan	1.000	S. America, Colombia	Jones and Jones 1991

Table A2. (cont.)

Language	Phylum	Genus	Weight value	Linguistic area, country	Sources
Basque	Basque	Basque	1.000	Eurasia, Spain	Lafitte 1962, Arotcarena 1976, Saltarelli 1988, King 1994
Bengali	Indo-European	Bengali-Assamese	0.031	Eurasia, Bangladesh	Dimock 1965, Radice 1994
Brahui	Dravidian	Dravidian, Northern	0.5	Eurasia, Pakistan	Andronov 1980, Bray 1986
Bukiyip	Torricelli	Torricelli	1.000	A-NG, Papua New Guinea	Conrad and Wogiga 1991
Bulgarian	Indo-European	Slavic	0.0105	Eurasia, Bulgaria	personal knowledge
Burmese	Sino-Tibetan	Lolo-Burmese	0.125	Eurasia, Burma/Myanmar	Okell 1994
Burushaski	Burushaski	Burushaski	1.000	Eurasia, Pakistan	Lorimer 1935, Berger 1998
Belorussian	Indo-European	Slavic	0.014	Eurasia, Belarus	Mayo 1976, Pashkevich 1978
Cahuilla	Uto-Aztecan	Takic	0.167	N. America, USA	Seiler 1977, Seiler and Hioki 1979
Canela-Kraho	Macro-Ge	Ge-Kaingang	1.000	S. America, Brazil	Popjes and Popjes 1986
Carib	Carib	Carib	0.25	S. America, Surinam	Hoff 1968
Cayuvava	Cayuvava	Cayuvava	1.000	S. America, Bolivia	Key 1967
Chamorro	Austronesian	Chamorro	0.1	SEA and Oceania, USA	Topping 1973
Chinantec (Lealao)	Oto-Manguean	Chinantecan	0.33	N. America, Mexico	Rupp 1989
Chinese (Cantonese)	Sino-Tibetan	Chinese	0.25	SEA and Oceania, China	Matthews and Yip 1994
Chinese (Mandarin)	Sino-Tibetan	Chinese	0.25	SEA and Oceania, China	Li and Thompson 1981
Chukchi	Chukotko-Kamchatkan	Chukotko-Kamchatkan	1.000	Eurasia, Russia	Dunn 1999
Comanche	Uto-Aztecan	Numic	0.083	N. America, USA	Robinson and Armagost 1990, Charney 1993
Cree (Plains)	Algic	Algonquian	0.5	N. America, Canada	Wolfart and Carroll 1981

Appendix 2. Languages in the WALS sample

Language	Family	Genus	Value	Region	Source
Czech	Indo-European	Slavic	0.007	Eurasia, Czech Republic	Sova 1962, Townsend 1981
Daga	Trans-New Guinea	Central and South Eastern New Guinea	0.083	A-NG, Papua New Guinea	Murane 1974
Dani (Lower Grand Valley)	Trans-New Guinea	Dani-Kwerba	0.042	A-NG, Irian Jaya	Bromley 1981
Diola-Fogny	Niger-Congo	Northern Atlantic	0.165	Africa, Senegal	Sapir 1965
Dutch	Indo-European	Germanic	0.0209	Eurasia, Netherlands	Donaldson 1981
English	Indo-European	Germanic	0.0208	Eurasia, UK	personal knowledge
Evenki	Altaic	Tungus	0.33	Eurasia, Russia	Nedjalkov 1997
Ewe	Niger-Congo	Kwa	0.033	Africa, Ghana	Westermann 1930
Fijian (Boumaa)	Austronesian	Oceanic	0.036	SEA and Oceania, Fiji	Dixon 1988
Finnish	Uralic	Finnic	0.25	Eurasia, Finland	Karlsson 1978 Päivi Juvonen, p.c.
French	Indo-European	Italic, Romance	0.0625	Eurasia, France	personal knowledge
Fur	Nilo-Saharan	Fur	0.17	Africa, Sudan	Jakobi 1993, Angelika Jakobi, p.c.
Garifuna	Arawakan	Maipuran	0.5	S. America, Honduras	Ronald Ross, p.c.
Garo	Sino-Tibetan	Baric	0.125	Eurasia, India	Burling 1961
Georgian	South Caucasian	South Caucasian	1.000	Eurasia, Georgia	Aronson 1982, Hewitt 1995
German	Indo-European	Germanic	0.0208	Eurasia, Germany	Lide and Magnusson 1970
Gooniyandi	Australian	Bunaban	0.143	A-NG, Australia	Gooniyandi
Grebo	Niger-Congo	Kru	0.033	Africa, Côte d'Ivoire	Innes 1966
Greek (Modern)	Indo-European	Greek	0.125	Eurasia, Greece	Christiades 1980, Mackridge 1985, Joseph and Philipaki-Warburton 1987
Greenlandic (West)	Eskimo-Aleut	Eskimo-Aleut	0.5	N. America, Denmark	Fortescue 1984
Guarani	Tupi	Tupi-Guarani	1.000	S. America, Paraguay	Guasch 1996
Hausa	Afro-Asiatic	West Chadic	0.1	Africa, Nigeria	Kraft 1973, Newman 2000
Hebrew (Modern)	Afro-Asiatic	Semitic	0.05	Africa, Israel	Glinert 1989
Hindi	Indo-European	Indic	0.031	Eurasia, India	Harley 1944

190 Suppletion in verb paradigms

Table A2. (cont.)

Language	Phylum	Genus	Weight value	Linguistic area, country	Sources
Hixkaryana	Carib	Carib	0.5	S. America, Brazil	Derbyshire 1979
Hopi	Uto-Aztecan	Hopi	0.167	N. America, USA	Albert and Shaul 1985, Seaman 1996
Hungarian	Uralic	Ugric	0.25	Eurasia, Hungary	Rice 1970, Benkö and Samu 1972, Olsson 1992, Törkenczy 1997
Hunzib	North Caucasian	Avaro-Andi-Didio	0.165	Eurasia, Dagestan	van den Berg 1995
Igbo	Niger-Congo	Igboid	0.0165	Africa, Nigeria	Green and Igwe 1963
Ika	Chibchan	Chibchan	0.5	S. America, Colombia	Frank 1990, Paul Frank, p.c.
Imonda	Trans-New Guinea	Northern Trans-New Guinea	0.33	A-NG, Papua New Guinea	Seiler 1985
Indonesian	Austronesian	Sundic	0.1	SEA and Oceania, Indonesia	Sneddon, 1996
Ingush	North Caucasian	Nax	0.33	Eurasia, Dagestan, Russia	Nichols 1994, Johanna Nichols, p.c.
Iraqw	Afro-Asiatic	Cushitic, Southern	0.05	Africa, Tanzania	Mous, 1992
Irish	Indo-European	Celtic	0.125	Eurasia, Ireland	Thurneysen 1946, Dillon and Ó Cróinin 1961, McCone 1987, Vendryes 1987, Elvira Veselinovic, p.c.
Jakaltek	Mayan	Mayan	1.000	N. America, Guatemala	Day 1973, Craig 1977
Japanese	Japanese	Japanese	1.000	Eurasia, Japan	Martin 1975, Hinds 1986, Martin 1987, Lange 1988, Chino 1996
Kannada	Dravidian	Dravidian Proper	0.5	Eurasia, India	Schiffman 1983, Sridhar 1990
Kanuri	Nilo-Saharan	Saharan	0.17	Africa, Nigeria	Hutchison 1981 John Hutchinson, p.c.
Kawesqar	Alacalufan	Alacalufan	1.000	S. America, Chile	Clairis 1985
Kayardild	Australian	Tangkic	0.036	A-NG, Australia	Evans 1995

Appendix 2. Languages in the WALS sample 191

Language	Family	Genus	Value	Region	References
Ket	Yenisei Ostyak	Ket	1.000	Eurasia, Russia	Dul'zon 1949, Ivanov et al. 1968, Krejnovich 1968, Vall and Kanakin 1988, Vall and Kanakin 1990
Kewa	Trans-New Guinea	East New Guinea Highlands	0.045	A-NG, Papua New Guinea	Franklin, 1971
Khalkha	Altaic	Mongolian	0.33	Eurasia, Mongolia	Grønbech and Krueger 1955, Poppe 1964
Khasi	Austro-Asiatic	Khasi	0.125	SEA and Oceania, India	Rabel 1961
Khmer (Central)	Austro-Asiatic	Khmer	0.125	SEA and Oceania, Cambodia	Noss et al. 1966, Jacob 1968, Ehrman 1972, Schiller 1985
Khoekhoe	Khoisan	Central Southern African Khoisan	0.5	Africa, Namibia	Hagman 1977
Kilivila	Austronesian	Oceanic	0.031	SEA and Oceania, Papua New Guinea	Senft 1986
Kiowa	Kiowa-Tanoan	Kiowa-Tanoan	1.000	N. America., USA	Watkins 1984
Koasati	Muskogean	Muskogean	1.000	N. America, USA	Booker 1980, Kimball 1991, Kimball 1993
Korean	Korean	Korean	1.000	Eurasia, N & S Korea	Sohn 1994
Krongo	Niger-Congo	Kadugli	0.34	Africa, Sudan	Reh 1985, Mechthild, p.c.
Kunama	Nilo-Saharan	Kunama	0.16	Africa, Eritrea	Bender 1996
Kuot	East Papuan	New Britain East Papuan	0.5	A-NG, Papua New Guinea	Lindström In preparation
Kutenai	Kutenai	Kutenai	1.000	N. America, Canada	Boaz 1927, Garvin 1948a, Garvin 1948b, Garvin 1948c
Ladakhi	Sino-Tibetan	Tibetan	0.125	SEA and Oceania, India	Koshal 1979
Lakhota	Siouan	Siouan	1.000	N. America, USA	Van Valin 1977, Berg 1981, Rood and Taylor 1996
Lango	Nilo-Saharan	Nilotic	0.04	Africa, Uganda	Noonan 1992
Latvian	Indo-European	Baltic	0.125	Eurasia, Latvia	Fennell and Gelsen 1980
Lavukaleve	East Papuan	Solomons East Papuan	0.5	A-NG, Solomon Islands	Terrill 1999

Table A2. (cont.)

Language	Phylum	Genus	Weight value	Linguistic area, country	Sources
Lezgian	North Caucasian	Lezgic	0.165	Eurasia, Dagestan, Russia	Haspelmath 1993
Luvale	Niger-Congo	Bantoid	0.0055	Africa, Zambia	Horton 1949, White 1949
Macushi	Carib	Carib	0.25	S. America, Guyana	Abbott 1991
Makah	Washakan	Washakan	1.000	N. America, USA	Matthew Davidson, p.c.
Makedonian	Indo-European	Slavic	0.0105	Eurasia, Macedonia	Lunt 1952, de Bray 1980b
Malagasy	Austronesian	Borneo	0.1	SEA and Oceania, Madagaskar	Domenichini-Ramiaramanana 1976, Dez 1980, Keenan and Polinsky 1998
Maltese	Afro-Asiatic	Semitic	0.025	Africa, Malta	Borg and Azzopardi-Alexander 1997
Mangarayi	Australian	Mangarayi	0.072	A-NG, Australia	Merlan 1982
Maninka (Western)	Niger-Congo	Mande	0.33	Africa, Mali	Delafosse 1929, Tokarskaja 1964, Creissels 1983
Maori	Austronesian	Oceanic	0.031	SEA and Oceania, New Zealand	Harlow 1996
Mapuche	Araucanian	Araucanian	1.000	S. America, Chile	Smeets 1989
Mara	Australian	Maran	0.143	A-NG, Australia	Heath 1981
Maranungku	Australian	Daly	0.142	A-NG, Australia	Tryon 1970
Maricopa	Hokan	Yuman	0.5	N. America, USA	Gordon 1986
Martuthunira	Australian	Pama-Nyungan	0.035	A-NG, Australia	Dench 1995
Mataco	Mataco-Guaicuru	Mataco	1.000	S. America, Bolivia	Urquiza and Mani 1974, Tovar 1981
Maung	Australian	Yiwaidjan	0.143	A-NG, Australia	Capell and Hinch 1970
Maybrat	West Papuan	Central Bird's Head	1.000	A-NG, Indonesia, Irian Jaya	Dol 1999
Meithei	Sino-Tibetan	Meithei	0.125	SEA and Oceania, India	Bhat and Ningomba 1997, Chelliah 1997
Miwok (Southern Sierra)	Penutian	Miwokan	1.000	N. America, USA	Broadbent 1964

Appendix 2. Languages in the WALS sample   193

Mixtec (Chalcatongo)	Oto-Manguean	Mixtec	0.33	N. America, Mexico	Macaulay 1982, Macaulay 1996
Mokilese	Austronesian	Micronesian	0.084	SEA and Oceania, Micronesia	Harrison 1976
Mundari	Austro-Asiatic	Munda	0.5	SEA and Oceania, India	Osada 1992
Mupun	Afro-Asiatic	West Chadic	0.1	Africa, Nigeria	Fraizyngier 1993
Murle	Nilo-Saharan	Surmic	0.08	Africa, Sudan, Ethiopia	Arensen 1982
Nahuatl (North Pueblo)	Uto-Aztecan	Aztecan	0.083	N. America, Mexico	Brockway 1984
Nahuatl (Tetelcingo)	Uto-Aztecan	Aztecan	0.083	N. America, Mexico	Tuggy 1977
Navajo	Na-Dene	Athapaskan-Eyak	0.5	N. America, USA	Haile 1926, Young 1992
Ndyuka	Creole	English based Creole	0.5	S. America, Surinam, Fr. Guiana	Huttar and Huttar 1994
Nenets	Uralic	Samoyedic	0.5	Eurasia, Russia	Salminen 1998
Ngiyambaa	Australian	Pama-Nyungan	0.036	A-NG, Australia	Donaldson 1980
Nivkh	Nivkh	Nivkh	1.000	Eurasia, Russia	Panfilov 1965, Otaina 1978, Gruzdeva 1998
Nunggubuyu	Australian	Nunggubuyu	0.072	A-NG, Australia	Heath 1982, Heath 1984
Oneida	Iroquoian	Iroquoian	0.5	N. America, Canada	Karin Michelson, p.c.
Oromo (Boraana)	Afro-Asiatic	Cushitic, Eastern	0.05	Africa, Kenya	Stroomer 1995
Oromo (Harar)	Afro-Asiatic	Cushitic, Eastern	0.05	Africa, Ethiopia	Owens 1985
Otomí (Ixtenco)	Oto-Manguean	Otomian	0.34	N. America, Mexico	Lastra 1998
Pashto	Indo-European	Iranian	0.031	Eurasia, Pakistan/Afghanistan	Henrik Liljegren, p.c.
Passamaquoddy	Algic	Algonquian	0.5	N. America, Canada	Sherwood 1986, Benjamin Bruening, p.c.
Persian	Indo-European	Iranian	0.031	Eurasia, Iran	Khanlari 1979, Lazard 1992, Mahootian 1997. Leila Naseh, p. c.
Pipil	Uto-Aztecan	Aztecan	0.084	N. America, El Salvador	Campbell 1985
Pirahã	Mura	Mura	1.000	S. America, Brazil	Everett 1986

Table A2. (cont.)

Language	Phylum	Genus	Weight value	Linguistic area, country	Sources
Polish	Indo-European	Slavic	0.014	Eurasia, Poland	Stone 1980, Mazur 1983, Marcin Kilarski, p.c.
Pomo (Eastern)	Hokan	Pomo	0.5	N. America, USA	McLendon 1975, McLendon 1996
Quechua (Imbabura)	Quechuan	Quechuan	1.000	S. America, Ecuador	Cole 1985
Rama	Chibchan	Rama	0.5	S. America, Nicaragua	Grinevald 1990
Rapanui	Austronesian	Oceanic	0.031	SEA and Oceania, Chile	Du Feu 1996
Russian	Indo-European	Slavic	0.014	Eurasia, Russia	Es'kova 1985, Pirogova 1991, Wade 2000, Maria Koptjevskaja-Tamm, p.c.
Samoan	Austronesian	Oceanic	0.036	SEA and Oceania, Samoa	Mosel and Hovhaugen 1994, Niklas and Aiga Jonsson, p.c.
Sango	Creole	Ngbandi based Creole	0.5	Africa, Central African Republic	Samarin 1967, Thornell 1997
Sanuma	Yanomam	Yanomam	1.000	S. America, Brazil	Borgman 1990
Selknam	Chon	Chon	1.000	S. America, Argentina	Najis 1973
Semelai	Austro-Asiatic	Aslian	0.125	SEA and Oceania, Malaysia	Kruspe 1999
Seneca	Iroquoian	Iroquoian	0.5	N. America, USA	Chafe 1996
Sentani	Trans-New Guinea	Sentani	0.045	A-NG, Indonesia, Iryan Jaya	Cowan 1965
Serbo-Croatian	Indo-European	Slavic	0.0105	Eurasia, Serbia, Croatia	Subotic and Forbes 1918, Partridge 1964, Elvira Veselinovic, Vladan Boskovic, p.c.
Shipibo-Konibo	Panoan	Panoan	1.000	S. America, Peru	Valenzuela 1997
Slave	Na-Dene	Athapaskan-Eyak	0.5	N. America, Canada	Rice 1989, Keren Rice, p.c.
Slovak	Indo-European	Slavic	0.007	Eurasia, Slovakia	De Bray 1980a, Mistrik 1981

Appendix 2. Languages in the WALS sample 195

Language	Family	Subgroup	Value	Area	References
Slovene	Indo-European	Slavic	0.0105	Eurasia, Slovenia	Derbyshire 1993, Albretti 1997, Herrity 2000
Songhay (Koyraboro Senni)	Nilo-Saharan	Songhai	0.17	Africa, Mali	Heath 1999
Sorbian (Upper)	Indo-European	Slavic	0.014	Eurasia, Germany	de Bray 1980a, Schuster-Shewc 1996
Sotho (Southern)	Niger-Congo	Bantoid	0.00275	Africa, Lesotho	Jacottet, 1927
Spanish	Indo-European	Italic	0.0625	Eurasia, Spain	Butt and Benjamin 1988
Squamish	Salish	Central Salish	1.000	N. America, Canada	Kuipers 1967, Peter Jacobs, p.c.
Suena	Trans-New Guinea	Binanderean	0.083	A-NG, Papua New Guinea	Wilson 1974
Supyire	Niger-Congo	Gur	0.033	Africa, Mali	Carlson 1994
Swahili	Niger-Congo	Bantoid	0.0055	Africa, Tanzania	Ashton 1947, Loogman 1965
Swedish	Indo-European	Germanic	0.0625	Eurasia, Sweden	personal knowledge
Taba	Austronesian	South Halmanera	0.251	SEA and Oceania, Indonesia	Bowden 1997
Tagalog	Austronesian	Meso-Philippine	0.1	SEA and Oceania, Philippines	Schachter 1972, McFarland 1976, Ramos and Bautista 1986
Tamazight (Central Atlas)	Afro-Asiatic	Berber	0.2	Africa, Morocco	Hamid Ouali, p.c.
Tepehuan (Northern)	Uto-Aztecan	Tepiman	0.125	N. America, Mexico	Bascom 1982
Thai	Tai-Kadai	Kam-Tai	1.000	SEA and Oceania, Thailand	Noss 1964, Yates and Tryon 1971
Tiwi	Australian	Tiwian	0.143	A-NG, Australia	Osborne 1974
Trumai	Trumai	Trumai	1.000	S. America, Brazil	Guirardello 1999
Tukang Besi	Austronesian	Sulawesi	0.1	SEA and Oceania, Indonesia, Sulawesi	Donohue 1999, Mark Donohue, p.c.
Turkana	Nilo-Saharan	Nilotic	0.04	Africa, Kenya	Heine 1980, Dimmendaal 1983
Turkish	Altaic	Turkic	0.34	Eurasia, Turkey	Lewis 1967, Underhill 1976, Kari Fraurud, p.c.
Ukrainian	Indo-European	Slavic	0.014	Eurasia, Ukraine	Medushevsky and Zyatovska. 1963, Humesky 1980, Pugh and Press 1999

Table A2. (cont.)

Language	Phylum	Genus	Weight value	Linguistic area, country	Sources
Usan	Trans-New Guinea	Adelbert Range	0.165	A-NG, Papua New Guinea	Reesnik 1987, Ger Reesnik, p.c.
Ute	Uto-Aztecan	Numic	0.083	N. America, USA	Givón and Southern Ute Tribe 1980
Vietnamese	Austro-Asiatic	Viet-Muong	0.125	SEA and Oceania, Viet Nam	Thompson 1965, Nguyen 1997
Warao	Warao	Warao	1.000	S. America, Venezuela	Romero-Figeroa 1997
Wari'	Chapacura-Wanham	Chapacura-Wanham	1.000	S. America, Brazil	Everett and Kern 1997
Wichita	Caddoan	Caddoan	1.000	N. America, USA	Rood 1976
Wolaytta	Afro-Asiatic	Omotic	0.2	Africa, Ethiopia	Lamberti and Sottile 1997
Yagua	Peba-Yaguan	Peba-Yaguan	1.000	S. America, Peru	Payne and Payne 1990
Yaqui	Uto-Aztecan	Cahita	0.125	N. America, Mexico	Johnson 1962, Dedrick and Casad 1999
Yimas	Sepik-Ramu	Nor-Pondo	0.5	A-NG, Papua New Guinea	Foley 1991
Yoruba	Niger-Congo	Defoid	0.033	Africa, Nigeria	Ward 1952, Bamgbose 1966
Yukaghir	Yukaghir	Yukaghir	1.000	Eurasia, Russia	Maslova 1999
Yup'ik, Central	Eskimo-Aleut	Eskimo-Aleut	0.5	N. America, USA	Jacobson and Jacobson 1995
Zulu	Niger-Congo	Bantoid	0.00275	Africa, Malawi	O'Neil 1913, Ziervogel et al. 1967
Zuni	Zuni	Zuni	1.000	N. America, USA	Newman 1996

APPENDIX 3

Additional data

Table A3. Verb-meaning index

Verb meaning	Non-categorial suppletion Lgs	Non-categorial suppletion W	Tense suppletion Lgs	Tense suppletion W	Aspect suppletion Lgs	Aspect suppletion W	Suppletion in several tense–aspect categories Lgs	Suppletion in several tense–aspect categories W	Suppletive perfect Lgs	Suppletive perfect W	Suppletive imperative Lgs	Suppletive imperative W	Suppletion in verbal number Lgs	Suppletion in verbal number W
be big	–	–	–	–	–	–	–	–	–	–	–	–	3	1.84
be long	–	–	–	–	–	–	–	–	–	–	–	–	1	1
be short	–	–	–	–	–	–	–	–	–	–	–	–	1	1
be small	–	–	–	–	–	–	–	–	–	–	–	–	2	1.34
aim	–	–	–	–	1	0.014	–	–	–	–	–	–	–	–
arrive	–	–	–	–	–	–	–	–	–	–	–	–	3	0.452
be/exist	31	7.29	22	4.03	–	–	3	0.26	8	0.171	3	1.253	2	1.5
be lost	–	–	–	–	–	–	–	–	–	–	–	–	1	1
beat	–	–	–	–	1	0.011	–	–	–	–	–	–	1	0.1
become	–	–	1	0.17	2	0.29	–	–	–	–	–	–	–	–
become cold	–	–	–	–	1	0.165	–	–	–	–	–	–	–	–
become, happen, go	–	–	–	–	1	0.5	–	–	–	–	–	–	–	–
belong to	–	–	–	–	–	–	–	–	–	–	–	–	1	0.5
bet	–	–	–	–	–	–	–	–	–	–	–	–	1	0.125
bite off	–	–	–	–	–	–	–	–	–	–	–	–	1	0.34
break	–	–	–	–	–	–	–	–	–	–	–	–	2	1
bring/carry	–	–	–	–	3	0.58	–	–	–	–	–	–	–	–
catch	–	–	–	–	2	0.028	–	–	–	–	–	–	–	–
come out (in quality)	–	–	–	–	–	–	–	–	–	–	–	–	1	0.5
come/go	12	2.03	17	2.29	16	4.176	12	1.56	3	0.03	34	8.28	14	6.033
cry	–	–	–	–	1	0.125	–	–	–	–	–	–	–	–
cut	–	–	–	–	–	–	–	–	–	–	–	–	1	1
die[a]	2	0.5	3	0.83	2	0.495	–	–	–	–	–	–	12	4.253

Note: Lgs = number of languages where verb X shows a particular king of tense-aspect suppletion; W = weight value sum of these languages
[a] In Lezgian this verbs means also 'kill'.

Table A3. (cont.)

Verb meaning	Non-categorial suppletion Lgs	Non-categorial suppletion W	Tense suppletion Lgs	Tense suppletion W	Aspect suppletion Lgs	Aspect suppletion W	Suppletion in several tense–aspect categories Lgs	Suppletion in several tense–aspect categories W	Suppletive perfect Lgs	Suppletive perfect W	Suppletive imperative Lgs	Suppletive imperative W	Suppletion in verbal number Lgs	Suppletion in verbal number W
do	1	0.06	1	0.083	6	1.051	2	1.33	–	–	2	0.33	–	–
do while walking, walk	–	–	–	–	–	–	–	–	–	–	–	–	1	0.5
drink	–	–	–	–	1	–	–	–	–	–	–	–	–	–
drive something out	–	–	–	–	–	–	–	–	–	–	–	–	1	0.083
dwell	1	–	–	–	–	–	–	–	–	–	–	–	–	–
eat	2	1.01	1	0.5	4	0.54	–	–	–	–	–	–	3	–
fall	–	–	–	–	–	–	–	–	–	–	1	0.165	7	4.455
fall in water	–	–	–	–	–	–	–	–	–	–	–	–	1	0.5
fly	–	–	–	–	–	–	–	–	–	–	–	–	1	0.083
get	–	–	2	0.188	–	–	–	–	–	–	–	–	1	0.17
get up	–	–	–	–	–	–	–	–	–	–	–	–	2	0.625
give	3	1.23	4	0.68	3	1.29	1	0.33	–	–	5	0.795	3	1.005
go about	–	–	–	–	–	–	–	–	–	–	–	–	1	1
go along doing X	–	–	–	–	–	–	–	–	–	–	–	–	1	0.167
go around something out of sight	–	–	–	–	–	–	–	–	–	–	–	–	1	0.167
grasp	–	–	–	–	–	–	–	–	–	–	–	–	1	0.125
have	3	0.38	2	1.01	–	–	–	–	–	–	–	–	–	–
hear	–	–	–	–	2	0.048	–	–	–	–	–	–	–	–
hit	1	0.17	–	–	–	–	–	–	–	–	–	–	2	1.340
hold	–	–	–	–	–	–	–	–	–	–	–	–	2	1.083
injure	–	–	–	–	–	–	–	–	–	–	–	–	1	0.340
jump	–	–	–	–	–	–	–	–	–	–	–	–	1	0.330
kill	1	0.17	–	–	–	–	–	–	–	–	–	–	9	3.958
lay/put	–	–	–	–	6	0.181	–	–	–	–	–	–	5	3.830
lie	–	–	–	–	–	–	–	–	–	–	–	–	12	4.743

Appendix 3. Additional data

live	–	–	–	0.083	–	–	–	–
make netbag	–	–	1	–	–	–	–	1	0.330
make noise	–	–	–	–	–	–	–	1	1
move	–	–	–	–	0.007	–	–	1	1
negative auxliaries	–	–	–	–	–	–	2	0.750	–
not like	–	–	–	–	–	–	–	1	0.330
pick up	–	–	–	–	–	–	–	1	0.330
pull out	–	–	–	–	–	–	–	2	0.840
release	–	–	–	–	–	–	–	1	1
remove	–	–	–	–	–	–	–	1	0.083
return	–	–	–	–	–	–	–	2	0.423
rise	–	–	–	–	–	–	–	2	1
run	–	–	1	0.17	–	–	–	4	1.965
say/speak	5	2.42	3	0.3	9	0.845	1	–	2	0.415	1	0.083
see/watch/look	1	0.17	1	0.330	7	1.282	–	1	0.084	–	–
shoot	1	0.17	–	–	–	–	–	–	–
sit	–	–	2	0.670	–	–	–	1	0.167	14	8.038
sit, lie	–	–	–	–	–	–	–	1	0.340
sleep	–	–	–	–	–	–	–	6	2.336
stampede	–	–	–	–	–	–	–	1	0.330
stand	–	–	1	0.021	–	–	–	8	4.538
stay	–	–	3	0.542	–	–	–	–	–
start	–	–	–	–	–	–	–	3	0.830
store	–	–	–	–	–	–	–	1	0.5
strike, swear	1	0.17	–	–	–	–	–	–	–
swim	–	–	–	–	–	–	–	1	0.5
take	–	–	–	–	10	0.568	–	2	0.029	9	4.965
think so, hope	1	1	–	–	–	–	–	–	–
throw	–	–	–	–	2	0.025	–	–	5	3.840
visit	–	–	–	–	–	–	–	1	0.125
wake up	–	–	1	0.5	–	–	–	–	–
walk	–	–	1	0.5	–	–	–	2	0.5

Suppletion in verb paradigms

Table A4. Number of suppletive verbs per language

Language name	Tot	Non-categorial	Tense	Aspect	Several TA categories	Perfect only
Abkhaz	1		1 'be'			
Alamblak	1		1 'go'			
Armenian (Eastern)	10	1 'be'		9 'come', 'eat', 'give' 'do' 'put' 'carry' 'become' 'cry'		
Awa Pit	1	1 'be'				
Basque	1	1 'be'				
Bengali	2		1 'be'	1 'go'		
Brahui	2	1 'be'	1 'go'			
Bulgarian	3	1 'be'		1 'come'		1
Burushaski	2	1		1 'come'		
Belorussian	6		1 'exist, have'	3 'say' 'take' 'catch'	2 'go' 'come'	
Carib	1	1 'be'				
Chamorro	2		2 'be at' 'exist, have'			
Chinantec (Lealao)	2	1 ''go'		1 'come'		
Czech	5	1 'be'		2 'take' 'put'	2 'go' 'come'	
Dani (Lower Grand Valley)	1		1 'go'			
Dutch	2	1 'be'	1 'go'			
English	2	1 'be'	1 'go'			
Ewe	1		1 'be at'			
Finnish	1	1 'be'				
French	3	3[a] 'be', 'have' 'go'			3 'be', 'have', 'go'	
Fur	10	6 'be', 'die', 'go', 'kill', 'look', 'strike', 'swear'	4 'become' 'come' 'run' 'sit'			
Georgian	9		3 'be' 'give' 'have an inanimate object'	2 'see' 'drink'	4 'come' 'say' 'tell' 'do'	
German	3	1 'be'	2 'go' 'stay'			
Greek (Modern)	4	1 'be'		3 'say' 'see' 'eat'		1 'be'
Hebrew (Modern)	2		2 'exist, have' 'say'			
Hindi	2	1 'be'		1 'go'		
Hixkaryana		1 'be'				

Note: Tot = total of suppletive verbs according to tense and aspect; TA = tense–aspect; non-categorial = non-categorial suppletion

Table A4. (*cont.*)

Language name	Tot	Non-categorial	Tense	Aspect	Several TA categories	Perfect only
Hungarian		3 'be' 'go' 'come'				
Hunzib	1	1 'be'	1 'be'			
Ika	1			1 'go'		
Ingush	8	4 'come' 'go' 'die' 'speak'	1 'see'		3 'be' 'do' 'give'	
Irish	10	1 'be'	4 'say' 'eat' 'hear' 'see'	1 'carry'	4 'go' 'come' 'give' 'get'	
Kannada	1		1 'be at'			
Kanuri	3		3 'stay, live' 'come' 'die'			
Kewa	2		2 'go' 'come'			
Khoekhoe	1		1 'be (of property)'			
Koasati	4	4 'be (a member of a group), hold an office' 'say' 'dwell' 'think so hope'				
Kuot	4		4 'sit, live' 'walk' 'fall' 'wake up'			
Latvian	2	1 'be'	2 'go' 'give'			
Lakhota	1	1 'say'				
Lezgian	10		1 'be of identity'	9 'come' 'come again' 'do' 'give' 'eat' 'become' 'become cold' 'kill, die'		
Macushi	1	1 'be'				
Macedonian	2	1 'be'				1 'go'
Maltese	1	1 'say'				
Mara	3			3 'go/come' 'tell' 'take'		
Maung	1		1 'go'			
Mixtec (Chalcatongo)	3		1 'die'	2 'come' 'go'		
Mundari	2		2 'be of identity' 'be, exist'			
Nahuatl (North Pueblo)	2		2 'be' 'go'			
Nahuatl (Tetelcingo)	3		1 'be' 'come'	1 'see'		
Nunggubuyu	1			1 'go'		
Oneida	1			1 'say'		

Table A4. (cont.)

Language name	Tot	Non-categorial	Tense	Aspect	Several TA categories	Perfect only
Oromo (Harar)	1		1 'exist'			
Otomí (Ixtenco)	1			1 'go'		
Pashto	3	1 'be'		2 'go' 'come'		
Persian	3		1 'be'	2 'come' 'see'		
Pipil	2		1 'come'			1 'see'
Polish	6	1 'be'		4 'say' 'see' 'watch' 'take'	2 'go' 'come'	
Russian	6		1 'exist, have'	3 'say' 'take' 'put'	2 'go, walk' 'come'	
Serbo-Croatian	6	1 'be'		3 'say' 'look' 'hear'	2 'come' 'go'	2 'come' 'go'
Slave	3	1 'say'		2 'become, happen, go' 'do'		
Slovak	6	1 'be'		3 'take' 'put' 'move'	2 'go' 'come'	
Slovene	8	1 'be'		5 'say' 'do' 'take' 'throw' 'hit, beat'	2 'go' 'come'	
Sorbian (Upper)	6	1 'be'		4 'take' 'put' 'aim' 'throw'	2 'go' 'come'	
Spanish	6	6[a] 'be' 'go' 'do, make' 'give' 'have' 'say'	2 'do, make', 'give'		4 'be', 'go', 'have', 'say'	
Suena	6		6 'be' 'go' 'come' 'say' 'do' 'live'			
Supyire	3		1 'be'	2 'come' 'hear'		
Swedish	3		3 'be' 'go' 'get'			
Taba	1	1 'have'				
Tepehuan (Northern)	3	1 'come'		2 'do' 'eat'		
Tukang Besi	1		1 'give'			
Turkana	1		1 'be somewhere, have'			
Ukrainian	6		1 'exist, have'	3 'say' 'take' 'catch'	2 'come' 'go'	
Usan	4	2 'give' 'shoot' 'hit'	2 'say' 'stay'			
Wichita	1			1 'go'		
Yimas	1	1 'be'				

[a] These verbs are given dual classification in this table for the following reasons: all of them lack a stem for the present tense, so they are included in the group of verbs with non-categorial suppletion. Since they have stems for the remaining tense-aspect categories, they are shown their too. In all counts, I have counted them on the group of non-categorial suppletion only.

Appendix 3. Additional data 203

Table A5. Imperfective vs. perfective aspectual pairs in Slavic languages

Group	Language	'say/speak' IPFV	'say/speak' PFV	'take' IPFV	'take' PFV	'lay, put' IPFV	'lay, put' PFV
EAST	Russian	*govorit'*	*skazat'*	*brat'*	*vzjat'*	*klast'*	*položit'*
	Belorussian	*kazats'*	*skazats'*	*brats'*	*uzjats'*	*klas'tsy*	*paklas'tsy*
		gavaryt					
	Ukrainian	*kazati*	*skazati*	*brati*	*uzjati*	*klasti*	*poklasti*
		govorit					
WEST	Polish	*mówić*	*powiedzieć*	*brać*	*wziąć*	*klaść*	*położyć*
	Upper Sorbian	*prajić*	*prajić*	*brać*	*wzać*	*ktac*	*położyć*
			riesć / powěsć				
	Czech	*říkati*	*říci*	*bráti*	*vzíti*	*klasti*	*položiti*
		mluviti					
	Slovak	*vraviet'*	*povedat'*	*brat'*	*vzjat'*	*klast'*	*položit*
		hovorit'					
SOUTH	Slovene	*praviti* 'say'	*reči* 'say'	*jemati*	*vzeti*	*postavljati*	*postaviti*
		govoriti 'say, tell'	*povédati* 'tell'				*položiti*
	Serbo-Croatian	*reći*		*uzimati*	*uzeti*	*stavljati*	*staviti*
	Macedonian	*govoriti*	*izgovoriti*				
		zboruva		*zema*	*zeme*	*klava*	*klade*
		veli					*položi*
		kažuva	*kaže*				
			reče				
	Bulgarian	*govorja*		*vzemam*	*vzema*	*slagam*	*složa*
		(pri)kazvam	*kaža (reka)*[a]				
	OCS	*(rešti)*	*rešti*	*vazimati*	*vazęnti*	*polagati*	*položiti*
		glagolati				*klasti*	

[a] This latter verb is very rarely used, and stylistically marked.

Table A5. (Cont.)

Group	language	'see/look/watch' IPFV	PFV	'throw' IPFV	PFV	'catch' IPFV	PFV
EAST	Russian	videt'	uvidet'	metat'	metnut'/vymetat'	lovit'	poimat' (ulovit')
	Belorus'	smotret' bačic' nagljadac'	posmotret' ubačic' ugledec'	brocat' kidac' [b]	brosit' kinuc'	lavic'	ulavic'/zlavic'
	Ukrainian	bačiti ogljadati	ubačiti ugljaditi	kidati metati	kinuti metnuti	loviti	(s)piimati
WEST	Polish	widzieć oglądać spoglądać	zobaczyć obejrzeć spojrzeć	rzucac	rzucic	lapac	zlapac
	U. Sorbian	widźeć c hladać	pohladać	mjetac	cisnyc	lojic popadowac	popadnyc
	Czech	vidĕti hledĕti	uvidĕti [a] pohledĕti	házet	hodir	chytat	chytit
	Slovak	vidiet'	uvidiet' pozriet'	hadzat' metat'/vrhat'	hodit' metnut'/vrhnut'(sa)	chytat' lapat'/lovit'	chytit'(sa) ulapit'/ulovit'
SOUTH	Slovene	videti	uvideti	metati	vreči	loviti	uloviti
	Serbo-Croatian	videti gledati	videti pogledati	bacati	baciti	xvatati	uxvatiti
	Macedonian	viduva (se) gleda	vidi	metka frla	metne fŕli	(se) faka	(se) fali
	Bulgarian	viždam gledam	vidja pogledna	mjatam xvarljam	metna xvarlja	lovja xvaštam	ulovja xvana
	OCS	vidĕti	uzirĕti	metati	vrĕšti	loviti	uloviti

[b] A root consonant, especially the stops t and d can be lost before the perfectivizing suffix -nu-; thereby the pairs kidać vs. kinuti which might look like different or irregular formations to readers not familiar with Slavic morphology.
c Neither the grammar Schuster-Shewc (1996), nor the consulted dictionaries specify aspect for this verb. I think it might be a bi-aspectual verb judging by only sporadic examples but I am not certain.
[d] With a slight meaning change 'to catch sight of'.

Appendix 3. Additional data 205

Group	Language	'do' IPFV	'do' PFV	'beat' IPFV	'beat' PFV	'move' IPFV	'move' PFV
EAST	Russian	delat'	sdelat'	bit' udarjat'	pobit' udarit'	dvigat'(sja)	dvinut'(sja)
	Belorussian	rabic'	zrabic'	bic' udarjac'	pabic'	ruxac' perejaxdzac'	rušyc'
	Ukrainian	robiti	zrobiti	biti udarjat	pobiti	ruxati	ruxnuti
WEST	Polish	robić	zrobić	uderzac	uderzyc	ruszac (sie)	ruszyc (sie)
	U. Sorbian	činić dźělać 'work, make'	sćinić	bić	pobić dyrić	hibać	zhybać, hibyć na-/z-hnuć
	Czech	dělati	udělati	(roz)bijet	bit udeřit	hybat	hnout
	Slovak	robit'	urobit'	bit' mlatit'	zbit' namlatit'	hybat'	hnut'
SOUTH	Slovene	delati	storiti	tolči[e] biti	udariti	premikati	premakniti (se)
	Serbo-Croatian	početi, počenjati činiti	narediti učiniti	tući udarati	istući udariti	pomerati	pomeriti
	Macedonian	pravi	napravi	bie čuka	nabie čukne udri	(se) dvižI (se) mrdnuva	mrdne
	Bulgarian	pravja	napravja	bija 'beat' udrjam 'hit'	nabija udarja	dviža (se) mərdam	mrədna
	OCS	dělati tvoriti	sədělati sətvoriti	biti udarjati	pobiti udariti	dvižati sę	dvignǫti

[e] These verbs are listed as suppletive according to aspect only in (Albretti, 1997: 168); the latest grammar of Slovene, (Herrity, 2000) does not list them.

Table A6. Number of verbs with suppletive imperatives per language

Language	Number of verbs and verb meanings
!Xu	(2) 'come', 'go'
Acoma	(1) 'go'
Alagwa	(4) 'come', 'go', 'go, leave' 'give'
Arabic (Egyptian)	(1) 'come'
Arabic (Moroccan)	(1) 'go'
Arabic (Tunisian)	(1) 'come'
Armenian (Eastern)	(1) 'give'
Bulgarian	(1) 'come'
Carib	(2) 'go', 'say'
Finnish	(1) negative auxiliary
Georgian	(1) 'come'
Greek (Modern)	(1) 'come'
Guarani	(1) 'go'
Hopi	(1) 'sit down'
Hungarian	(1) 'come'
Ingush	(2) 'come', 'go'
Iraqw	(1) 'come'
Irish	(1) 'give'
Jakaltek	(2) 'come', 'go'
Kanuri	(1) 'come'
Krongo	(1) 'go'
Kunama	(3) 'come', 'go', 'enter'
Lezgian	(8) 'come', 'come back', 'go', 'go back', 'give', 'give temporarily', 'do again', 'eat'
Luvale	(1) 'come'
Makedonian	(1) 'come'
Maltese	(1) 'come'
Mataco	(1) 'be'
Mixtec (Chalcatongo)	(1) 'come'
Murle	(2) 'come', 'go'
Nahuatl (North Pueblo)	(3) 'come', 'go', 'be'
Nenets	(1) negative auxiliary
Oromo (Boraana)	(2) 'come', 'go'
Oromo (Harar)	(1) 'come'
Rama	(1) 'go'
Russian	(1) 'take'
Serbo-Croatian	(1) 'come'
Songhay (Koyraboro Senni)	(1) 'be'
Spanish	(1) 'go'
Swahili	(2) 'come', 'go'
Tamazight (Central Atlas)	(1) 'come'

Table A7. Number of verbal number pairs per language

Language Name	Number of verb pairs/triples[a] and verb meanings
!Xu	(18): 'be big', 'belong to', 'break' (intransitive), 'break' (transitive), 'come', 'come out, rise', 'descend', 'own', 'kill', 'pull down, place', 'rise, stand up', 'sit', 'stand', 'store', 'take out', 'die', 'lie d 'throw away', 'walk'
Ainu	(8): 'be', 'come', 'go', 'kill', 'place', 'sit', 'stand', 'take'
Amele	(2): 'go', 'get, take'
Barasano	(1): 'move'
Burushaski	(5): 'fall for class x nouns'[a]
Cahuilla	(3): 'die', 'kill', 'lie'
Canela-Kraho	(4): 'enter', 'kill', 'put', 'throw down'
Comanche	(11): 'die', 'drive out', 'enter/leave enclosed space', 'go inside', 'hold, carry', 'kill for food', 'lie down', 'remove', 'say', 'sleep', 'talk'
Georgian	(4): 'be seated', 'fall down', 'sit down', 'throw down'
Hopi	(4): 'arrive', 'be eating', 'go along doing X', 'go around doing X',
Imonda	(6): 'eat', 'lie', 'make netbag', 'not like', 'sleep', 'stand'
Ingush	(10): 'come', 'die', 'fall', 'jump', 'go', 'lie [animate SUBJ]', 'lie [inanimate SUBJ]', 'lie down', 'run off', 'sit', 'take'
Ket	(1): 'drowse'
Kiowa	(12): 'be big, impotant', 'be small, young', 'be tall, long', 'be short', 'be, be sitting', 'be lying', 'be sitting [inanimate SUBJ]', 'drop, fall', 'land, fall against', 'lay', 'set, put in', 'sever'
Koasati	(13): 'dwell' (3), 'stand' (3), 'sit' (3), 'go about' (3), 'be lost', 'come', 'go', 'die', 'hit', 'make noise', 'pick something up', 'release something', 'run',
Krongo	(14): 'be small', 'be big', 'bite off', 'call', 'die', 'give', 'hit', 'injure', 'pull out', 'put', 'return', 'run away', 'take', 'throw',
Kunama	(2): 'come', 'go there'
Maricopa	(4): 'be located' (3), 'lie' (3), 'sit' (3), stand (3)
Mupun	(3): 'fall', 'hit', 'put'
Murle	(1): 'go'
Navajo	(8): 'go/come' (3), 'come out (in quality)', 'die', 'die of old age, hunger', 'lie/lay down' (3), 'run for shelter '(3), 'sit' (3)
Passamaquoddy	(1): 'walk'
Pomo (Eastern)	(6): 'give', 'kill', 'pull out something that resists', 'sit', 'stand',
Samoan	(2): 'come', 'go'
Shipibo-Konibo	(2): 'come', 'go'
Slave	(11): 'be seated' (3), 'die', 'eat' (3), 'fall down' (3), 'fall in water' (3), 'fight' (3), 'kill', 'sleep', 'start out [controlled]' (3), 'start out [uncontrolled]' (3), 'swim' (3)
Tepehuan (Northern)	(12): 'bet', 'come', 'die', 'fall', 'get up', 'go up', 'grasp', 'kill', 'lie down', 'run', 'visit', 'walk around'
Usan	(3): 'give', 'hit' 'shoot'
Ute	(8): 'enter', 'fly', 'lie down', 'kill', 'return', 'sit', 'sleep', 'stand'
Wari	(2): 'go', 'throw'
Wichita	(1): 'go'
Yaqui	(6): 'go', 'die', 'lie', 'lie down', 'sit', 'stand'
Zuni	(4): 'be standing', 'be in a sitting position', 'hold', 'take'

[a] A triple is indicated by a digit 3 in brackets, following the verb meaning.
[b] In Burushaski, the nouns are divided into the following classes: human males (class m), human females (class f), other nouns denoting animates and most concrete specific count nouns (class x); abstract, non-count /mass nouns and only a few count nouns (class y) (Tiffou 1995: 417)

Table A8. Verbal number pais: lexemic groups and verb meanings

Leximic group	Verb meaning	No	%	Weight values	% of total weight values sum
MOTION (intransitive)	go	14	8	6.619	8
	fall	7	4	4.455	5
	come	4	2	3.036	4
	run	4	2	1.965	2
	arrive	3	2	0.452	1
	enter	3	2	1.243	1
	start	3	2	0.830	1
	get up	2	1	0.625	1
	return	2	1	0.423	0
	rise	2	1	1.000	1
	walk	2	1	0.625	1
	fall in water	1	1	0.500	1
	fly	1	1	0.083	0
	go about	1	1	1.000	1
	go along doing X	1	1	0.167	0
	go around something out of sight	1	1	0.167	0
	jump	1	1	0.330	0
	move	1	1	1.000	1
	stampede	1	1	0.330	0
	swim	1	1	0.500	1
	visit	1	1	0.125	0
	walk, do while walking	1	1	0.500	1
MOTION (transitive)	put	5	3	3.830	4
	throw	5	3	3.840	4
	take	3	2	2.500	3
	give	2	1	0.840	1
	drive something out	1	1	0.083	0
	get, take	1	1	0.170	0
	grasp	1	1	0.125	0
	pick up	1	1	0.330	0
	pull out	2	1	0.840	1
	release	1	1	1.000	1
	remove	1	1	0.083	0
	take out	1	1	0.500	1
POSITION	sit	13	7	7.538	10
	lie	11	6	4.576	6
	stand	8	5	4.538	5
	hold	1	1	1.000	1
	hold, carry	1	1	0.083	0
	lie, exist, be	1	1	0.167	0
	sit, dwell	1	1	0.500	1
	sit, lie	1	1	0.340	0
	store	1	1	0.500	1

Note: No = number of languages in which the a verbal number pair for a certain sense is observed

Table A8. (cont.)

Leximic group	Verb meaning	No	%	Weight values	% of total weight values sum
DIE/INJURE	die	11	6	3.753	4
	kill	9	5	3.958	5
	break	2	1	1.000	1
	hit	2	1	1.340	2
	beat	1	1	0.100	0
	bite off	1	1	0.340	0
	cut	1	1	1.000	1
	die of old age/hunger	1	1	0.500	1
	injure	1	1	0.340	0
STATIVE VERBS	sleep	6	3	2.336	3
	big	3	2	1.840	2
	small	2	1	1.340	2
	be LOC	1	1	0.500	1
	be lost	1	1	1.000	1
	be, exist	1	1	1.000	1
	long	1	1	1.000	1
	short	1	1	1.000	1
OTHER	eat	3	2	0.997	1
	belong to	1	1	0.500	1
	bet	1	1	0.125	0
	come out (in quality)	1	1	0.500	1
	make netbag	1	1	0.330	0
	make noise	1	1	1.000	1
	not like	1	1	0.330	0
	say	1	1	0.083	0

210 Suppletion in verb paradigms

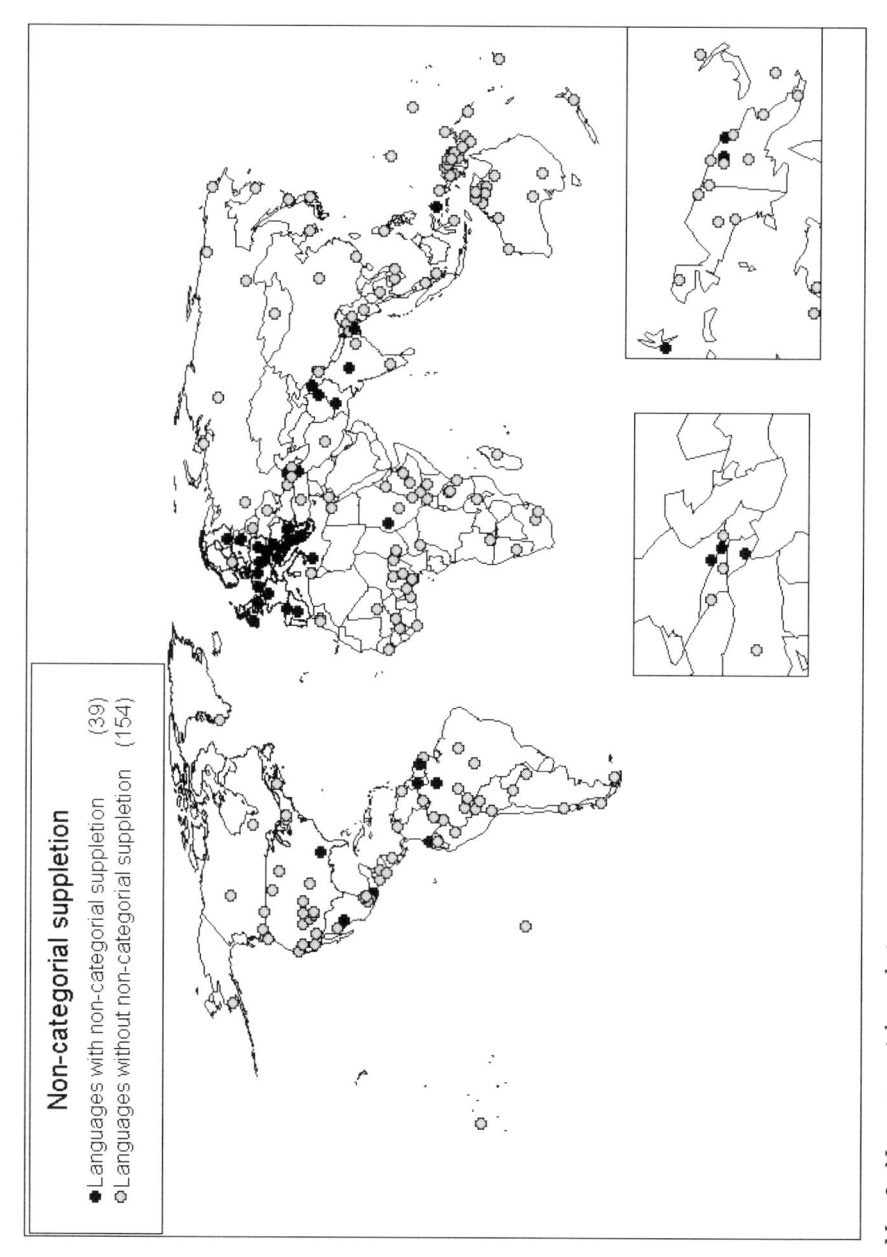

Map 2. Non-categorial suppletion

Appendix 3. Additional data   211

Categorial tense-aspect suppletion

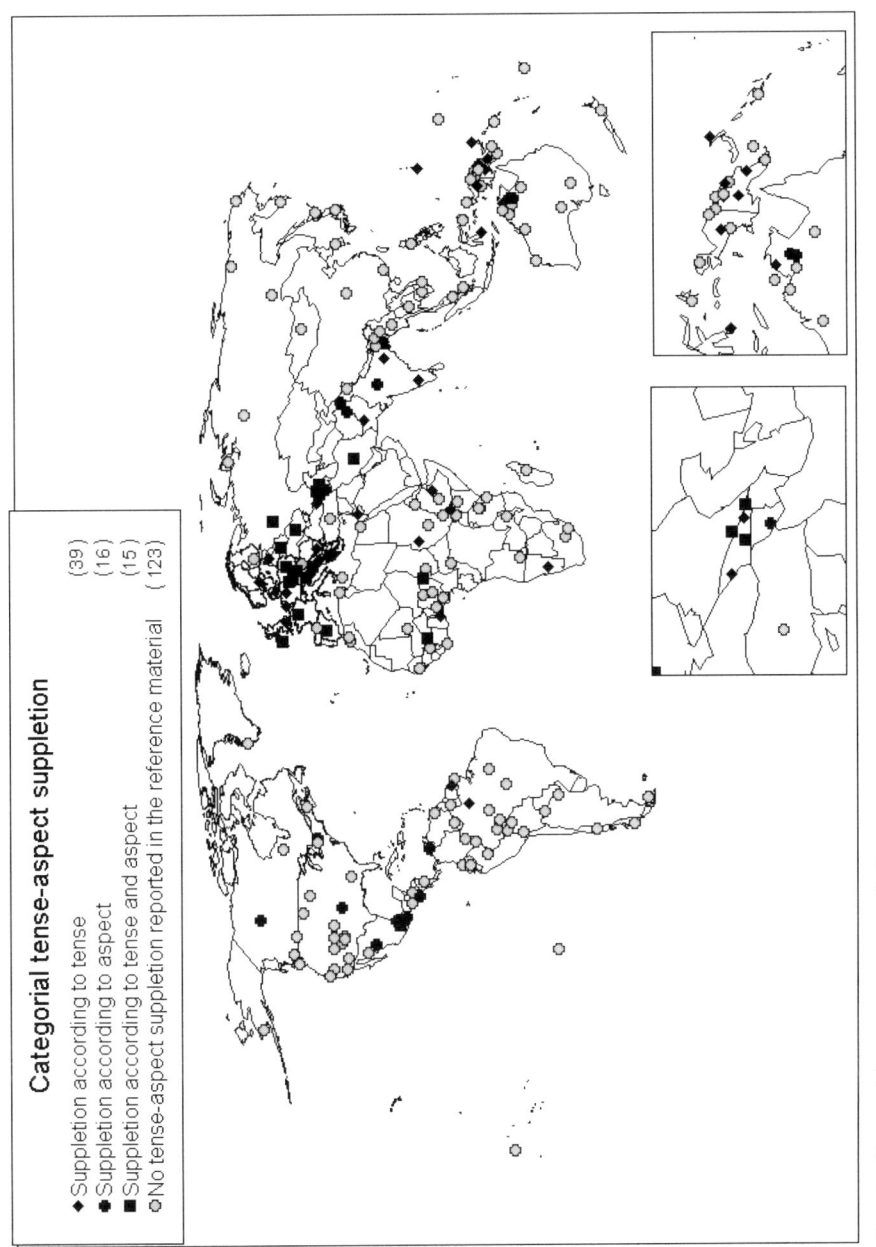

◆ Suppletion according to tense   (39)
✦ Suppletion according to aspect   (16)
■ Suppletion according to tense and aspect   (15)
○ No tense-aspect suppletion reported in the reference material (123)

Map 3. Categorial tense-aspect suppletion

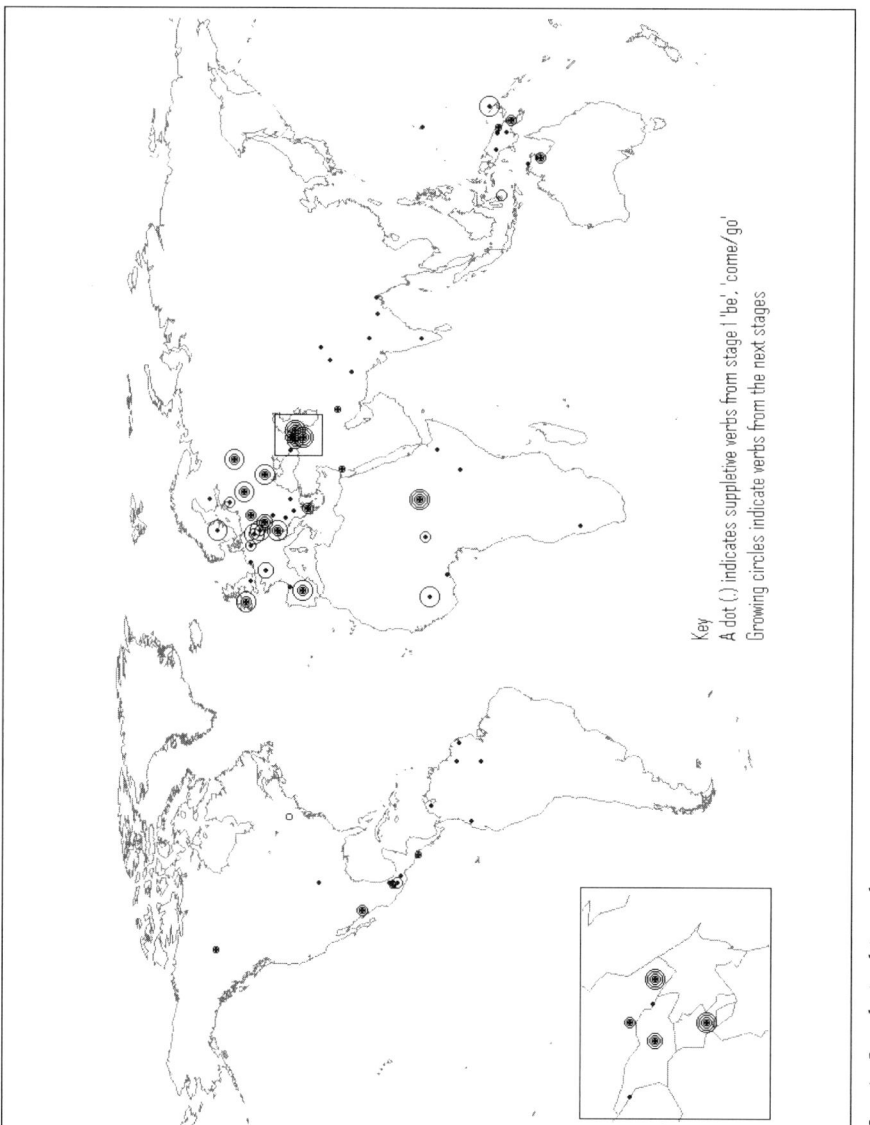

Map 4. Suppletive hierarchy

Appendix 3. Additional data 213

Suppletive Imperatives
▲ A regular and a suppletive imperative (8)
● Suppletive imperatives (33)
♦ Suppletive hortative (2)
○ No suppletive imperative in the reference material (154)

Map 5. Suppletive imperatives

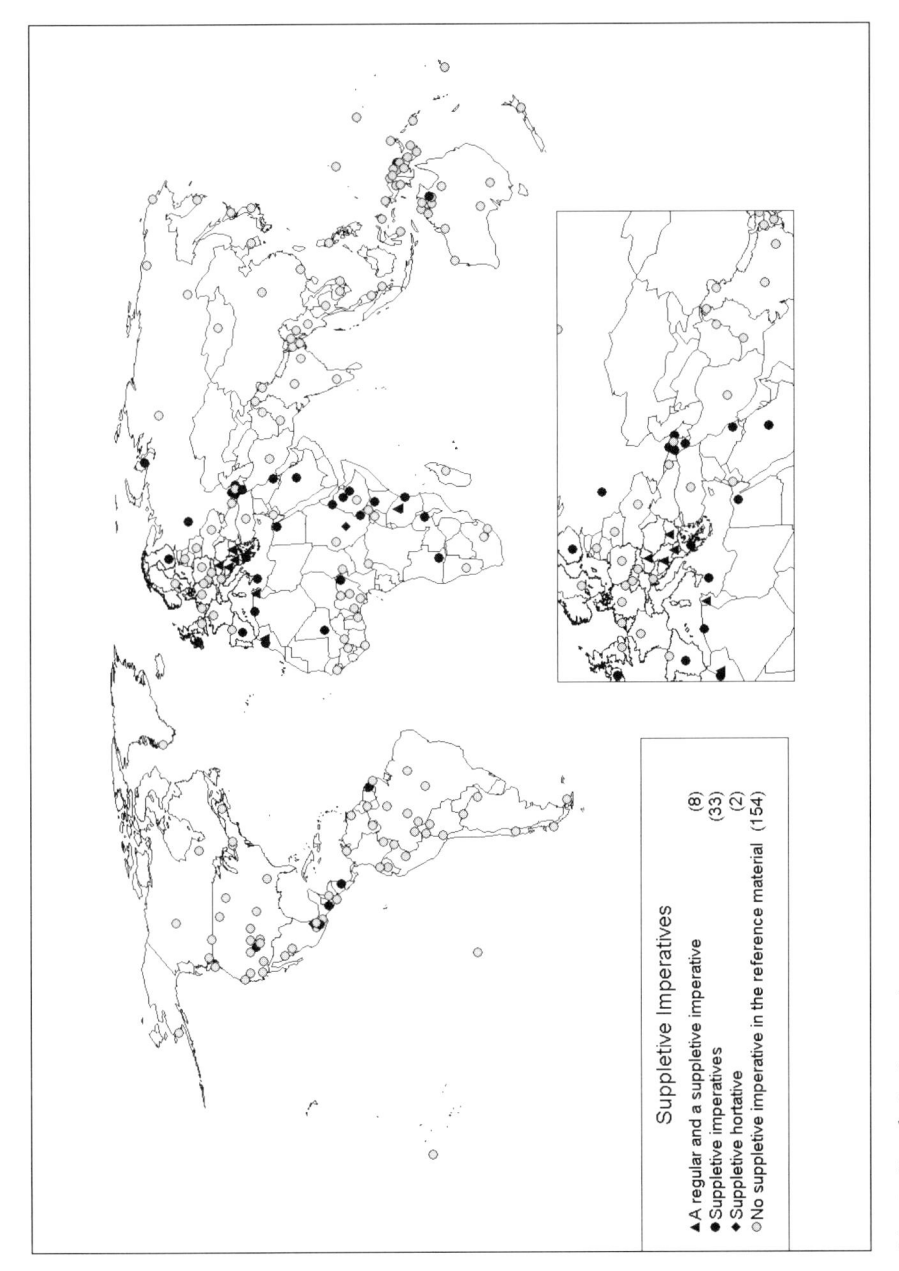

214 Suppletion in verb paradigms

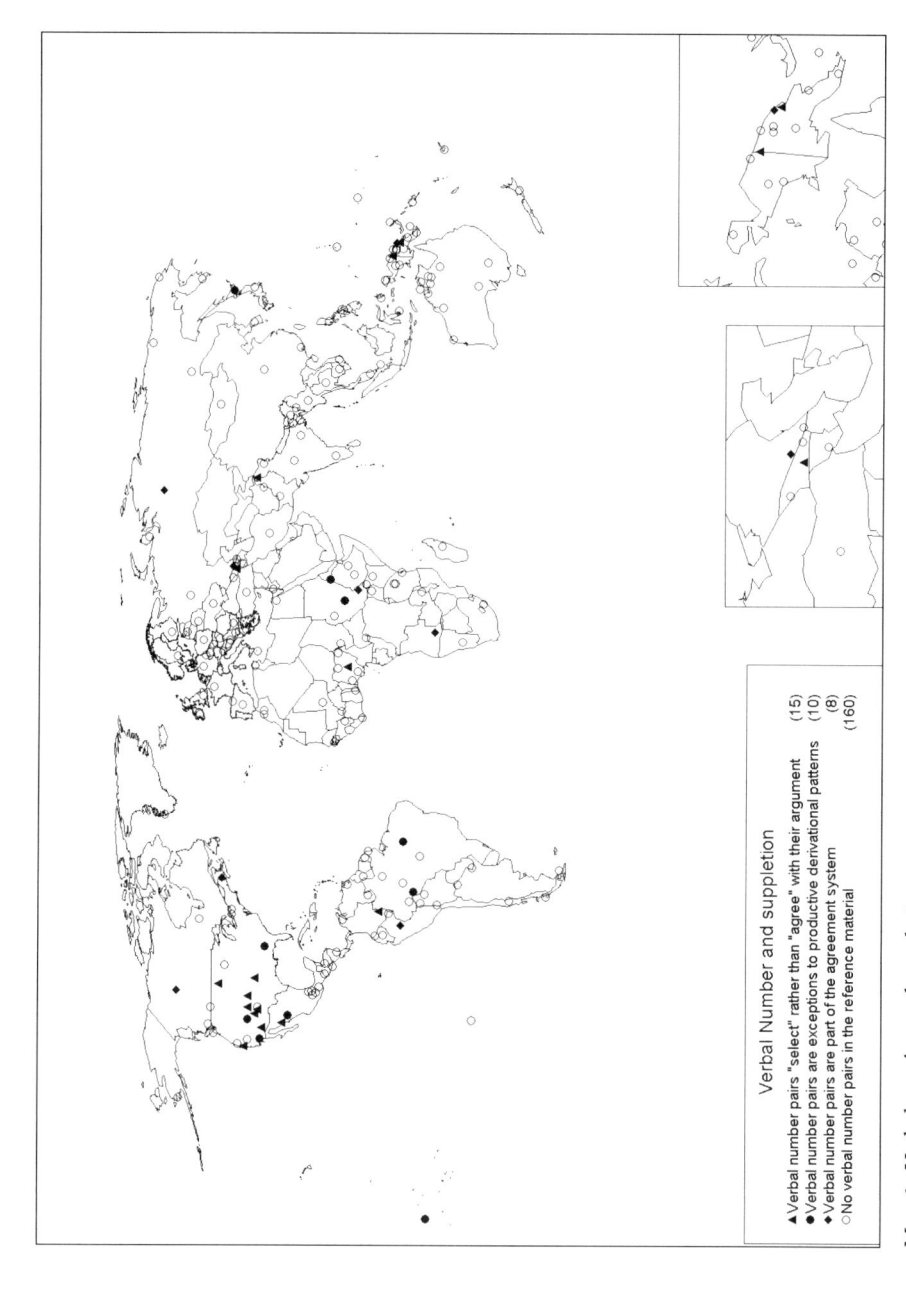

Map 6. Verbal number and suppletion

References

Abott, Miriam. 1991. Macushi. In *Handbook of Amazonian Languages,* Vol. 3, Desmond C. Derbyshire and Geoffrey Pullum (eds), 23–160. Berlin: Mouton de Gruyter.
Albert, Roy and Shaul, David Leedom. 1985. *A Concise Hopi and English Lexicon.* Amsterdam: John Benjamins.
Albretti, Andrea. 1997. *Slovene. A complete course for beginners.* London: Teach Yourself Books.
Anderson, Stephen. 1985. Inflectional morphology. In *Language Typology and Syntactic Description,* Timothy Shopen (ed.), 151–201. Cambridge: Cambridge University Press.
Andronov, M. S. 1980. *The Brahui Language.* Moscow: Nauka.
Arensen, Jon. 1982. *Murle Grammar*: Occasional Papers in the Study of Sudanese Languages. Sudan: Juba: College of Education, University of Juba and SIL.
Aronoff, Mark. 1976. *Word Formation in Generative Grammar.* Cambridge MA: The MIT Press. (Reprinted in 1979).
Aronoff, Mark and Anshen, Frank. 1998. Morphology and the lexicon: Lexicalization and productivity. In *The Handbook of Morphology,* Andrew Spencer and Arnold Zwicky (eds), 237–47. Oxford: Blackwell.
Aronson, Howard. I. 1982. *Georgian: A reading grammar.* Columbus OH: Slavica Publishers.
Arotcarena, Abbé. 1976. *Grammaire basque (Dialectes Navarro-Labourdins).* Bayonne: Librarie Jakin.
Asher, S. and Simpson, F. (eds). 1994. *The Encyclopedia of Language and Linguistics.* Oxford: Pergamon.
Ashton, E. O. 1947. *Swahili Grammar. (Including intonation).* London: Longman.
Aski, Janice. 1995. Verbal suppletion: An analysis of Italian, French, and Spanish to go. *Linguistics* 33: 403–32.
Bamgbose, Ayo. 1966. *A Grammar of Yoruba.* Cambridge: Cambridge University Press.
Bascom, Burton. 1982. Northern Tepehuan. In *Studies in Uto-Aztecan Grammar,* Vol.3, Ronald W. Langacker, 267–393. Arlington TX: SIL and the University of Texas at Arlington.
Battistella, Edwin. 1996. *The Logic of Markedness.* New York NY: Oxford University Press.
Bell, A. 1978. Language samples. In *Universals of Human Language,* J. Greenberg (ed.), 123–56. Stanford CA: Stanford University Press.
Bender, Lionel M. 1996. *Kunama* [Languages of the World/Materials 59]. Munich: Lincom.
Benkö, Loránd and Samu, Imre. 1972. *The Hungarian Language.* The Hague: Mouton.
Benmamoun, Elabbas. 1996. The derivation of the imperative in Arabic. In *Perspectives on Arabic Linguistcs IX,* Mushira Eid and Dilworth Parkinson (eds), 151–64. Amsterdam: John Benjamins.
Berg, Ragnar. 1981. *Dakota/Lakota norsk grammatikk og ordbok.* Kongsberg: Berg og Berg.
Berger, Hermann. 1998. *Die Burushaski-Sprache von Hunza und Nager.* Wiesbaden: Harrassowiz.
Bhat, D. N. S. and Ningomba, M. S. 1997. *Manipuri Grammar* Vol. 04 [Lincom Studies in Asian Linguistics]. Munich: Lincom.
Birjulin, Leonid A. and Xrakovskij, Victor S. 2001. Imperative sentences: Theoretical problems. In *Typology of Imperative Constructions,* Victor S. Xrakovskij (ed.), 3–50. Munich: Lincom.

Bittner, Andreas. 1988. Reguläre Irregularitäten. *Zeitschrift für Phonetik, Sprachwissenschaft und Kommunikationsforschung* 41: 416–25.

Bittner, Andreas. 1996. *Starke "schwache" Verben-schwache "starke" Verben. Deutsche Verbflexion und Natürlichkeit* [Studien zur deutschen Grammatik 51]. Tübingen: Stauffenburg.

Bloomfield, Leonard. 1926. A set of postulates for the science of language. *Language* 2: 153–64.

Bloomfield, Leonard. 1933. *Language*. London: Ruskin House, George Allen & Unwin. (Reprinted in 1962).

Boaz, Franz. 1927. Additional notes on the Kutenai language. *International Journal of American Linguistics* 4: 85–104.

Booker, Karen. 1980. Comparative Muskogean: Aspects of Proto-Muskogean verb morphology. PhD dissertation, University of Kansas.

Bopp, Franz. 1845–1853. *A Comparative Grammar of Sanscrit, Zend, Greek, Latin, Lithuanian, Gothic, German and Slavonic Languages*. London: Madden and Malcolm. (Reprinted in Hildesheim: Olms 1985).

Borg, Albert and Azzopardi-Alexander, Marie. 1997. *Maltese*. London: Routledge.

Borgman, Donald M. 1990. Sanuma. In *Handbook of Amazonian Languages*, Desmod C. Derbyshire and Geoffrey Pullum (eds), 15–248. Berlin: Mouton de Gruyter.

Bosworth, Joseph and Toller, T. Northcote (eds). 1882–1898. *An Anglo-Saxon Dictionary Based on the Manuscript Collections of Joseph Bosworth*. Oxford: At the Clarendon Press.

Bowden, John. 1997. Taba (Makian Dalam), Department of Linguistics and Applied Linguistics. PhD dissertation, University of Melbourne.

Bray, Denys. 1986. *Brahui Language Introduction and Grammar*. New Delhi: Asian Educational Services.

Bright, William (ed.). 1992. *International Encyclopedia of Linguistics*. Oxford: Oxford University Press.

Broadbent, Sylvia M. 1964. *The Southern Sierra Miwok Language* [University of California Publications in Linguistics 38]. Berkeley CA: University of California Press.

Brockway, Earl. 1984. North Pueblo Nahuatl. In *Studies in Uto-Aztecan Grammar*, Ronald W. Langacker (ed.). Dallas TX: SIL and the University of Texas at Arlington.

Bromley, H. Myron. 1981. *A Grammar of Lower Grand Valley Dani* [Pacific Linguistics 63]. Canberra: Department of Linguistics, Research School of Pacific Studies, The Australian National University.

Bruce, Les. 1984. *The Alamblak Language of Papua New Guinea (East Sepik)*. Canberra: Pacific Linguistics.

Buck, Carl D. 1915. Words of speaking and saying in the Indo-European languages: First paper. *American Journal of Philology* 36(1): 1–18.

Buck, Carl D. 1949. *A Dictionary of Selected Synonyms in the Principal Indo-European Languages*. Chicago IL: University of Chicago Press.

Burling, Robbins. 1961. *A Garo Grammar* [Deccan College Monograph Series 25]. Poona: Deccan College Postgraduate and Research Institute.

Butt, John and Benjamin, Carmen. 1988. *A New Reference Grammar of Modern Spanish*. London: Edward Arnold.

Bybee, Joan. 1985. *Morphology* [Typological Studies in Language 9]. Amsterdam: John Benjamins.

Bybee, Joan. 1988. Morphology as lexical organization. In *Theoretical Morphology*, Michael Hammond and Michael Noonan (eds), 119–42. San Diego CA: Academic Press.

Bybee, Joan, Perkins, Revere and Pagliuca, William. 1994. *The Evolution of Grammar*. Chicago IL: The University of Chicago Press.

Cabrera, Juan C. Moreno. 1998. On the relationships between grammaticalization and lexicalization. In *The Limits of Grammaticalization*, Anna Giacalone Ramat and Paul Hopper (eds), 211–27. Amsterdam: John Benjamins.

Campbell, Lyle. 1985. *The Pipil Language of El Salvador*. Berlin: Mouton de Gruyter.

Capell, A. and Hinch, H. E. 1970. *Maung Grammar: Texts and vocabulary*. The Hague: Mouton.

Carlson, Robert. 1994. *A Grammar of Supyire*. Berlin: Mouton de Gruyter.

Carstairs-McCarthy, Andrew. 1990. Phonologically conditioned suppletion. In *Contemporary Morphology*, Wolfgang Dressler (ed.), 17–23. Berlin: Mouton de Gruyter.

Carstairs-McCarthy, Andrew. 1992. *Current Morphology*. London: Routledge.

Carstairs-McCarthy, Andrew. 1994. Suppletion. In *The Encyclopedia of Language and Linguistics*, S. Asher and F. Simpson (eds), 4410–4411. Oxford: Pergamon.

Carstairs-McCarthy, Andrew. 1998. Paradigmatic Structure: Inflectional Paradigms and Morphological Classes. In *The Handbook of Morphology*, Andrew Spencer and Arnold Zwicky (eds), 322–34. Oxford: Blackwell.

Casad, Eugeme. H. 1984. Cora. In *Studies in Uto-Aztecan grammar 4: Southern Uto-Aztecan grammatical sketches*, Ronald W. Langacker (ed.), 153–459. Dallas TX: SIL and the University of Texas at Arlington.

Chafe, Wallace. 1996. Sketch of Seneca, an Iroquoian Language. In *Handbook of North American Indians: Languages*, Ives Goddard (ed.), 551–79. Washington DC: Smithsonian Institution.

Charney, Jean Ormsbee. 1993. *A Grammar of Comanche*. Lincoln NB: University of Nebraska Press.

Chelliah, Shobhana L. 1997. *A Grammar of Meithei* [Mouton Grammar Library 17]. Berlin: Mouton de Gruyter.

Chino, Naoko. 1996. *Japanese Verbs at a Glance*. Tokyo: Kodansha International.

Christiades, Vassilios. 1980. *201 Greek Verbs Fully Conjugated in all the Tenses*. New York NY: Barron.

Clairis, Christos. 1985. *El Qawasqar*. Valdivia, Chile: Faculdad de Filosofía y Humanidades.

Cole, Peter. 1985. *Imbabura Quechua* [Croom Helm Descriptive Grammars]. London: Croom Helm.

Conrad, Robert J. and Wogiga, Kepas. 1991. *An outline of Bukiyip grammar* [Pacific Linguistics, Series C No. 113]. Canberra: Australian National University.

Comrie, Bernard. 2003. Recipient Person Suppletion in the Verb 'Give'. In *In Language and Life: Essays in Memory of Kenneth L. Pike*, eds. Mary Ruth Wise, Thomas N. Headland and Ruth M. Brend, 265–81. Dallas, TX: SIL International and the University of Texas at Arlington.

Corbett, Greville, Hippisley, Andrew, Brown, Dunstan and Marriott, Paul. 2001. Frequency, regularity and the paradigm: A perspective from Russian on a complex relation. In *Frequency and the Emergence of Linguistic Structure*, Joan Bybee and Paul Hopper (eds), 201–27. Amsterdam: John Benjamins.

Corbett, Greville G. 2000. *Number* [Cambridge Textbooks in Linguistics]. Cambridge: Cambridge University Press.

Cowan, H. K. J. 1965. *Grammar of the Sentani Language*. Gravenhage: Martinus Nijhoff.

Craig, Colette G. 1977. *The Structure of Jacaltec*. Austin TX: University of Texas Press.

Creissels, Denis. 1983. *Eléments de Grammaire de la Langue Mandinka*. Grenoble: Publications de l'Université des Langues et Letttres.

Crimmins, M. 1994. Type/token distinction. In *The Encyclopedia of Language and Linguistics.* S. Asher and F. Simpson (eds), Vol. 9, 4800–1. Oxford: Pergamon.

Croft, William. 1990. *Typology and Universals.* Cambridge: Cambridge University Press.

Croft, William. 1991. The evolution of negation. *Journal of Linguistics* 27: 1–27.

Curnow, Timothy Jowan. 1997. A grammar of Awa Pit (Cuaiquer): An indigenous language of south-western Colombia, Linguistics. PhD dissertation, Australian National University.

Dahl, Östen. 1985. *Tense and Aspect Systems.* Oxford: Blackwell.

Dahl, Östen. 2000. Verbs of becoming as future copulas. In *Tense and Aspect in the Languages of Europe*,Östen Dahl (ed.), 351–61. Berlin: Mouton de Gruyter.

Dahl, Östen. 2005. *The Growth and Maintenance of Linguistic Complexity.* Amsterdam: John Benjamins.

Davies, Mark. 2004. Corpus del Español: http://www.corpusdelespanol.org.

Day, Christopher. 1973. *The Jacaltec Language*: Indiana University Publications.

de Bray, Reginald George Arthur. 1980a. *Guide to the West Slavonic Languages.* London: J. M. Dent & Sons.

de Bray, Reginald George Arthur. 1980b. *Guide to the South Slavonic Languages.* Columbus OH: Slavica Publishers.

de Haan, Ferdinand. 1997. *The Interaction of Negation and Modality: A typological study* [Outstanding Dissertations in Linguistics Series] New York NY: Garland.

Dedrick, J. M. and Casad, Eugene. H. 1999. *Sonora Yaqui Language Structures.* Tuscon AZ: University of Arizona Press.

Delafosse, Maurice. 1929. *La Langue Mandingue et ses dialectes.* Paris: Librairie Orientaliste Paul Geuthner.

Delbrück, Bertold. 1888. *Altindische Syntax.* Darmstadt: Wissenschaftliche Buchgesellschaft. (Reprinted in 1968).

Dench, Alan. 1995. *Martuthunira. A language of the Pilbara region of Western Australia.* Canberra: Pacific Linguistics.

Derbyshire, Desmod C. 1979. *Hixkaryana* [Lingua Descriptive Series 1]. Amsterdam: North-Holland.

Derbyshire, William W. 1993. *A Basic Reference Grammar of Slovene.* Columbus OH: Slavica Publishers.

Deshpande, Madhav M. 1992. Justification for verb-root suppletion in Sanskrit. *Historische Sprachforschung* 105: 18–49.

Dez, Jacques. 1980. *Structures de la langue Malgache.* Paris: Publications Orientalistes de France.

Dickey, Stephen M. 2000. *Parameters of Slavic Aspect: A cognitive approach.* Stanford CA: CSLI Publications.

Dillon, Myles and Ó Cróinin, Donsha. 1961. *Teach Yourself Irish.* London: The English Universities Press.

Dimmendaal, Gerrit Jan. 1983. *The Turkana Language.* Dordrecht: Foris.

Dimock, Edward C. 1965. *Introduction to Bengali.* Honolulu HI: East-West Center Press.

Dixon, Robert M. W. 1988. *A Grammar of Boumaa Fijian.* Chicago IL: University of Chicago Press.

Dixon, Robert M. W. 2002. Copula clauses in Australian languages. *Anthropological Linguistics* 44(1): 1–37.

Dol, Philomena Hedwig. 1999. A Grammar of Maybrat. PhD dissertation, Rijksuniversiteit Leiden

Domenichini-Ramiaramanana, Bakoly. 1976. *Le Malgache*. Paris: Centre National de la Recherche Scientifique et du Conseil International de la Langue Française.
Donaldson, B. C. 1981. *Dutch Reference Grammar*. The Hague: Martinus Nijhoff.
Donaldson, Tamsin. 1980. *Ngiyambaa: The language of the Wangaaybuwan*. Cambridge: Cambridge University Press.
Donohue, Mark. 1999. *A Grammar of Tukang Besi*. Berlin: Mouton de Gruyter.
Dressler, W. 1985. Suppletion in Word-Fomation. In *Historical Morphology*, J. Fisiak (ed.), 97–112. The Hague: Mouton.
Dressler, Wolfgang U., Mayerthaler, Willi, Panagl, Oswald and Wurzel, Wolfgang U. (eds). 1987. *Leitmotifs in Natural Morphology*. Amsterdam: John Benjamins.
Dryer, Matthew S. 1989. Large linguistic areas and language sampling. *Studies in Language* 13(2): 257–92.
Dryer, Matthew S. 1992. The Greenbergian word order correlations. *Language* 68: 81–138.
Du Feu, Veronica. 1996. *Rapanui* [Descriptive Grammars]. London: Routledge.
Dul'zon, A. P. 1949. *Ketskii jazyk*. Tomsk: Izdatel'stvo Tomskogo Universiteta.
Dunn, Michael John. 1999. A Grammar of Chukchi, PhD dissertation, Australian National University.
Durie, Mark. 1986. The grammaticization of number as a verbal category. In *Proceedings of the Twelfth Annual Meeting of the Berkeley Linguistic Society, 15–17 February 1986*, Vassiliki Nikiforidou, Mary VanClay, Mary Niepokuj and Deborah Feder (eds), 355–70. Berkeley CA: CLS.
Dvoreckij, I. N. 1958. *Drevnogrecesko-russkoj slovar'*. Moskva: Gosudarstvennoe Izdatel'stvo Inostrannyx i Nacional'nyx Slovarej.
Ehrman, Madeline E. 1972. *Contemporary Cambodian: Grammatical sketch*. Washington DC: Department of State, Foreign Service Institute.
Es'kova, N. A. 1985. K morfologii russkogo imperativa (Forma vtorogo lica edinstvennogo chisla). *Russian Linguistics* 9: 149–63.
Evans, Nicholas D. 1995. *A Grammar of Kayardild*. Berlin: Mouton de Gruyter.
Everett, Daniel L. 1986. Piraha. In *Handbook of Amazonian Languages*, Desmod C. Derbyshire and Geoffrey Pullum (eds), 200–325. Berlin: Mouton de Gruyter.
Everett, Daniel L. and Kern, Barbara. 1997. *Wari': The Pacaas Novos language of Western Brazil* [Descriptive Grammars]. London: Routledge.
Facundes, Sidney da Silva. 2000. The Language of the Apurina People of Brazil. PhD dissertation, University of New York at Buffalo.
Fennell, Trevor G. and Gelsen, Henry. 1980. *A Grammar of Modern Latvian*. The Hague: Mouton.
Fertig, David. 1998. Suppletion, natural morphology, diagrammaticity. *Linguistics* 36(6): 1065–1091.
Foley, William A. 1991. *The Yimas Language of New Guinea*. Stanford CA: Stanford University Press.
Fortescue, Michael. 1984. *West Greenlandic* [Croom Helm Descriptive Grammars]. London: Croom Helm.
Frajzyngier, Zygmunt. 1986. From preposition to copula. In *Proceedings of the Twelfth Annual Meeting of the Berkeley Linguistics Society*, Vassiliki Nikiforidou, Mary VanClay, Mary Niepokuj and Deborah Feder (eds), 371–87. Berkeley CA: BLS.
Frajzyngier, Zygmunt. 1993. *A Grammar of Mupun*. Berlin: Dietrich Reimer.

Frank, Paul. 1990. *Ika Syntax* [Studies in the Languages of Colombia]. Dallas TX: SIL and University of Texas at Arlington.
Franklin, K.J. 1971. *A Grammar of Kewa, New Guinea* [Series C No. 16]. Canberra: Pacific Linguistics, Australian National University.
Garvin, Paul L. 1948a. Kutenai: Phonemics. *International Journal of American Linguistics* 14: 37–8.
Garvin, Paul L. 1948b. Kutenai II: Morpheme Variations. *International Journal of American Linguistics* 14: 86–90.
Garvin, Paul L. 1948c. Kutenai III: Morpheme distributions (prefix, theme, suffix). *International Journal of American Linguistics* 14: 171–87.
Givón, T. and Southern Ute Tribe. 1980. *Ute Reference Grammar*. Ignacio CO: Ute Press.
Glinert, Lewis. 1989. *The Grammar of Modern Hebrew*. Cambridge: Cambridge University Press.
Gorbachevskij, A. A. 1967. *K voprosy o putjax vozniknovlenija suppletivnyx form v slavjanskix jazykax*. Dushanbe: Tadjikskij Gosudarstvenyj Universitet im. V. I. Lenina.
Gordon, Lynn. 1986. *Maricopa Morphology and Syntax* [University of California Publications in Linguistics 108]. Berkeley CA: University of California Press.
Green, M. M. and Igwe, Rev. G. E. 1963. *A Descriptive Grammar of Igbo*. Berlin: Akademie Verlag.
Greenberg, Joseph (ed.). 1966. *Language Universals*. The Hague: Mouton.
Grimes, Barbara (ed.). 1988. *Ethnologue: Languages of the world (plus supplement: Ethnologue index)*. Dallas TX: Summer Institute of Linguistics.
Grinevald, Colette. 1990. A grammar of Rama. Ms., *Report to the National Science Foundation, BNS 8511156*. n/a.
Grønbech, Kaare and Krueger, John R. 1955. *An Introduction to Classical (Literary) Mongolian*. Wiesbaden: Otto Harrasowitz.
Gruzdeva, Ekaterina. 1998. *Nivkh* [Languages of the World/Materials 111]. Munich: Lincom.
Guasch, Antonio, S. I. 1996. *El Idioma Guaraní*. Asunción: Cepag.
Guirardello, Raquel. 1999. A Reference Grammar of Trumai. PhD dissertation, Rice University.
Haas, Mary. 1948. Classificatory verbs in Muskogee. *International Journal of American Linguistics* XIV: 4(4): 244–6.
Hagman, Roy. 1977. *Nama Hottentott Grammar* [Indiana University Publications, Language Science Monographs]. Bloomington IN: Indiana University.
Haile, Berard. 1926. *A Manual of Navaho Grammar*. St. Michael's AZ: Franciscan Fathers.
Haiman, John. 1983. Iconic and Economic Motivation. *Language* 59: 781–819.
Halle, Morris. 1973. Prolegomena to a theory of word formation. *Linguistic Inquiry* 4(1): 3–16.
Hammond, Michael and Noonan, Michael (eds). 1988. *Theoretical Morphology*. San Diego CA: Academic Press.
Hardman, M. J. 2001. *Aymara* [Lincom Studies in Native American Linguistics 35]. Munich: Lincom.
Harley, A. H. 1944. *Colloquial Hindustani*. London: Kegan Paul, Trench, Trubner & Co.
Harlow, Ray. 1996. *Maori*. [Languages of the World/Materials 20]. Munich: Lincom.
Harrison, Sheldon, P. 1976. *Mokilese Reference Grammar*. Honolulu HI: The University Press of Hawaii.
Hartmann, R. R. K. and Stork, F. C. 1972. *Dictionary of Language and Linguistics*. London: Applied Science Publishers.
Haspelmath, Martin. 1993. *A Grammar of Lezgian*. Berlin: Mouton de Gruyter.
Haspelmath, Martin. 2000. The agglutination hypothesis: A belated empirical investigation. Ms., Paper presented at the International Typology Meeting, Vienna, February 25, 2000. Vienna.

Haviland, John. 1979. Guugu Yimidhirr. In *Handbook of Australian Languages* I, Robert M. W. Dixon and Barry J. Blake (eds), 26–180. Canberra: Australian National University Press.
Heath, Jeffrey. 1981. *Basic Materials in Mara: Grammar, texts and dictionary*. Canberra: The Australian National University, Research School of Pacific Studies.
Heath, Jeffrey. 1982. *Nunggubuyu Dictionary*. Canberra: Australian Institute of Aboriginal Studies.
Heath, Jeffrey. 1984. *Functional Grammar of Nunggubuy*. Canberra: Australian Institute of Aboriginal Studies.
Heath, Jeffrey. 1999. *A Grammar of Koyra Chiini. The Songhay of Timbuktu*. Berlin: Mouton de Gruyter.
Heine, Bernd. 1980. Turkana. In *The Non-Bantu Languages of Kenya*, Bernd Heine and Wilhelm Möhlig (eds), 37–97. Berlin: Dietrich Reimer.
Heine, Bernd, Claudi, Ulrike and Hünnemeyer, Frederike. 1991. *Grammaticalization. A conceptual framework*. Chicago IL: The University of Chicago Press.
Heine, Bernd and Kuteva, Tania. 2002. *World Lexicon of Grammaticalization*. Cambridge: Cambridge University Press.
Hercus, Luise A. 1994. *A Grammar of the Arabana-Wangkanguru Language, Lake Eyre Basin, South Australia*. Canberra: Pacific Linguistics, Australian National University
Herman, Louis Jay. 1975. *A Dictionary of Slavic Word Families*. New York NY: Columbia University Press.
Herrity, Peter. 2000. *Slovene: A comprehensive grammar*. London: Routledge.
Hewitt, B. G. 1989. *Abkhaz* [Croom Helm Descriptive Grammars]. London: Routledge.
Hewitt, B. G. 1995. *Georgian: A structural reference grammar*. Amsterdam: John Benjamins.
Hinds, John. 1986. *Japanese*. London: Croom Helm.
Hoff, Berend Jacob. 1968. *The Carib Language*. The Hague: N. V. Nederlandsche boek- en steendrukkerij v/h H. L. Smits.
Hoijer, Harry. 1945. Classificatory verbs in the Apalachean languages. *International Journal of American Linguistics* XI(1): 13–23.
Hopper, Paul and Traugott, Elizabeth. 1993. *Grammaticalization*. Cambridge: Cambridge University Press.
Horton, A. E. 1949. *A Grammar of Luvale*. Johannesburg: Witwaterstrand University Press.
Humesky, Assya. 1980. *Modern Ukrainian*. Edmonton: Canadian Institute of Ukrainian Studies.
Hutchison, John P. 1981. *The Kanuri Language: A reference grammar*. Madison WI: African Studies Program, University of Wisconsin.
Huttar, George L. and Huttar, Mary L. 1994. *Ndyuka* [Descriptive Grammars]. London: Routledge.
Hyltenstam, Kenneth and Viberg, Åke. 1993. *Progression and Regression in Language*. Cambridge: Cambridge University Press.
Innes, Gordon. 1966. *An introduction to Grebo*. London: School of Oriental and African Studies, University of London.
Ivanov, V. Vs., Todorov, V. N. and Uspensky, B. A. 1968. *Ketskii sbornik*. Moskva: Nauka.
Jacob, Judith M. 1968. *Introduction to Cambodian*. Oxford: Oxford University Press.
Jacobson, Steven A. and Jacobson, Anna W. 1995. *A Practical Grammar of the Central Alaskan Yup'ik Eskimo Language*. Fairbanks AK: Alaska Native Language Center and Program, University of Alaska Fairbanks.

Jakobi, Angelika. 1993. *A Fur Grammar*. Hamburg: Buske.
Jakobson, Roman. 1939. Signe zéro. In *Roman Jakobson, Selected Writings* II, 211–19. The Hague: Mouton.
Jakobson, Roman. 1971. *Selected Writings* II: *Word and language*. The Hague: Mouton.
Jeanne, LaVerne, Hale, Kenneth and Pranka, Paula. 1984. Where is suppletion? Paper presented at *GLOW, 1984*.
Johnson, Jean B. 1962. *El Idioma Yaqui*. Mexico: Instituto Nacional de Antropologia e Historia.
Jones, Wendell and Jones, Paula. 1991. *Barasano Syntax* [Studies in the Languages of Colombia 2]. Dallas TX: SIL and the University of Texas at Arlington.
Joseph, Brian D. and Philipaki-Warburton, Irene. 1987. *Modern Greek*. London: Croom Helm.
Karlsson, Fred. 1978. *Finsk Grammatik*. Helsingin: Suomalaisen kirjallisuuden Seura.
Keenan, E. L. and Polinsky, Maria. 1998. Malagasy. In *Handbook of Morphology*, Andrew Spencer and Arnold Zwicky (eds), 563–624. Oxford: Blackwell.
Keller, Rudi. 1994. *On Language Change: The invisible hand in language*. London: Routledge.
Key, Harold. 1967. *Morphology of Cayuvava*. The Hague: Mouton.
Khanlari, P. N. 1979. *A History of the Persian Language*. Delhi: Idarah-i Adabiyat-i Delli.
Kimball, Geoffrey D. 1991. *Koasati Grammar*. Lincoln NB: University of Nebraska Press in co-operation with the American Indian Studies Research Institute, Indiana University.
Kimball, Geoffrey D. 1993. Two hunters, two wives, two dogs and two clawed witches: The use of the dual in a Koasati narrative. *International Journal of American Linguistics* 59: 473–88.
King, Alan R. 1994. *The Basque Language. A practical introduction*. Reno NV: University of Nevada Press.
Koneckaja, Vera P. 1973. *Suppletivism v germanskix jazykax*. Moskva: Izdatel'stvo Nauka.
König, Christa and Heine, Bernd. 2001a. *The !Xun of Ekoka: A demographic and linguistic report* [Khoisan Forum 17]. Cologne: University of Cologne.
König, Christa and Heine, Bernd. 2001b. *The !Xun of Ekoka: A demographic and linguistic report* [Khoisan Forum 17]. Cologne: University of Cologne.
Koshal, Sanyukta. 1979. *Ladakhi Grammar*. Delhi: Motilal Banarsidass.
Kozintseva, Natalia. 1995. *Modern Eastern Armenian* [Languages of the Word/Materials 22]. Munich: Lincom.
Kraft, Charles. 1973. *Hausa*. London: English University Press.
Krejnovich, E. A. 1968. *Glagol Ketskogo jazyka*. Leningrad: Izdatelstvo Nauka. Leningradskoe otdelenie.
Kruspe, Nicole. 1999. Semelai. PhD dissertation, University of Melbourne.
Kuipers, Aert H. 1967. *The Squamish Language: Grammar, texts and dictionary*. The Hague: Mouton.
Lafitte, Pierre. 1962. *Grammaire Basque*. Bayonne: Des Amis du musée basque et Ikas.
Lamberti, Marcello and Sottile, Roberto. 1997. *The Wolaytta language*. Köln: Köppe.
Langdon, Margaret. 1992. Yuman Plurals: From derivation to inflection to noun agreement. *International Journal of American Linguistics* 58: 405–24.
Lange, Ronald A. 1988. *501 Japanese Verbs Fully Described in all Inflections, Moods, Aspects and Formality Levels*. New York NY: Barron.
Lass, Roger. 1990. How to do things with junk: Exaptation in language evolution. *Journal of Linguistics* 26: 79–102.
Lastra, Yolandra. 1998. *Ixtenco Otomí* [Languages of the World/Materials 19]. Munich: Lincom.
Lazard, Gilbert. 1992. *A Grammar of Contemporary Persian*. Costa Meca CA: Mazda Publishers in association with Bibliotheca Persica.

Leech, Geoffrey, Rayson, Paul, and Wilson, Andrew. 2001. *Word Frequencies in Written and Spoken English*. Harlow: Longman.
Lewis, G. L. 1967. *Turkish Grammar*. Oxford: Clarendon Press.
Lewis, Robert E., Kurath, Hans and Kuhn, Sherman M. (eds). 1952-present. *Middle English Dictionary*. Ann Arbor MI: University of Michigan Press.
Li, Charles N. and Thompson, Sandra A. 1981. *Mandarin Chinese: A functional reference grammar*. Berkeley CA: University of California Press.
Lide, Sven and Magnusson, Rudolf. 1970. *Tysk grammatik*. Stockholm: Språkförlaget.
Lidell, Henry, S. and Scott, Robert. 1871. *Greek-English Lexicon*. Oxford: Clarendon Press.
Lindström, Eva. In preparation. *A Descriptive Grammar of Kuot. A non-Austronesian language of New Ireland, Papua New Guinea*.
Loogman, Alfons. 1965. *Swahili Grammar and Syntax*, Vol. 1 [Duquesne Studies, African Series]. Pittsburgh PA: Duquesne University Press.
Lorimer, D. L. 1935. *The Burushaski Language* [Serie B: Skrifter XXIX]. Oslo: Institutet for Sammenlignende Kulturforskning.
Lunt, Horace. 1952. *A Grammar of the Macedonian Literary Language*. Skopje: Macedonian State Press.
Macaulay, Monica. 1982. Verbs of motion and arrival in Mixtec. In *Proceedings of the Eighth Annual Meeting of the Berkeley Linguistics Society*, Monica Macaulay et al., 414–26. Berkeley CA: BLS.
Macaulay, Monica. 1996. *A Grammar of Chalcatongo Mixtec*. Berkeley CA: University of California Press.
Mackridge, Peter. 1985. *A Descriptive Analysis of Standard Modern Greek*. Oxford: Oxford University Press.
Mahootian, Shahrzad. 1997. *Persian*. London: Routledge.
Malkjær, Kirsten and Anderson, James M. (eds). 1991. *The Linguistics Encyclopedia*. London: Routledge.
Manczak, Witold. 1966. La nature du suppletivisme. *Linguistics* 28: 82–9.
Maring, Joel M. 1967. Grammar of Acoma Keresan. PhD dissertation, Indiana University.
Markey, T. L. 1985. On suppletion. *Diachronica* 11(1): 51–66.
Martin, Samuel E. 1975. *A Reference Grammar of Japanese*. New Haven CT: Yale University Press.
Martin, Samuel E. 1987. *The Japanese Language Through Time*. New Haven CT: Yale University Press.
Maslov, Juri. 1984. *Ocherki po aspektologii*. Leningrad: Izdatel'stvo Leningradskogo universiteta.
Maslova, Elena. 1999. A Grammar of Kolyma Yukaghir, University of Bielefeld: Habilitation Thesis.
Maslova, Elena. 2000. A dynamic approach to the verification of distributional universals. *Linguistic Typology* 4-3(3): 307–33.
Matthews, Peter H. 1974. *Morphology: An introduction to the theory of word structure*. Cambridge: Cambridge University Press.
Matthews, Steven and Yip, Virginia. 1994. *Cantonese: A comprehensive grammar*. London: Routledge.
Mayerthaler, Willi. 1981. *Morphological Naturalness*. Ann Arbor MI: Karoma.
Mayo, Peter J. 1976. *A Grammar of Byelorussian*. Sheffield: The Anglo-Byelorussian Society in association with the Department of Russian and Slavonic Studies, University of Sheffield.

Mazur, B. W. 1983. *Colloquial Polish*. London: Routledge.
McCone, Kim. 1987. *The Early Irish Verb*. Maynooth: An Sagart.
McFarland, Curtis D. 1976. *A Provisional Classification of Tagalog Verbs* [Study of Languages and Cultures of Asia & Africa Monograph Series 8]. Tokyo: Tokyo University of Foreign Studies.
McIntosh, Angus, Samuels, M. L., Benskin, Michael, Laing, Margaret and Williamson, Keith (eds). 1986. *A Linguistic Atlas of Late Mediaeval English*. Aberdeen: Aberdeen University Press.
McLendon, Sally. 1975. *A Grammar of Eastern Pomo*. Berkeley CA: University of California Press.
McLendon, Sally. 1996. Sketch of Eastern Pomo, a Pomoan Language. In *Handbook of North American Indians*, Ives Goddard (ed.), 507–50. Washington DC: Smithsonian Institution.
Medushevsky, A. and Zyatovska., R. 1963. *Ukrainian Grammar*. Kiev: State Textbook Publishing House Radyanska Shkola.
Melcuk, Igor. 1976. On Suppletion. *Linguistics* 170: 45–90.
Melcuk, Igor. 1994. Suppletion: Toward a logical analysis of the concept. *Studies in Language* 18(2): 339–410.
Merlan, Francesca. 1982. *Mangarayi* [Lingua Descriptive Series]. Amsterdam: North-Holland.
Miller, Wick. 1965. *Acoma Grammar and Texts* [University of California Publications in Linguistics 40] Berkeley CA: University of California Press.
Mistrik, Jozef. 1981. *Basic Slovak*. Bratislava: Slovenské Pedagogiské Nakladatel'stvo.
Mitchell, T. F. 1962. *Colloquial Arabic: The living language of Egypt* [Teach Yourself Books]. London: The English Universities Press.
Mithun, Marianne. 1988. Lexical categories and the evolution of verbal number. In *Theoretical Morphology*, Hammond Michael and Michael Noonan (ed.), 211–33.
Mohanan, K. P. 1986. *The Theory of Lexical Phonology*. Dordrecht: Reidel.
Mosel, Ulrike and Hovhaugen, Even. 1994. *A Reference Grammar of Samoan*. Scandinavian University Press, The Institute for Comparative Research Human Culture.
Mous, Maarten. 1992. *A Grammar of Iraqw*. PhD dissertation, Rijksuniversiteit Leiden.
Mous, Maarten. In Preparation. *Alagwa: Grammar, text and lexicon*.
Mugdan, J. 1994. Morphological Units. In *The Encyclopedia of Language and Linguistics*, S. Asher and F. Simpson (eds), 2543–2553. Oxford: Pergamon.
Murane, Elizabeth. 1974. *Daga Grammar: From morpheme to discourse*. Norman OK: SIL, University of Oklahoma Press.
Najis, E. 1973. *Lengua Selknam* [Filologia y Linguistica 3]. Buenos Aires: Universidad del Salvador.
Nedjalkov, Igor. 1997. *Evenki* [Descriptive Grammars]. London: Routledge.
Newman, John. 1997. *The Linguistics of Giving* [Typological Studies in Language 36]. Amsterdam: John Benjamins.
Newman, Paul. 2000. *The Hausa language: An encyclopedic reference grammar*. New Haven CT: Yale University Press.
Newman, Stanley. 1996. Sketch of the Zuni Language. In *Handbook of North American Indians: Languages*, Ives Goddard (ed.), 483–506. Washington DC: Smithsonian Institution.
Nguyen, Dinh-Hoa. 1997. *Vietnamese* [London Oriental and African Language Library 9]. Amsterdam: John Benjamins.
Nichols, Johanna. 1994. Ingush. In *Indigenous Languages of the Caucasus*, Riek Smeets (ed.), 79–146. Delmar NY: Caravan Books.

Nida, Eugene. 1963. The identification of morphemes. In *Readings in Linguistics*, Martin Joos (ed.), 255–71. New York NY: American Council of Learned Societies.
Noonan, Michael. 1992. *Lango* [Mouton Grammar Library]. Berlin: Mouton de Gruyter.
Noss, Richard, Proum, Im, Purtle, David and Sous, Someth. 1966. *Cambodian: Basic course*, Vol. 1. Washington DC: Department of State, Foreign Service Institute.
Noss, Richard B. 1964. *Thai Reference Grammar*. Washington DC: Foreign Service Institute, Department of State.
Okell, John. 1994. *Burmese: An introduction to the spoken language*, Vol. 1 [Southeast Asian Language Text Series]. DeKalb IL: Northern Illinois University, Center for Southeast Asian Studies.
Olsson, Magnus. 1992. Hungarian Phonology and Morphology. PhD dissertation, Lund University.
O'Neil, J. 1913. *A Grammar of the Sindebele Dialect of the Zulu*. London: Simpkin, Marshall, Hamilton, Kent & Co Ltd.
Osada, Toshiki. 1992. *A Reference Grammar of Mundari*. Tokyo: Institute for he Study of Languages and Cultures of Asia and Africa.
Osborne, Charles Roland. 1974. *The Tiwi Language* [AAS 55]. Canberra: Australian Institute of Aboriginal Studies.
Osthoff, Hermann. 1899. *Vom Suppletivwesen der indogermanischen Sprachen*. Heildelberg: J. Hörning.
Otaina, G. A. 1978. *Kachestvennye glagoly v nivhskom jazyke*. Moskva: Izdatel'stvo Nauka.
Owens, Jonathan. 1985. *A Grammar of Harar Oromo*. Hamburg: Buske.
Palmer, F. R. 1995. Negation and the modals of possibility and necessity. In *Modality in Grammar and Discourse*, Joan Bybee and Suzanne Fleischman (eds), 453–71. Amsterdam: John Benjamins.
Panfilov, Vladimir. 1965. *Grammatika nivhskogo jazyka*. Moskva: Izdatel'stvo Nauka.
Partridge, Monica. 1964. *Serbo-Croatian*. London: McGraw-Hill.
Pashkevich, V. 1978. *Fundamental Byelorussian*. Toronto: Byelorussian Community.
Payne, Doris L. and Payne, Thomas E. 1990. Yagua. In *Handbook of Amazonian Languages*, Desmod C. Derbyshire and Geoffrey Pullum (eds), 249–474. Berlin: Mouton de Gruyter.
Perkins, Revere D. 1989. Statistical techniques for determining language sample size. *Studies in Language*. 13(2): 293–315.
Pierce, Joe E. 1963. *Turkish Frequency Counts* [American Council of Learned Societies: Research and Studies in Uralic and Altaic Languages]. Cleveland OH: Micro Photo Division, Bell & Howell.
Pirogova, L.I. 1991. *Complete Handbook of Russian Verbs*. Lincolnwood IL: Passport Books.
Pitman, Donald. 1980. *Bosquejo del Gramatica Araona*, Vol. 9: Notas Linguisticas de Bolivia. La Paz.
Popjes, Jack and Popjes, Jo. 1986. Canela-Kraho. In *Handbook of Amazonian Languages* 1, Desmod C. Derbyshire and Geoffrey Pullum (eds), 128–99. Berlin: Mouton de Gruyter.
Poppe, Nicholas. 1964. *Grammar of Written Mongolian*. Wiesbaden: Otto Harrassowitz.
Prokosch, Eduard. 1939. *A Comparative Germanic Grammar*. Philadelphia PA: Linguistic Society of America, University of Pennsylvania.
Pugh, Stefan M. and Press, Ian. 1999. *Ukrainian*. London: Routledge.
Quirk, Randolph and Wrenn, C. L. 1971. *An Old English Grammar*. London: Methuen.
Rabel, Lili. 1961. *Khasi, A language of Assam*. Baton Rouge LA: Louisiana State University Press.

Radice, William. 1994. *Bengali. A complete course for beginners* [Teach Yourself Books]. London: Hoddler Headline.
Ramos, Teresita V. and Bautista, Maria Lourdes S. 1986. *Handbook of Tagalog Verbs: Inflections, modes and aspects*. Honolulu HI: University of Hawaii Press.
Reesnik, Ger P. 1987. *Structures and Their Functions in Usan. A Papuan language of Papua New Guinea*. Amsterdam: John Benjamins.
Reh, Mechthild. 1985. *Die Krongo-Sprache*. Berlin: Dietrich Reimer.
Rice, Keren. 1989. *A Grammar of Slave*. Berlin: Mouton de Gruyter.
Rice, Lester A. 1970. *Hungarian Morphological Irregularities*. Cambridge MA: Slavica Publishers.
Rijkhoff, Jan, Bakker, Dik, Hengeveld, Kees and Kahrel, Peter. 1993. A method of language sampling. *Studies in Language*. 17 (1): 169–203.
Rijkhoff, Jan and Bakker, Dik. 1998. Language sampling. *Linguistic Typology* 2–3(3): 263–314.
Roberts, John. 1987. *Amele*. London: Croom Helm.
Robinson, Lila Wistrand and Armagost, James. 1990. *Comanche Dictionary and Grammar*. Dallas TX: SIL and the University of Texas at Arlington.
Rolfs, Gerhard. 1968. *Grammatica storica della lingua italiana e dei suoi dialetti: Morfologia*. Turin: Einaudi.
Romero-Figeroa, Andrés. 1997. *A Reference Grammar of Warao*. Munich: Lincom.
Ronnerberger-Sibold, Elke. 1980. *Sprachverwendung-Sprachsystem Ökonomie und Wandel* [Linguistische Arbeiten 87]. Tübingen: Niemeyer.
Ronnerberger-Sibold, Elke. 1987. A performance model for a natural theory of linguistic change. In *Papers from the 7th International Conference on Historical Linguistics*, Anna Giacalone Ramat, Onofrio Carruba and Giuliano Bernini (eds), 517–33. Amsterdam: John Benjamins.
Rood, David. 1976. *Wichita Grammar*. New York NY: Garland.
Rood, David S. and Taylor, Allan R. 1996. Sketch of Lakhota, a Siouan Language. In *Handbook of North American Indians: Languages*, Ives Goddard (ed.), 440–82. Washington DC: Smithsonian Institution.
Roseborough, Margaret. 1938. *An Outline of Middle English Grammar*. Toronto: The Macmilllan Company of Canada Limited, at St Martin's House.
Rosén, Hannah. 2000. Preclassical and classical Latin precursors of Romance verb-stem suppletion. *Indogermanische Forschungen* 105: 270–83.
Rudes, Blair. 1980. On the nature of verbal suppletion. *Linguistics* 18: 655–76.
Ruhlen, Merritt. 1987. *A Guide to the World's Languages*. Stanford CA: Stanford University Press.
Rupp, James E. 1989. *Lealao Chinantec Syntax*. Dallas TX: SIL and University of Texas at Arlington.
Salminen, Tapani. 1998. Nenets. In *The Uralic Languages*, Daniel Abondolo (ed.), 516–47. London: Routledge.
Saltarelli, Mario. 1988. *Basque*. London: Croom Helm.
Samarin, William J. 1967. *A Grammar of Sango*. The Hague: Mouton.
Sapir, J. David. 1965. *A Grammar of Diola-Fogny*, Vol. 3 [West African Language Monographs]. Cambridge: Cambridge University Press.
Scalise, Sergio. 1986. *Generative Morphology*. Dordrecht: Foris.
Schachter, Paul. 1972. *Tagalog Reference Grammar*. Berkeley CA: University of California Press.

Schiffman, Harold F. 1983. *A Reference Grammar of Spoken Kannada*. Seattle WA: University of Washington Press.
Schiller, Eric. 1985. Forward into the past: A look at Khmer morphology. In *Proceedings of the Conference on Participant Roles: South Asia and Adjacent Areas*, Arlene Zide, David Magier and Eric Schiller (eds), 82–91. Bloomington IN: Indiana University Linguistics Club.
Schuster-Shewc, H. 1996. *Grammar of the Upper Sorbian Language*. Munich: Lincom.
Schuyt, Roel. 1990. *The Morphology of Slavic Verbal Aspect. A descriptive and historical study*. Amsterdam: Rodopi.
Seaman, P. David. 1996. *Hopi Dictionary: Hopi-English, English-Hopi with grammatical appendix*. Flagstaff AZ: Department of Anthropology, Northern Arizona University.
Seiler, Hansjakob. 1977. *Cahuilla Grammar*. Morongo Indian Reservation, Banning CA: Malki Museum Press.
Seiler, Hansjakob and Hioki, Kojiro. 1979. *Cahuilla Dictionary*. Morongo Indian Reservation, Banning CA: Malki Museum Press.
Seiler, Walter. 1985. *Imonda, a Papuan Language*. Canberra: Pacific Linguistics.
Senft, Gunter. 1986. *Kilivila: The language of the Trobriand islanders*. Berlin: Mouton de Gruyter.
Sherwood, David Fairchild. 1986. *Maliseet-Passamaquoddy Verb Morphology*. Ottawa: National Musems of Canada/Musées nationaux du Canada.
Shields, Kenneth. 1992. *A History of Indo-European Verb Morphology*. Amsterdam: John Benjamins.
Singh, Rajendra. 1996. Natural phono(morpho)logy: A view from the outside. In *Natural Phonology: The State of the Art*, Bernhard Hurch and Richard A. Rhodes (eds), 1–38. New York NY: New York University Press.
Smeets, Catharina J.M.A. 1989. A Mapuche Grammar. PhD dissertation, Rijksuniversiteit Leiden.
Snapp, Allen, Anderson, John and Anderson, Joy. 1984. Northern Paiute. In *Studies in Uto-Aztecan Grammar*, Ronald W. Langacker, 1–92. Dallas TX: SIL.
Sohn, Ho-min. 1994. *Korean*. London: Routledge.
Sova, Milosh. 1962. *A Practical Czech Course for English-Speaking Students*. Praha: Statni Pedagogické Nakladatelství.
Spencer, Andrew. 1991. *Morphological Theory*. Oxford: Blackwell.
Spencer, Andrew and Zwicky, Arnold eds. 1998. *The Handbook of Morphology*. Oxford: Blackwell.
Sridhar, S. N. 1990. *Kannada* [Croom Helm Descriptive Grammars]. London: Routledge.
Stassen, Leon. 1997. *Typology of Intransitive Predication*. Oxford: Clarendon Press.
Steinfeldt, E. 1965. *Russian Word Count*. Moscow: Progress Publishers.
Stevenson, R.G. 1969. *Bagirmi Grammar*, Vol. 3 [Linguistic Monograph Series]. Khartum: Faculty of Arts, University of Khartum.
Stone, Gerald. 1980. *An Introduction to Polish*. Oxford: Clarendon Press.
Stroomer, Harry. 1995. *A Grammar of Boraana Oromo (Kenya)*. Köln: Köppe.
Stump, Gregory. 2001. *Inflectional Morphology*. Cambridge: Cambridge University Press.
Subotic, Dragotin and Forbes, Nevill. 1918. *Grammar of Serbian*. Oxford: At the Clarendon Press.
Suen, Ching Y. 1986. *Computational Studies of the Most Frequent Chinese Words and Sounds*. Singapore: World Scientific.

Tamura, Suzuko. 1988. *The Ainu Language*. Tokyo: Sanseido. [Reprinted in 2000, translated from Japanese to English by Sanseido Co. Ltd].
Tanaka, Toshiya. 2002. The origin and development of the *es vs. *wes suppletion in the Germanic copula: From a non-Brugmannian standpoint. NOWELE 40, April, 3–27.
Tekavcic, Pavao. 1972. *Grammatica storica dell'italiano*. Bologna: Mulin.
Terrill, Angela. 1999. A grammar of Lavukaleve: A Papuan language of the Solomon Islands, Linguistics, PhD dissertation, Australian National University.
Thomas, Calvin. 1899. *A Practical German Grammar*. New York NY: Henry Holt.
Thompson, Laurence C. 1965. *A Vietnamese Grammar*. Seattle WA: University of Washington.
Thornell, Christina. 1997. *The Sango Language and its Lexicon*, Vol. 32 [Travaux de L'Institut de Linguistique de Lund]. Lund: Lund University Press.
Thurneysen, Rudolf. 1946. *A Grammar of Old Irish*. Dublin: The Dublin Institute for Advanced Studies.
Tiffou, Étienne and Patry, Richard. 1995. La notion de pluralité verbale: Le cas du bourouchaski du Yasin. *Journal Asiatique* 282 (2): 407–44.
Tokarskaja, V.P. 1964. *Jazyk Malinke (Mandingo)*. Moskva: Izdatel'stvo Nauka.
Topping, Donald. 1973. *Chamorro Reference Grammar*. Honolulu HI: The University of Hawaii Press.
Törkenczy, Miklós. 1997. *Hungarian: Verbs & essentials of grammar*. Chicago IL: Passport Books, NTC Contemporary Publishing Group.
Tovar, Antonio. 1981. *Relatos y dialogos de los Matacos. Seguidos de una grammatica de su lengua*. Madrid: Ediciones Cultura Hispanica del Instituto de Cooperacion Iberoamericana.
Townsend, Charles E. 1981. *Czech through Russian*. Columbus OH: Slavica Publishers.
Townsend, Charles E. and Janda, Laura A. 1996. *Common and Comparative Slavic*. Columbus OH: Slavica Publishers.
Trask, R. L. 1993. *A Dictionary Of Grammatical Terms in Linguistics*. London: Routledge.
Trubezkoy, Nicholas. 1969. *Principles of phonology*. Berkeley CA: University of California Press. (First publ. 1939).
Tryon, D. T. 1970. *An Introduction to Maranungku (Northern Australia)*. Canberra: Pacific Linguistics.
Tuggy, David H. 1977. Tetelcingo Nahuatl. In *Studies in Uto-Aztecan grammar*, ed. Ronald W. Langacker, 1–140. Arlington TX: SIL and University of Texas at Arlington.
Underhill, Robert. 1976. *Turkish Grammar*. Cambridge MA: The MIT Press.
Urquiza, Vinaz and Mani, Teresa. 1974. *Lengua Mataca*. Buenos Aires: Centro de Estudios Linguisticos.
Valenzuela, Pilar M. 1997. Basic Verb Types and Argument Structures in Shipibo-Conibo, Linguistics, MA thesis, University of Oregon.
Vall, M. N. and Kanakin, I. A. 1988. *Kategorrii glagola v ketskom jazyke*. Novosibirsk: Nauka, Sibirskoe otdelenie.
Vall, M. N., and Kanakin, I. A. 1990. *Ocherk fonologii i grammatiki ketskogo jazyka*. Novosibirsk: Nauka, Sibirskoe otdelenie.
van den Berg, Helma. 1995. *A Grammar of Hunzib (with Texts and Lexicon)* [Lincom Studies in Caucasian Linguistics 01]. Munich: Lincom.
van der Auwera, Johan, Lejeune, Ludo, Umarani, Pappuswamy and Goussev, Valentin. 2005. The morphological imperative. In *World Atlas of Language Structures*, Matthew S. Dryer, Martin Haspelmath, David Gil and Bernard Comrie (eds). Oxford: Oxford University Press.

Van Valin, Robert D. 1977. Aspects of Lakhota Syntax, Linguistics. PhD dissertation, University of California.
Varro, Marcus Terentius. 1958. *On the Latin Language*. Cambridge MA: Harvard University Press. (Reprinted in translation by Ronald G. Kent).
Vasmer, Max. 1964–1973. *Etymologicheskij slovar' russkogo jazyka*. Moskva: Izdatel'stvo Progress.
Vendryes, J. 1987. *Lexique Étymologique de l'Irlandais Ancien*. Paris: CNRS.
Viberg, Åke. 1993. Crosslinguistic perspectives on lexical organization and lexical progression. In *Progression and Regression in Language*, Kenneth Hyltenstam and Åke Viberg (eds), 340–85. Cambridge: Cambridge University Press.
Vincent, Nigel, and Börjars, Kersti. 1998. Suppletion and syntactic theory. Ms.
Voegelin, C. F. and Voegelin, F. M. 1978. *Classification and Index of the World's Languages*. New York NY: Elsevier.
Voorhoeve, Clemens Lambertus. 1965. *The Flamingo Bay Dialect of the Ásmat language*. The Hague: N. V. Nederlandsche boek- en steendrukkerij v/h H. L. Smits.
Wade, Terence. 2000. *A Comprehensive Russian Grammar*. Oxford: Blackwell.
Ward, Ida C. 1952. *An Introduction to the Yoruba Language*. Cambridge W. Heffer & Sons. (Reprinted in 1956).
Watkins, Laurel. 1984. *A Grammar of Kiowa*. Lincoln NB: University of Nebraska Press.
Wełna, Jerzy. 2001. Suppletion for suppletion, or the replacement of eode by went in English. *Studia Anglica Posnaniensia* 36: 95–110.
Werner, Otmar. 1987. Natürlichkeit und Nutzen morphologischer Irregularität. In *Beiträge zum 3. Essener Kolloquium über Sprachwandel und seine bestimmenden Faktoren*, Norbert Boretzky, Werner Enninger and Thomas Stolz (eds), 289–316. Bochum: Brockmeyer.
Westermann, Diedrich. 1930. *A Study of the Ewe Language*. London: Oxford University Press.
Whaley, Lindsay. 1997. *Introduction to Typology: The unity and diversity of language*. Thousand Oaks CA: Sage.
White, C.M.N. 1949. *A Short Lwena Grammar*. London: Longman, Greens & Co.
Wilson, Darryl. 1974. *Suena Grammar* [Workpapers Papua New Guinea Languages 8]. Ukarumpa, Papua New Guinea: SIL.
Wolfart, H. Christoph and Carroll, Janet F. 1981. *Meet Cree: A guide to the Cree language*. Lincoln NB: University of Nebraska Press.
Wurzel, Wolfgang U. 1990. Gedanken zu Suppletion und Natürlichkeit. *Zeitschrift für Phonetik, Sprachwissenschaft und Kommunikationsforschung* 43: 86–91.
Yates, Warren G. and Tryon, Absorn. 1971. *Thai. Basic course*, Vol. 1. Washington DC: Foreign Service Institute, Department of State.
Young, Robert W. 1992. *Analytical Lexicon of the Navajo Language*. Albuquerque NM: University of New Mexico Press.
Zaliznjak, A. A. 1995. *Drevne-Novgorodskij Dialekt*. Moskva: Shkola Jazyku Russkoj Kul'tury.
Ziervogel, D., Louw, J. A. and Ngidi, J. 1967. *A Handbook of the Zulu Language*. Pretoria: J. L. Van Schaik.
Zigmond, Maurice, Booth, Curtis and Munro, Pamela. 1990. *Kawaiisu: Dictionary, grammar and texts* [University of California Publications in Linguistics 119]. Berkeley CA: University of California Press.

Index of languages

!Xu 153

Abkhaz 44
Acoma 141
Afro-Asiatic languages 59, 85, 94, 119, 136, 138, 140–3, 147, 149, 150, 157, 176
Ainu 118, 152, 157, 166
Alagwa 141, 142
Alamblak 66
Altaic languages 43
Amele 120
Amharic 143
Arabic
   Algerian Arabic 141–5
   Classical Arabic 144
   Egyptian Arabic 59, 136, 143–4
   Iraqi Arabic 143
   Lebanese Arabic 143
   Moroccan Arabic 143
   Standard Arabic 136, 144
   Syrian Arabic 143
   Tunisian Arabic 143–5
Armenian
   Modern Eastern 68, 72, 82
Austro-Asiatic languages 38, 39, 94, 124
Austronesian languages 39, 43, 60, 94, 141, 157, 167, 169

Barasano 152, 169
Basque 38, 79, 83, 94
Belorussian 127, 129, 130
Bengali 65, 72
Brahui 65, 82
Bukiyip 60
Bulgarian 48, 77, 78, 126, 127, 130, 131, 145, 146
Burushaski 68, 72, 94, 122, 157, 165, 166

Canela-Kraho 167
Cantonese 46, 47
Carib 80, 94, 95, 133, 140, 141, 175
Chamorro 67
Cherokee 163
Chukchi 122
Comanche 164, 170, 171
Cora 171
Czech 127–9, 131

Daga 59
Diola-Fogny 85
Dutch 78–80, 120

English 1, 3–16, 19, 23, 36, 38, 46, 48, 49, 63, 64, 78, 80, 98–100, 104–6, 120, 133, 164, 171
   American English 22
   Middle English 20, 112–15
   Old English 27, 112, 113
   Scottish English 114
Evenki 44

Finnish 22, 30, 49, 60, 82, 138
French 11, 13, 15–18, 28, 58, 76, 78, 80, 106–8, 110, 111, 120, 149
   Old French 110, 111
Fur 82–6

Geez 143
Georgian 5, 65, 75, 76, 77, 88, 159, 161
German 3, 14, 17, 18, 80, 84, 120
Germanic languages 12, 14, 15, 17, 33, 35, 41, 78, 80, 88, 97, 105, 112, 121, 122, 125
Gothic 120, 125
Greek 1, 2, 40, 58, 59, 68, 69, 77, 78, 82, 87, 112, 125, 127, 136, 137, 142, 144, 146
   Classical Greek 1, 142, 144
Guugu Yimidhirr 123

Hebrew 40
Hindi 72, 80, 120
Hopi 153
Hungarian 22, 30, 83, 84
Hunzib 44

Icelandic 84
Ika 47, 48
Imbabura Quechua 118
Indo-European 3, 8, 14, 15, 17, 25, 30, 40, 41, 47, 58, 59, 65, 69, 70, 72, 75–88, 94, 95, 105, 112, 120–2, 125, 127, 133, 137, 140, 146, 149, 175
Ingush 44, 76, 77, 83, 84, 137
Iraqw 118, 138, 143
Irish 8, 22, 58, 67, 76, 120
Italian 106–8

Jakaltek 136, 137
Japanese 122

Kanuri 59
Kapingamarangi 157, 169
Kawaiisu 169, 170
Ket 38, 155, 162, 163
Khalkha 44
Khmer 39

Index of languages

Kiowa 152, 157
Koasati 38, 151, 167
Korean 61
Krongo 59, 137, 151, 152, 165–7, 173
Kunama 167

Lango 124, 125
Latin 1–3, 28, 84, 106–8, 119, 120, 127, 128
Latvian 120
Lezgian 22, 44, 72, 135

Macedonian 77, 78, 126, 127, 130–2
Macushi 80, 141, 142
Makedonian *see* Macedonian
Malagasy 60
Maltese 83, 85, 143, 144
Mandarin Chinese 102, 104
Mara 73
Maricopa 151
Martuthunira 123
Mataco 140
Mixtec
   Chalcatongo Mixtec 73, 75, 141, 142
Mixtec languages
Mon-Khmer languages 39
Mongolian 43, 118
Moses-Columbian 169
Munda languages 39, 124
Mundari 67, 124, 125
Mupun 119, 149, 150
Murle 152, 161–3

Navajo 152, 159, 160, 161, 173
Ndyuka 38
Nenets 138
Niger-Congo languages 39, 43, 59, 85, 94, 137, 140, 151, 157
North-Caucasian languages 44, 83
Nunggubuyu 141, 142

Old Church Slavonic 120, 126
   OCS 126–8, 130–2
Old Icelandic 84
Oneida 38, 92
Oromo
   Boraana 143
   Harar 143

Paiute
   Northern Paiute 170
Pashto 75
Pipil 77, 78
Polish 5, 127–31

Pomo
   Eastern Pomo 152
Popoluca
   Texistepec Popoluca 172
Portuguese 84

Romance languages 15, 17, 28, 35, 41, 58, 76, 106–7, 115
Russian 8–13, 16–18, 53, 71, 75, 98–100, 104, 116, 127–33, 164–5

Samoan 157, 167
Sango 118
Sanskrit 1, 2, 27, 112, 127
Serbo-Croatian 76–78, 127–31, 144, 145
Shipibo-Konibo 162, 163, 173
Slave 159–61
Slavic languages 17, 33, 46, 68, 69–82, 120, 126–33, 146, 168, 177
Slovak 127, 129, 131
Slovene 69–71, 80–83, 127–29, 131
Somali 143
Sorbian
   Upper Sorbian 127, 129, 131
Spanish 54–56, 76, 82, 84, 99, 100, 104–8, 120
Suena 67
Supyire 122
Swahili 139
Swedish 15, 47, 48, 88, 120–2

Taba 141–2
Tagalog 5
Tamazight 143
Tepehuan
   Northern Tepehuan 83, 167, 171
Tigre 40
Tongan 157
Turkish 22, 30, 44, 99, 102, 104, 122, 144, 145

Ukrainian 127, 129, 130
Usan 60
Ute 151, 152, 160–1

Warao 118
Wari' 167
Wichita 72, 152
Wolaytta 122

Yimas 79
Yukaghir 118
Yup'ik
   Central Yup'ik 38

Zuni 157

Index of authors

Anderson, Stephen 4
Anshen, Frank 4, 20
Arensen, Jon 161
Aronoff, Mark 4, 19, 20
Asher, S. 1, 4
Aski, Janice 25, 28, 105–15

Bakker, Dik 34, 36, 37
Bell, A. 34
Birjulin, Leonid A. 135
Bittner, Andreas 21, 26
Bloomfield, Leonard 3, 4, 9, 14
Booker, Karen 155
Bopp, Franz 2
Börjars, Kersti 25, 29
Bosworth, Joseph 113
Bright, William 1, 4
Brown, Dunstan 98
Buck, Carl D. 106, 121, 127, 132
Bybee, Joan 6–11, 22, 24, 28, 30, 33, 37, 38, 40, 51–8, 63, 74, 78, 82, 84–5, 98, 121, 135, 137, 168, 171, 172, 176

Cabrera, Juan C. Moreno 145
Carstairs-McCarthy, Andrew 7–9, 20, 22, 51
Corbett, Greville G. 98, 149, 150, 155, 158, 163, 164, 167
Crimmins, M. 23
Croft, William 52, 53

Dahl, Östen 18, 36, 40–3, 49, 69, 71, 72, 104, 116, 121, 122, 168, 178
Davies, Mark 99
Delbrück, Bertold 2
Deshpande, Madhav M. 1, 2, 27, 28
Dickey, Stephen M. 69
Dixon, Robert M. W. 116, 118, 119, 123
Dressler, Wolfgang U. 15, 21–6, 29, 30, 98
Dryer, Matthew S. 34–6, 40–2, 66, 93, 139, 175, 176
Durie, Mark 30, 157, 159, 169
Dvoreckij, I. N. 142

Fertig, David 21, 23–6, 28, 104
Foley, William A. 79

Gorbachevskij, A. A. 26–7
Goussev, Valentin 136
Greenberg, Joseph 53, 54
Grimes, Barbara 34
Grønbech, Kaare 118

Halle, Morris 19
Hammond, Michael 19
Hartmann, R. R. K. 1, 4
Haspelmath, Martin 14, 22, 35
Haviland, John 124
Heine, Bernd 121, 122, 171
Hengeveld, Kees 34, 37
Herman, Louis Jay 128
Hippisley, Andrew 98
Hopper, Paul 171

Jakobson, Roman 21, 52–5
Janda, Laura A. 127

Kahrel, Peter 34, 37
Keller, Rudi 132
Koneckaja, Vera P. 27
Krueger, John R. 118
Kuteva, Tania 121, 122, 171

Lass, Roger 23
Leech, Geoffrey 99
Lejeune, Ludo 136
Lewis, Robert E. 112
Lidell, Henry, S. 142
Lorimer, D. L. 166

McIntosh, Angus 114
Macaulay, Monica 142
Malkjær, Kirsten 4
Manczak, Witold 106
Markey, T. L. 26
Marriott, Paul 98
Martin, Samuel E. 14, 35
Maslov, Juri 69
Maslova, Elena 34, 36
Matthews, Peter H. 4, 9, 20
Mayerthaler, Willi 21, 84
Mithun, Marianne 150, 158, 163, 164, 167, 172
Mohanan, K. P. 19
Mous, Maarten 118
Mugdan, J. 5, 6

Nida, Eugene 23
Noonan, Michael 19

Osthoff, Hermann 2, 3, 25, 26, 27

Pagliuca, William 33, 37
Patry, Richard 165, 166

Perkins, Revere D. 33, 34, 37
Pierce, Joe E. 23, 99
Poppe, Nicholas 118
Prokosch, Eduard 112

Rayson, Paul 99
Rice, Keren 150, 160
Rijkhoff, Jan 34, 36, 37
Rolfs, Gerhard 106
Ronnerberger-Sibold, Elke 24
Rosén, Hannah 107
Rudes, Blair 9, 14, 30, 106
Ruhlen, Merritt 34

Scalise, Sergio 19
Schuyt, Roel 69
Scott, Robert 142
Shields, Kenneth 121
Simpson, F. 1, 4
Singh, Rajendra 23
Spencer, Andrew 20
Stassen, Leon 116–21
Steinfeldt, E. 99
Stork, F. C. 1, 4
Stump, Gregory 4, 54
Suen, Ching Y. 99

Tekavcic, Pavao 106

Thomas, Calvin 3
Tiffou, Étienne 165–6
Toller, T. Northcote 113
Townsend, Charles E. 127
Trask, R. L. 1, 4
Traugott, Elizabeth 171

Umarani, Pappuswamy 136

Valenzuela, Pilar M. 162
van der Auwera, Johan 136
Varro, Marcus Terentius 2
Viberg, Åke 93
Vincent, Nigel, 25, 28, 29, 108
Voegelin, C. F. 34, 37, 39
Voegelin, F. M. 34, 37, 39

Wełna, Jerzy 114–15
Werner, Otmar 24
Whaley, Lindsay 24
Wilson, Andrew 99
Wurzel, Wolfgang U. 21, 26

Xrakovskij, Victor S. 135

Zaliznjak, A. A. 133
Zigmond, Maurice 170
Zwicky, Arnold 20

Index of subjects

analogy 23, 42, 106, 113
autonomous forms 56, 57, 78, 79, 82, 83, 84, 85

blocking 19, 20, 115

classificatory verbs 163
communicative maxims
    dynamic 116, 121, 126, 128, 132, 135, 178
    static 115, 132

derivation 2, 4, 6, 10, 11, 12, 13, 19, 46, 54, 56, 79, 128, 130, 158, 163–7, 173
Dryer Distribution 42, 66, 73, 86, 93, 139, 140, 156, 175, 176

frequency
    token 23–5, 29, 97, 104–5
    type 105

grammaticalization 31, 97, 115–16, 121–6, 134, 171, 177

hierarchy
    semantic relevance 11, 28, 57
    lexical/suppetive

imperative-only verbs 141–2
inflection 2, 4, 6, 8, 10, 11, 16, 19, 20, 53, 54, 57, 68, 93, 98, 161, 168
intransitive predication 116, 117
    locational encoding 117, 120
    nominal encoding 117–20, 150, 152
    strategy switching 119

language genus/genera
lexicalization 31, 92, 93, 97, 107, 126, 133, 134, 145, 155, 158, 164, 168, 177

markedness 21, 26, 30, 52, 57, 84

productivity 7, 12, 13, 97, 164, 165, 173

replacement 9, 106, 108, 125
    pragmatically driven 132

samples used
suppletion
    alternation 14–16, 20, 25, 48, 64, 98, 109, 111, 135, 138, 152, 159, 164
    borderline 47, 48, 158
    categorial 18, 48, 49, 58, 64, 66, 67, 73, 74, 78, 79, 83–92, 98, 133, 134, 140, 156, 177
    less prototypical 47, 168
    major types 58, 175
    minor types 58, 175
    non-categorial 18, 48, 49, 58, 64, 78, 79, 83–92, 98, 133, 134, 177
    prototypical 47, 48, 61, 135, 152, 165, 168, 173
    strong
    syntactic
    weak

template
    morphonological 28, 108, 109, 110, 111, 113, 115

weight value 42–4, 64, 66–8, 73, 74, 86, 90, 93–5, 139, 140, 154–7, 177, 178

Typological Studies in Language

A complete list of titles in this series can be found on the publishers' website, www.benjamins.com

68 ABRAHAM, Werner and Larisa LEISIÖ (eds.): Passivization and Typology. Form and function. viii, 530 pp. + index. *Expected September 2006*
67 VESELINOVA, Ljuba N.: Suppletion in Verb Paradigms. Bits and pieces of the puzzle. 2006. xvii, 235 pp.
66 HICKMANN, Maya and Stéphane ROBERT (eds.): Space in Languages. Linguistic Systems and Cognitive Categories. 2006. x, 362 pp.
65 TSUNODA, Tasaku and Taro KAGEYAMA (eds.): Voice and Grammatical Relations. In Honor of Masayoshi Shibatani. 2006. xviii, 342 pp.
64 VOELTZ, F. K. Erhard (ed.): Studies in African Linguistic Typology. 2006. xiv, 426 pp.
63 FILIMONOVA, Elena (ed.): Clusivity. Typology and case studies of the inclusive–exclusive distinction. 2005. xii, 436 pp.
62 COUPER-KUHLEN, Elizabeth and Cecilia E. FORD (eds.): Sound Patterns in Interaction. Cross-linguistic studies from conversation. 2004. viii, 406 pp.
61 BHASKARARAO, Peri and Karumuri Venkata SUBBARAO (eds.): Non-nominative Subjects. Volume 2. 2004. xii, 319 pp.
60 BHASKARARAO, Peri and Karumuri Venkata SUBBARAO (eds.): Non-nominative Subjects. Volume 1. 2004. xii, 325 pp.
59 FISCHER, Olga, Muriel NORDE and Harry PERRIDON (eds.): Up and down the Cline – The Nature of Grammaticalization. 2004. viii, 406 pp.
58 HASPELMATH, Martin (ed.): Coordinating Constructions. 2004. xcv, 578 pp.
57 MATTISSEN, Johanna: Dependent-Head Synthesis in Nivkh. A contribution to a typology of polysynthesis. 2003. x, 350 pp.
56 SHAY, Erin and Uwe SEIBERT (eds.): Motion, Direction and Location in Languages. In honor of Zygmunt Frajzyngier. 2003. xvi, 305 pp.
55 FRAJZYNGIER, Zygmunt and Erin SHAY: Explaining Language Structure through Systems Interaction. 2003. xviii, 309 pp.
54 AIKHENVALD, Alexandra Y. and R.M.W. DIXON (eds.): Studies in Evidentiality. 2003. xiv, 349 pp.
53 GIVÓN, T. and Bertram F. MALLE (eds.): The Evolution of Language out of Pre-language. 2002. x, 394 pp.
52 GÜLDEMANN, Tom and Manfred von RONCADOR (eds.): Reported Discourse. A meeting ground for different linguistic domains. 2002. xii, 425 pp.
51 NEWMAN, John (ed.): The Linguistics of Sitting, Standing and Lying. 2002. xii, 409 pp.
50 FEIGENBAUM, Susanne and Dennis KURZON (eds.): Prepositions in their Syntactic, Semantic and Pragmatic Context. 2002. vi, 304 pp.
49 WISCHER, Ilse and Gabriele DIEWALD (eds.): New Reflections on Grammaticalization. 2002. xiv, 437 pp.
48 SHIBATANI, Masayoshi (ed.): The Grammar of Causation and Interpersonal Manipulation. 2002. xviii, 551 pp.
47 BARON, Irène, Michael HERSLUND and Finn SØRENSEN (eds.): Dimensions of Possession. 2001. vi, 337 pp.
46 AIKHENVALD, Alexandra Y., R.M.W. DIXON and Masayuki ONISHI (eds.): Non-canonical Marking of Subjects and Objects. 2001. xii, 364 pp.
45 BYBEE, Joan and Paul J. HOPPER (eds.): Frequency and the Emergence of Linguistic Structure. 2001. vii, 492 pp.
44 VOELTZ, F. K. Erhard and Christa KILIAN-HATZ (eds.): Ideophones. 2001. x, 436 pp.
43 GILDEA, Spike (ed.): Reconstructing Grammar. Comparative Linguistics and Grammaticalization. 2000. xiv, 269 pp.
42 DIESSEL, Holger: Demonstratives. Form, function and grammaticalization. 1999. xii, 205 pp.
41 FRAJZYNGIER, Zygmunt and Traci S. CURL (eds.): Reciprocals. Forms and functions. Volume 2. 2000. xii, 201 pp.
40 FRAJZYNGIER, Zygmunt and Traci S. CURL (eds.): Reflexives. Forms and functions. Volume 1. 2000. xiv, 286 pp.
39 PAYNE, Doris L. and Immanuel BARSHI (eds.): External Possession. 1999. ix, 573 pp.
38 SIEWIERSKA, Anna and Jae Jung SONG (eds.): Case, Typology and Grammar. In honor of Barry J. Blake. 1998. 395 pp.

37 GIACALONE-RAMAT, Anna and Paul J. HOPPER (eds.): The Limits of Grammaticalization. 1998. vi, 307 pp.
36 NEWMAN, John (ed.): The Linguistics of Giving. 1998. xv, 373 pp.
35 GIVÓN, T. (ed.): Grammatical Relations. A functionalist perspective. 1997. viii, 350 pp.
34 GIVÓN, T. (ed.): Conversation. Cognitive, communicative and social perspectives. 1997. viii, 302 pp.
33 FOX, Barbara A. (ed.): Studies in Anaphora. 1996. xii, 518 pp.
32 BYBEE, Joan and Suzanne FLEISCHMAN (eds.): Modality in Grammar and Discourse. 1995. viii, 575 pp.
31 GERNSBACHER, Morton Ann and T. GIVÓN (eds.): Coherence in Spontaneous Text. 1995. x, 267 pp.
30 DOWNING, Pamela A. and Michael NOONAN (eds.): Word Order in Discourse. 1995. x, 595 pp.
29 KAHREL (PJK), Peter and René van den BERG (eds.): Typological Studies in Negation. 1994. x, 385 pp.
28 GIVÓN, T. (ed.): Voice and Inversion. 1994. viii, 402 pp.
27 FOX, Barbara A. and Paul J. HOPPER (eds.): Voice: Form and Function. 1994. xiii, 377 pp.
26 LORD, Carol: Historical Change in Serial Verb Constructions. 1993. x, 273 pp.
25 SVOROU, Soteria: The Grammar of Space. 1994. xiv, 290 pp.
24 PERKINS, Revere D.: Deixis, Grammar, and Culture. 1992. x, 245 pp.
23 KEMMER, Suzanne: The Middle Voice. 1993. xii, 300 pp.
22 PAYNE, Doris L. (ed.): Pragmatics of Word Order Flexibility. 1992. viii, 320 pp.
21 DOWNING, Pamela A., Susan D. LIMA and Michael NOONAN (eds.): The Linguistics of Literacy. 1992. xx, 334 pp.
20 CROFT, William, Suzanne KEMMER and Keith DENNING (eds.): Studies in Typology and Diachrony. Papers presented to Joseph H. Greenberg on his 75th birthday. 1990. xxxiv, 243 pp.
19:2 TRAUGOTT, Elizabeth Closs and Bernd HEINE (eds.): Approaches to Grammaticalization. Volume 2: Types of grammatical markers. 1991. xii, 558 pp.
19:1 TRAUGOTT, Elizabeth Closs and Bernd HEINE (eds.): Approaches to Grammaticalization. Volume 1: Theoretical and methodological issues. 1991. xii, 360 pp.
18 HAIMAN, John and Sandra A. THOMPSON (eds.): Clause Combining in Grammar and Discourse. 1988. xiii, 428 pp.
17 HAMMOND, Michael, Edith MORAVCSIK and Jessica WIRTH (eds.): Studies in Syntactic Typology. 1988. xiv, 380 pp.
16 SHIBATANI, Masayoshi (ed.): Passive and Voice. 1988. x, 706 pp.
15 AUSTIN, Peter (ed.): Complex Sentence Constructions in Australian Languages. 1988. vii, 289 pp.
14 HINDS, John, Shoichi IWASAKI and Senko K. MAYNARD (eds.): Perspectives on Topicalization. The case of Japanese WA. 1987. xi, 307 pp.
13 Never published.
12 NEDJALKOV, Vladimir P. (ed.): Typology of Resultative Constructions. Translated from the original Russian edition (1983). Translation edited by Bernard Comrie. 1988. xx, 573 pp.
11 TOMLIN, Russell S.: Coherence and Grounding in Discourse. Outcome of a Symposium, Eugene, Oregon, June 1984. 1987. viii, 512 pp.
10 RANSOM, Evelyn N.: Complementation: its Meaning and Forms. 1986. xii, 226 pp.
9 BYBEE, Joan: Morphology. A Study of the Relation between Meaning and Form. 1985. xii, 235 pp.
8 SLOBIN, Dan I. and Karl ZIMMER (eds.): Studies in Turkish Linguistics. 1986. vi, 294 pp.
7 CRAIG, Colette G. (ed.): Noun Classes and Categorization. Proceedings of a symposium on categorization and noun classification, Eugene, Oregon, October 1983. 1986. vii, 481 pp.
6 HAIMAN, John (ed.): Iconicity in Syntax. Proceedings of a symposium on iconicity in syntax, Stanford, June 24–26, 1983. 1985. vi, 402 pp.
5 RUTHERFORD, William E. (ed.): Language Universals and Second Language Acquisition. 1984. ix, 264 pp.
4 CHISHOLM, William, Louis T. MILIC and John A.C. GREPPIN (eds.): Interrogativity. A colloquium on the grammar, typology and pragmatics of questions in seven diverse languages, Cleveland, Ohio, October 5th 1981-May 3rd 1982. 1984. v, 302 pp.
3 GIVÓN, T.: Topic Continuity in Discourse. A quantitative cross-language study. 1983. vi, 492 pp.
2 HAIMAN, John and Pamela MUNRO (eds.): Switch Reference and Universal Grammar. Proceedings of a symposium on switch reference and universal grammar, Winnipeg, May 1981. 1983. xv, 337 pp.
1 HOPPER, Paul J. (ed.): Tense-Aspect. Between semantics & pragmatics. 1982. x, 350 pp.